THE Secrets OF
Unlimited
Energy

SAL RACHELE

Other Books by Sal Rachele

Earth Awakens: Prophecy 2012–2030
Earth Changes and Beyond: Messages from the Founders
Life on the Cutting Edge
The Mystery of Time
The Real History of Earth
Soul Integration

For print books, visit our online bookstore at LightTechnology.com.

eBooks are available from Amazon, Apple iTunes, Google Play, Barnes & Noble, and Kobo.

THE Secrets OF
Unlimited
Energy

SAL RACHELE

Light Technology PUBLISHING

For information about special discounts for bulk purchases, please contact Light Technology Publishing Special Sales at 1-800-450-0985 or publishing@LightTechnology.com.

ISBN-13: 978-1-62233-083-6
ebook ISBN: 978-1-62233-823-8

Light Technology Publishing, LLC
Phone: 1-800-450-0985
1-928-526-1345
Fax: 928-714-1132
PO Box 3540
Flagstaff, AZ 86003
LightTechnology.com

Contents

PART 1: THE SCIENCE SECTION

Chapter 15: More Information on How We Dissipate Energy

Chapter 16: Even More Subtle Aspects of Energy Dissipation

Chapter 17: How to Increase the Flow of Energy into Your Physical Body and Other Levels

Chapter 18: A Review of How to Move from Entropy to Centropy

Chapter 19: The Necessary Changes in Society

Definition of Terms
Used in this Book

Aether, Ether, Etheric Plane: A higher dimension of the universe that contains nearly infinite energy. The universe "blinks" on and off millions of times per second, giving rise to Zero-Point fluctuations. During the "off" phase, energy moves from the physical to the etheric state, producing negative entropy. The aether itself is similar to a fluid, but it is not a fluid; it exists within and beyond our physical universe. Aetheric energy influences electromagnetic energy. It is a prime ingredient of dark energy and dark matter. The effects of the aether are what balances the Law of Conservation of Energy in so-called "over-unity" devices, since energy is merely being transferred between levels.

Awareness: The active state of consciousness in which beings are aware of themselves and their relationship to the universe. Awareness may contain thought, but it is beyond thought.

Black Hole: A region of space wherein the gravitational field is so strong that not even light can escape. Linked to white holes through a connector called a wormhole. At the very center of the black hole is a singularity.

Big Bang: A holographic projection of a singularity that resulted in the birth of our universe, approximately 14.2 billion years ago.

Big Crunch: The end point of universal contraction; the opposite of Big Bang; the returning of the holographic projection to its singularity state.

Bose-Einstein Condensate: The static state of the universe operating at zero degrees Kelvin.

Consciousness: A field of intelligence that permeates the universe. Spirit that is aware of itself. Measured in consciousness units (CU), ultra-tiny particle/waves that are everywhere present. When consciousness moves or is directed toward an outcome, it becomes the primary force of Creation. All other forces are derived from consciousness. Also known as the Mind of God, it exists in all life forms and a rudimentary version exists within inanimate objects.

Dark Energy, Dark Matter: Names for phenomena belonging to the etheric and higher dimensions of time/space. Approximately 96% of the universe is composed of dark energy and dark matter. Related to Zero-Point Energy.

Duality: A state of opposing forces, comparisons or contrasts, such as light vs. dark, good vs. evil, knowledge vs. ignorance, happiness vs. sadness, etc. The most prevalent state of consciousness in the world today. In science, can be analogous to a dipole or positively and negatively charged particles.

Energy: Defined in numerous ways as the force behind the ability to perform work, as a product of mass and the velocity of light squared, and as stored (potential) energy or active (kinetic) energy. Described in detail in the following sections.

Electromagnetic Null Zone: A region of space (within or without an atomic structure) wherein the polarities are exactly balanced, creating no movement of electrons. A means of creating resonant fields and superconductors.

God: Everything that is, and what is beyond everything that is. Undifferentiated source energy.

Godhead: The aspect of God that resides beyond the 12th dimension of our local universe.

Holographic Universe: The state of our universe after the Big Bang, where everything is a projection of a single point (singularity). Within each part of the universe is contained the whole of the universe. The mass of the entire universe is found inside every proton.

Illusions: Things which appear to be true as long as you believe in them, but which disappear once belief is removed.

Intelligence, Intelligent Beings: Spirit capable of knowing itself. Entities capable of reason, logic, creative and critical thinking.

Monatomic Resonant Field: A molecular state of certain elements wherein the nuclear forces form coherence through a superconducting nonpolarized field.

Nonduality: A state of undifferentiated reality where everything is unified and whole (oneness). A higher state of consciousness beyond the realms of duality.

Nonpolarized Field: A field wherein the electrons (and positrons) are perfectly balanced so as to have a zero difference in potential. A field where the electrons are not flowing (unipole vs. dipole) but are in a sort of stasis that forms a resonant field. A superconductor forms a nonpolarized field and vice versa.

Polarized Field: A field of electrons and positrons with an unbalanced load (potential), such as a typical electrical circuit. Any field wherein electrons flow from the negative to positive pole.

Quantum Fluctuations: Energy that "blinks" on and off once every Planck second, found in the vacuum of space at zero degrees Kelvin. Also known as Zero-Point Energy.

Quantum Coherence: A state of the quantum flux during the "blinking off" phase of the universe, whereby centropy (reverse entropy) occurs. This is when energy flows from the physical to the etheric state.

Resonant Field: A field of energy wherein the components (sub-atomic particles/waves) form a coherence (negentropy, centropy or nonpolarized field). This is the opposite of entropy. The energy of a resonant field is in a higher state than that of random space. Resonant fields are associated with superconductors since there is ultra-low resistance within the resonance.

Radiant Energy: Energy in the form of quantum fluctuations that emanates from within an atomic structure into the vacuum of space that exists outside of an atomic structure. Also known as "bleed-through." Somewhat synonymous with scalar electromagnetic energy. Not to be confused with the classical physics definition that refers to heat generated by electrical circuits, either intentionally (a space heater) or unintentionally (a computer console that gets hot when in constant use). Note: Our sun gives off both kinds of Radiant Energy.

Scalar Electromagnetic Energy, Scalar Waves: Nonpolarized EM waves that emanate from the Zero Point in the form of Radiant Energy. One of the forms of such radiance.

Singularity: A point in time/space that has no magnitude and infinite mass. The state of the universe before the Big Bang. However, singularities exist throughout the fabric of time/space, and every point is the exact same point.

Spirit: The intelligent energy that permeates all time/space and beyond. The main attribute of God.

Superconductor: A device that facilitates extremely low resistance; a field of extremely low resistance caused by atomic particles/waves forming resonance (affinity) with each other.

Superconducting Field: A resonant field wherein resistance approaches zero and current approaches infinity at a constant voltage. Created by removing polarization from a field (which creates scalar waves). Atomic particle/waves within a superconducting field have "affinity" for one another, which opens up a portal to the etheric dimensions (similar to the principle of a tunneling diode).

Superposition: The ability for particles to be simultaneously in more than one location at the same time. Similar to the wave principle.

Superstring Theory: A theory that postulates the universe is composed of "strings" of vibrating energy involving numerous dimensions of time/space.

Truth: That which is actually so regardless of what you believe.

Zero-Point Energy (ZPE): Quantum fluctuations in the vacuum of space that normally occur at zero degrees Kelvin but can be brought to room temperature by creating an electromagnetic structure amounts to about 5.1×10^{124} joules/cm^3. ZPE outside an atomic structure (in the vacuum of empty space) amounts to about 1.0×107^7 joules/cm^3. This background amount is the result of radiant energy "bleeding through" from within atomic structures into the nearby space around the atoms.

Preface

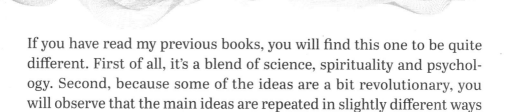

If you have read my previous books, you will find this one to be quite different. First of all, it's a blend of science, spirituality and psychology. Second, because some of the ideas are a bit revolutionary, you will observe that the main ideas are repeated in slightly different ways at different times throughout the book.

The vast majority of this material is given to me by my spirit guides and higher-dimensional beings. I've drawn from a few scientists and spiritual leaders, but over 80% of the material is "original." This word is in quotes because there really isn't such a thing as original material. Everything is available through the Universal Mind, or Mind of God, as you prefer. The real question is how to access the information and then, once accessed, how to apply it in your daily life.

Some of the information has been proven using rigorous scientific method, and some has not. For example, the idea that the universe blinks on and off, that the universe is a hologram, or that you can tap the field of negative entropy, are controversial ideas. Although there is strong evidence in the scientific world, many so-called "authorities" are going to criticize, or even ridicule, the information in this book.

I urge you to read through this book slowly and carefully, keeping an open mind at all times. That means not flatly rejecting anything just because it doesn't agree with your belief systems or the beliefs of prominent scientists and religious figures.

If you are not scientifically minded, you can read through the first part quickly and spend more time on the spiritual and psychological sections. We've kept the mathematics on an extremely basic level and there's not much of it. The writing style is a bit condensed, meaning that there is a tremendous amount of information on each page. Stop frequently when a specific paragraph resonates powerfully within you. Then apply the ideas in practical situations whenever possible.

"No one can fail who seeks to reach the truth."

— *A Course in Miracles*

A Summary of the Properties of the Universe

1. The universe is a singularity. A singularity has infinite mass and no space.

2. The universe we experience is holographic. Everything we see, hear, feel, touch and measure is part of the holographic "expansion" or projection of this singularity. In physics, the analogy of a balloon is used to describe the holographic expansion of the universe. Before the balloon is blown up, it exists (as a singularity). As the balloon is being blown up, it expands until eventually it reaches the maximum point of expansion. According to higher sources, the point of maximum acceleration of the expansion will occur approximately 25 billion years after the Big Bang. This will mark the halfway point of the entire expansion.

3. The Big Bang is the process whereby our universe holographically projected itself outward from the singularity. It is currently about 14.2 billion years into its expansion phase.

4. The universe expands and contracts much like a breathing cycle. When you first start exhaling, the expansion accelerates, then slows and stops at the peak of the exhale, before accelerating inward, then slowing and stopping at the peak of the inhale. The maximum point of expansion is approximately 50 billion years from the maximum point of contraction (the singularity before and between each Big Bang).

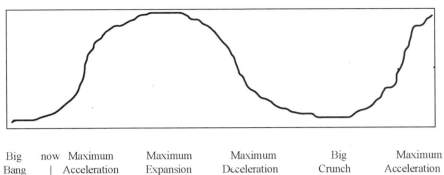

Big	now	Maximum	Maximum	Maximum	Big	Maximum
Bang	|	Acceleration	Expansion	Deceleration	Crunch	Acceleration

0 5 10 15 20 25 30 35 40 45 50 55 60 65 70 75 80 85 90 95 100 105 110 115 120

Billions of Years

5. There are an infinite number of Big Bangs, one approximately every 100 billion years.

6. Everything we experience in this universe is contained within the exact same point. There is no separation whatsoever. Every point is all points and vice versa.

7. Since there is really only one point in Creation, every point in time/space is the same point. This is the meaning of "everything is One."

8. Because the universe is holographic, the parts contain the whole and the whole contains the parts. God is within each one of us, and each one of us is within God.

9. All time/space is contained within the singularity of the universe and is out-pictured holographically as a realm of time/space that is about 14.2 billion years old.

10. Our universe is a mirror opposite of a "sister" universe that has opposite polarity. Our universe is mostly electrons with a few positrons. Our sister universe is mostly positrons with a few electrons.

11. Our universe "blinks on and off" once every Planck second (about 10-44 seconds).

12. During the "blinking on" phase, energy moves from the etheric into the physical planes through a process called "entropy."

13. During the "blinking off" phase, energy moves from the physical to the etheric planes in a process known as "centropy."

14. Past, present and future exist within this timeless moment we call now.

15. All time is connected. The past is happening now. The future is happening now.

16. There is nearly infinite energy within the structure of time/space.

17. There are 12 dimensions to the universe in this author's model system.

18. The higher dimensions consist primarily of centropy while the lower dimensions consist primarily of entropy.

19. Each human being has 12 dimensions or aspects of Self. In most souls, only three or four of these aspects are "activated." Activation means directing one's energy and attention into that level or dimension. Human beings are preoccupied with the lower four levels of being and so in most souls, the upper levels exist in potential only.

20. God's love radiates continuously throughout the universe. It is omnipresent, omniscient and omnipotent.

A Summary of What's in this Book

∞ Going Beyond Newton

From a mechanical (Newtonian) point of view, energy is defined as a product of power, work and force. It exists in two states, potential and kinetic (stored energy and energy in motion).

$E = mc^2$ is Einstein's famous equation that links matter and energy. Essentially, it states that matter is merely a form of energy existing at a certain vibration.

Everything is vibration. Superstring theory is based on this axiom. All the levels and dimensions of the universe exist within certain domains of vibration. The visible light spectrum, for example, exists within a narrow band of frequencies (vibrations). The spiritual universe is infinitely larger than the physical universe, by definition, since the visible light spectrum is just a tiny band between the infrared and ultraviolet spectrums.

There is an etheric dimension with nearly unlimited energy. This is one of the central premises of this book and is disputed by many scientists, yet it's easily proven if one puts aside the prejudices of Newtonian mechanics and considers all the related fields of study. The closest mainstream science has come to acknowledging the ether in modern times is the realization that about 96% of the universe consists of dark matter and dark energy. This currently unmeasurable realm is a combination of the long-sought etheric plane and influences from dimensions beyond the etheric.

The universe is holographic — the whole is contained in the parts. Not only is the universe a holographic projection of a single point (the Big Bang), but the entirety of the universe is contained in its parts. We will have a lot more to say about this further into the book.

∞ Everything Is Consciousness

Even a rock has consciousness, although in a form not normally recognized by human beings. This is not exactly pantheism because not all consciousness can be likened to an intelligent being. Nevertheless, there is consciousness in everything, and everything is in consciousness.

Light belongs to a higher dimension. In science this is evident in Einstein's Special Theory of Relativity. The central premise involves the observation that no matter how fast you are moving, the speed of light remains a constant. For example, if you are traveling at 99% the speed of light, Newtonian logic would say that if something passes you going the speed of light, it will appear to be moving 1% faster than you. Yet that is not what really happens. The object going the speed of light still appears to be going the speed of light relative to you. Consequently, you cannot accelerate to the speed of light in normal time/space. As you approach the speed of light, your mass approaches infinity, which means it will take an infinite amount of energy to push you into the speed of light.

The above paragraph implies it is not possible to go from sub-light speed to light speed. It must be, therefore, that since there is light everywhere in the universe, that that light is part of an eternal, unchanging realm that has always been and always will be. This also implies that the world of sub-light-speed objects is not inherently real, but merely a shadow of the real world, a world that travels at the speed of light.

In eastern philosophy, the world of sub-light objects is referred to as "maya" or "illusion." It is contained within the real world, or non-dual reality of God.

∞ The Observer Is the Observed

This famous statement from J. Krishnamurti and Dr. David Bohm has raised a few eyebrows. What does it really mean? Is it possible that there is no "inner" and "outer" reality and just reality itself?

The so-called world outside is not really separate from the perceiver. In actuality, there is no proof of a world "out there." Everything you think you see is being interpreted by the brain based on a series of perceptive mechanisms.

There is also no proof of an "inner" world. Where is it? What do you find if you cut open the brain or the heart, looking for it? Perhaps it is in the aura. But where?

A Course in Miracles states, "Everything exists within the Mind of God." If this is true, then there is truly no separation at all, even between bodies. If you look with the proper camera, you can see a spiderweb or network of energy connecting everything in the universe. In the science section of this book, we will demonstrate that everything in the cosmos consists of a single point, or singularity. The universe is a holographic projection of this single point.

∞ We Live in a Matrix

Call it a simulation, if you wish. This is a hugely popular idea recently suggested by top scientists in the artificial-intelligence field. And yes, it is possible to prove this, although currently there is no instrumentation that can measure in detail every fluctuation in the quantum vacuum.

The universe blinks on and off once every Planck second (10 to 44 seconds). We live in an extremely high-resolution movie (a 3D holographic projection). What happens during each blinking-off phase is not understood by scientists, yet this is the key to unlimited energy, as we shall see later.

∞ The Power of Belief

Your beliefs are extremely powerful. They are so powerful that you can seem to create unlike the Creator of the universe. For example, if you believe you are separate from God, you will seem to have that experience. This is like putting your hands up in front of the sun and then claiming that the sun is not shining or thinking the sun is not shining when it is nighttime. (In this case, the Earth is blocking the sun because you are turned away from it.) Or on a cloudy or foggy day, you think the sun is not shining. (Of course, it is shining above the clouds and fog.)

∞ Truth and Illusion

Let us now redefine two of the basic terms given in the Overview. Truth is that which is actually so on all levels and dimensions. Illusion is that which only seems to be true based on your beliefs (individually and/or collectively). When the belief ends, the illusion disappears.

Truth is eternal and unchanging but may have aspects that are constantly changing within the eternality. This can be likened to the fractal, which is constantly changing. Yet the function that generates the fractal remains unchanged.

The world is based on illusions. It appears the way our perception dictates. Our minds are like radio receivers. The channel we are tuned to dictates our reality. If we are tuned to the love channel, the world is a place of love. To one who is tuned to the fear channel, the world is a fearful place. In truth, there is only energy and vibration. We qualify that energy by our beliefs. We "activate" our beliefs by focusing repeatedly on them. Whatever we give time, energy, focus and attention to becomes our personal reality. We call this "activating" a particular level of consciousness.

∞ Fields of Consciousness and the Quantum Field

The main question asked and answered in this book is: "What is this nearly unlimited field of energy, and how do we tap into it to supply our energy needs for the foreseeable future?"

The missing ingredient in modern alternative-energy research is consciousness. Inventors want to know why Zero-Point Energy devices sometimes work and sometimes don't, or rather why they seem to work fine in the presence of their inventors and a few close friends, but do not work well in the presence of skeptics and the general public.

The short answer is that thoughts and beliefs create a field of consciousness, which in turn determines the nature of the quantum field in the vicinity of the consciousness. The size of the field of consciousness is determined by many complex factors, including the level of vibration of the observers of the Zero-Point Energy device. In other words, a resonant field is set up around the experiment or demonstration that is based on the aggregate level of vibration of the observers. If the field is predominantly negative, it creates a negative resonant field in the vicinity of the device, which counteracts the effects of the positive resonant field of the inventor and close friends. We will have more to say about this later.

∞ A Metaphysical Problem — The Law of Attraction

The metaphysical way of saying the above is that belief creates your experience of reality. If you believe in scarcity and lack and therefore think that Zero-Point Energy is unreal or cannot work in this world, you set up a resonant field based on those beliefs. A world that believes in scarcity cannot and will not experience the unlimited abundance of Zero-Point Energy as long as the belief in scarcity remains intact. To experience Zero-Point Energy under these conditions would violate the Law of Attraction. This is also why attempts to tap into the unlimited field of energy have been opposed by seemingly powerful forces. The belief in lack and scarcity (separation consciousness) is precisely why the world has an economic system that effectively prevents new energy technologies from being introduced successfully.

∞ The Zero-Point Energy Field

Zero-Point Energy (ZPE) is defined as the energy inherent within the static state of the universe (at zero degrees Kelvin). This energy consists of quantum fluctuations that "blink" on and off once every Planck second. In the following chapters, we will go into depth on the nature of the Zero-Point field — what it is and how to access it.

∞ Levels of Vibration Required for Proliferation of Zero-Point Energy Fields

The mathematics necessary to determine the precise level of vibration of consciousness necessary for Zero-Point Energy fields to proliferate on Earth is too complex to include in this material. Suffice to say, the higher your vibration, the more you can contribute to the spread of unlimited energy technologies on Earth. If a large group of souls raise their consciousness vibration sufficiently, new energy technologies will finally find their way into the everyday lives of people on Earth.

∞ Current Projects Involving Zero-Point Energy

In the Appendix, we will list some of the current projects employing Zero-Point technology. The list is extremely short and not very inclusive. This is because we have handpicked a few inventors and devices that we feel are legitimate, authentic and hold promise for future development.

∞ A Timeline for Implementation of Zero-Point Devices

This author's spirit guides originally predicted that Zero-Point Energy would enter mass production around the year 2020. Due to exceptionally strong negative beliefs still plaguing much of humanity, that estimate is now 2025. We are assured by higher beings that the delay is very minor and that within one generation, these devices will be commonplace. It depends entirely on how fast human beings raise their level of consciousness.

∞ Applications of Zero-Point Devices

The obvious applications include home and commercial power, agricultural operations, transport, medical, and space exploration. Imagine being able to grow food in one corner of the world for practically no expense, then ship it anywhere for a few pennies, taking only a few hours from harvest to shelf in the supermarket even if the destination is located on the opposite side of the Earth. Imagine homes, cars, factories and businesses with unlimited energy at almost no cost. This can be reality within one generation.

∞ The Unified Field Theory (Theory of Everything)

In the science section, we will explain the Unified Field Theory and how it will change everything in the world as we know it.

∞ ∞ ∞

Let us now go into depth on many of the topics introduced above. Throughout all three sections of this book (Scientific, Spiritual and

Psychological), we will be repeating many concepts in slightly differ-ent ways each time. If you read something that is repeated several times, there is a good reason. Part of our intention in writing this book is to reprogram the subconscious minds of humanity, and that often requires repetition and reinforcement.

Let's begin our exploration into the fascinating world of unlimited energy.

Some Common Myths about Energy

Before we commence the subject of energy in more detail, presenting the scientific, spiritual/metaphysical and psychological viewpoints, let us begin by dispelling some common myths about energy.

∞ Myth #1: There Is an Energy Shortage on Earth

Nothing could be further from the truth, and there is scientific proof. We live in a sea of nearly infinite energy. The problem is in how to harness that energy. The so-called "powers that be" have no real desire to discover the means of tapping this vast reservoir of renewable energy because it means losing their monopoly on fossil and nuclear fuels. Inventor after inventor has been harassed, killed, or had their inventions stolen and suppressed. Those that survive have often had great difficulty getting funding for their projects.

There is another reason free renewable-energy sources are not able to proliferate on Earth at this time. In the science and metaphysical sections of this book, we will look at the role the inventor plays in his/her experiments with Zero-Point Energy and how the consciousness of the creators of devices affects the outcome of experiments. We will see that it is necessary for humanity to raise its consciousness sufficiently to overcome the belief in lack and scarcity.

∞ Myth #2: Human Beings Are Inherently Primitive and Will Always Be Ruled by Overlords

While history seems to bear this out, the real history of the Earth has been suppressed, mainly by those who are also suppressing new inventions. A primitive species would indeed be incapable of cleaning up the planet and providing cheap, renewable energy to all its residents. Believing that we evolved from the ape is one of the cornerstones of the belief system that says humankind is unable to rise above the laws of entropy and decay. It is relatively easy to prove that we did not evolve from the ape. The short answer is that when a species mutates, eventually all members of that species are activated by the mutation. So then why are there still primates on Earth?

If you can get humans to believe they are little more than glorified apes, then you can get them to believe they need masters to take care of them, to make rules, and to create order and regulation. This Freudian worldview is a major reason there are not more human beings breaking out of the so-called "matrix" of societal controls and programs. Why Freudian? Because in the adult population, government and authority end up taking the place of mommy and daddy. We want mommy government to give us handouts (social programs) and daddy government to keep us safe (with a strong military).

This belief in the need for authorities to take care of us and watch over us manifests in various ways, including the two-party system of government in the Western world. The Democrats typically represent the mommy side of the equation and the Republicans usually represent the daddy side of things.

A small number of people control the drama from behind the scenes. All major political parties are puppets on a string, guided by a "priest class" of souls who understand the psychology of society and use it for their selfish purposes. Such souls are addicted to their sense of power (which is not true power but a false sense of superiority based on a deep-seated belief in inferiority). Ask yourself a basic question: "Why would truly powerful persons feel the need to control and manipulate others? Why would they need huge armies and institutions to suppress, control and enslave other human beings?"

The truth is, human beings have risen to seemingly great heights numerous times in the last ten million years, only to experience destruction, sometimes by nature, often by interference from other intelligent races, and even more often from their own ignorance (refusal to accept higher spiritual truths in favor of barbaric religious beliefs). In other words, the human ego has ruled the roost throughout most of humanity's journey on Earth, sabotaging the efforts of those who are truly loving and compassionate. A spiritually immature race cannot overcome the negative belief systems responsible for keeping humanity imprisoned in a world of war, poverty, misery and suffering.

Nevertheless, recent advances in telecommunications and medical technology make it possible for human beings to rise above their primitive belief systems and take their rightful place in the cosmos. This means more and more souls will come to the realization that humanity does not need to be ruled by an elite group who claim to be God's chosen ones. People will realize that energy belongs to everyone and is freely available throughout the cosmos.

∞ Myth #3: There Is No Such Thing as Perpetual Motion; You Cannot Get Something from Nothing

This is true up to a point, because the Law of Conservation of Energy is a prime principle of the universe. However, the vast majority of energy in the cosmos is contained in what scientists call "dark energy" and "dark matter." These together make up over 96% of total measurable energy. This energy/matter matrix includes what early scientists called the "aether."

In the early 20th century, physicists began discounting the existence of aether in favor of other theories and principles. This was a scientific mistake and a lot of them ended up "throwing the baby out with the bathwater." The "solution" has often manifested as using incorrect mathematics or inventing new mathematical ideas in order to explain the universe without aether.

In addition to the aether, there are other subtle energy fields, or what this author calls the "intermediate planes," defined as dimensions 4 through 6 in the 12-dimensional model system given in earlier books. The higher dimensions/levels (far beyond what can be measured with current scientific instruments) are called the "celestial planes" (dimensions 7 through 9) and "God planes" (dimensions 10 through 12). You can read about these higher dimensions in the book, *Soul Integration.*

Tapping just a tiny portion of the energy of the aether, or an even tinier part of these higher dimensions, would provide enough energy to fuel all enterprises on Earth for millions of years. Some simple mathematics will be explored in a later chapter that helps illustrate this. (Relax, it's extremely basic.)

∞ Myth #4: It's Too Expensive to Retool Everything to Accommodate New Sources of Energy

This is just plain *false.* Of course, at first there will be investment required. However, if you took the money from a few years' military budgets of the major nations on Earth, probably within 10 or 15 years at most you would have an infrastructure capable of retooling existing manufacturing. Yes, in the beginning you would still need fossil fuels to fabricate many of the machines needed for tapping the Zero-Point Energy. However, it is estimated that the total cost to provide continuous renewable energy could eventually be as low as $10,000 per household or $50,000 per small business. In many places, people pay that much in taxes to fund new military toys every year. In the case of the numbers above, these machines would be capable of running for 50 to 100 years without the need to replace worn-out parts, so this is essentially a one-time investment. Compare that to the cost of maintaining fossil-fuel refineries and nuclear reactors.

Like so many worthwhile things in life, an initial investment is required, but in this case, the investment's returns are beyond anything that can be achieved even with solar, wind, hydro or hydrogen energy systems. Once again, in a later section, we will go into a few of the details of how this is possible.

∞ Myth #5: People Are Used to Their Internal Combustion Engines and Will Not Change Quickly

This is an ego problem. Most human beings do not change until there is a crisis. They remain in denial even when there is ample evidence of danger, waiting until the problem can no longer be ignored. By that time, it is often too late to avoid the nasty consequences of this denial. Even if the world were able to function reasonably well for another 50 to 100 years using fossil fuels, the consciousness of Earth is rising, especially since the use of the Internet began less than 40 years ago. Several inventors have even published schematics of their Zero-Point Energy machines. The cat is out of the bag, as the saying goes. You cannot put the genie back into the bottle. Some new ideas are "going viral." Despite apparent management issues and bugs in the designs, companies like Tesla are producing electric cars, although this represents a bridge technology, one that is temporarily useful until the retooling for Zero-Point is completed.

More and more people are becoming aware of how advances in technology have been suppressed (unless it benefits the military, as in the case of computers, AI and surveillance). Although robotic systems are being heavily promoted at present, at some point there will be a "revolt against the machine," so to speak. As souls become aware of the higher dimensions of reality, they will realize that more sophisticated machines are not the answer to the deeper problems in the world. Yes, technology is capable of making life easier physically, but obviously it can be used to enslave as well as liberate.

Current technology is contributing greatly to the pollution on our world. As clean, renewable sources are brought forth, people will no longer be willing to accept that they must live in a polluted world of oil, plastics and outdated technologies.

∞ Myth #6: The "Powers that Be" Are Just Too Strong and Will Squelch any Real Progress

This is a variation on Myth #2 above. Yes, it's scary to speak out and express revolutionary ideas, but if everyone just went along with the status quo, we would still be living in the age of the horse and buggy. As we said earlier, the genie is out of the bottle. No amount of suppression and threats against inventors will cause new ideas to be extinguished from the minds of curious experimenters. Will this mean violent revolution? Perhaps. People are waking up — more slowly than desired, but nevertheless waking up. The crisis experienced by not adapting will spur many to take risks.

For some it will start with political rebellion — in fact that has already begun in certain Western countries. Regardless of what you think of the former U.S. president Donald Trump, for example, he was elected because about half of Americans were fed up with the power structure represented by the two-party system. This was a tiny first step, but an important one, nevertheless.

If you fail to take risks, you are like the tiny frog beside the river that enjoys the comforts of a stagnant warm pool of water until it dries up and the frog cannot find its way to the running water necessary to sustain its life — and it dies. Even if you manage to eke out a mediocre life by refusing to change, is that really living?

About 80% of the world is struggling just to meet their daily needs (food, clean water, housing, sanitation, etc.). Is this any way to live? Is it necessary? Without a few brave souls willing to challenge the status quo, war, poverty, misery and suffering on Earth will continue. If you are reading this, you are undoubtedly among the 20% that has enough leisure time to investigate what is being said in these pages. It is up to you. As the Hopi elders once said, "We are the ones we have been waiting for." No savior, religious or scientific, is going to solve our problems for us. It's time to take responsibility for our own thoughts, feelings, beliefs and actions, and become part of the solution, not part of the problem.

The so-called "powers that be" depend on you believing you are powerless to change the status quo. Their ownership of most media and financial institutions allows them to present a highly distorted perception of reality that engenders fear and mistrust — ideal conditions for continuing the strengthening of the military-industrial complex, as it is often called.

People are taught in the indoctrination centers called schools that we need government and the military to keep us safe from all sorts of imagined dangers. If you travel the world, you will see that the problems humanity faces are pretty much the same everywhere. There is no enemy just across the border of another country (unless you believe there is).

∞ Myth #7: Living a Life of Unlimited Energy and Prosperity Is for the Super Intelligent, or the Super Spiritually Evolved, Not for Me

Perhaps you believe you must become another Einstein or Tesla, or another Jesus or Buddha, before you can make any real difference in the world. That is just plain wrong. Both science and spirituality are in the process of proving that "the Kingdom of Heaven is within." As stated numerous times throughout this book, it is now provable that the entire universe exists holographically within every human being. Not only are we contained within God, but God is contained within us.

God created every one of us in His/Her image and likeness. What does this mean? It means we have the same creative attributes as our Creator. It means we are inherently super intelligent.

Quantum physics has shown (through the Nonlocality Principle) that everything is connected. Spiritual teachers say everything is One. Therefore, it is possible to tap into the unlimited field of intelligence (pure spirit) contained within all things. If you are equal to Mother Theresa, Gandhi, or the great inventors of times past and present, then the only difference between them and you is that you have not accessed your creative potential as fully as they did. It is there, waiting to be harnessed.

Understanding the nature of consciousness and how belief systems color your perception of reality is the starting point. Socrates said, "Know thyself." This two-word teaching should be required of every student in every school on Earth. "Know the truth and the truth shall set you free," is another great statement of wisdom. Education of self (and the world) should be first priority for every human being. It is time to stop living in ignorance or blindly believing what the so-called "authorities" tell you.

∞ Myth #8: If Unlimited Energy Were Possible, We Would Have Been Told About It

Who runs the media? What are journalists and newscasters told to say? What happens when they go against the status quo? What happens to your funding if you stray too far from the party line in the halls of research? How many scientists will continue to receive support from large corporations if they start talking about reverse entropy? Not many.

Most of what we have been told by the media is a lie. The media (all mainstream and most alternative) is owned by those who have an agenda. You are not going to get the whole picture. Take medicine, for example. If you were to get cancer, most of your family and friends would want you to get chemotherapy and radiation treatment. Yet these are toxic procedures that kill both healthy and diseased cells. About 90% of all cancer patients who undergo these procedures have the cancer reappear in another part of the body within ten years.

What about vaccines? Some of them have indeed been helpful in eradicating disease. But now most of them are outdated (are not effective anymore) and are full of harmful additives, plus multiple serums are being combined into a single shot, greatly multiplying the chance of side effects. There is huge money being made in the vaccine industry. Yet governments are forcing people to vaccinate their children or are strongly urging them by keeping them in fear and ignorance. As an example, the flu vaccine last year was declared to be about 1.5% effective, meaning that it prevented flu in about 15 out of every 1,000 people.

Viruses mutate constantly, and it takes a lot of research and money to keep up with the mutations. How much research has gone into the effects of combining up to *five* different serums in one injection? And why in the world does an infant need a Hepatitis B vaccine (unless the mother is a heroin addict or a prostitute)?

The two above examples (influenza and Hepatitis B) involve blatant lies being propagated by the so-called "authorities" of medicine, along with some well-meaning but ignorant doctors.

We all know there is propaganda being spoon fed to the gullible public in other areas such as government, finance and the military. How many more ill-designed, over-priced weapons do we need to feel safe and secure? Until we start questioning *everything* we see or hear in the media, we are unlikely to realize that we live in a sea of nearly unlimited energy.

Free, renewable Zero-Point Energy is not profitable for the major corporations. It does not keep people dumbed down and compliant to the so-called "powers that be." It is not politically correct. It represents freedom from authority and control, oppression and slavery. The so-called "Dark Lords" who think they run this world will not maintain their illusion of power if Zero-Point Energy finds its way into the mainstream.

∞ Myth #9: People Believe in Scarcity, and so They Will Not Benefit from Unlimited Energy

Unfortunately, this is not a myth, but a reality. The myth is that we are living in scarcity. An illusion is something that appears true only if you believe in it. As long as people believe the illusion of scarcity/lack, they will have that experience. Once this belief is removed, souls will realize they have been living in a sea of abundance all along but were blinded by their belief. It is like holding your hands up to block the sun and claiming that the sun is not shining, then later realizing what you are doing and removing your hands.

To remove the myth that we are living in lack and scarcity, we must stop believing in lack and scarcity. The latest breakthroughs in science have proven that there is more than enough energy in the vacuum of so-called "empty" space to supply our needs essentially forever. Spirituality teaches that God's limitless love and compassion pours itself out upon all living things. These are two ways of saying the same thing. Our number-one priority is letting go of the belief in lack and limitation and embracing what has already been proven by those scientists brave enough to stop believing in the status quo.

∞ Myth #10: This All Sounds Great, But I Have Bills to Pay and Mouths to Feed

Nobody said life was supposed to be easy. You might have to make some hard choices regarding your future. It may be time to stop supporting corrupt industries and governments to the greatest extent possible (without endangering your life or those of your children). Do the research, even if it is in your very limited spare time. Talk to those who know about these things. Read and re-read this book. Educate others about the myths and solutions offered herein. Make real education your top priority. Sift through the millions of articles and blogs on the Internet and get a broad picture of what is happening in science and spirituality. As hard as it may be, let go of your religious upbringing, including the religions of economics and consumerism. Let go of old belief systems, such as "Life is a struggle," and "There's not enough." Do the work on yourself that is required. Heal your grievances and judgments. Explore alternative medicine, holistic healing and new therapies. Ask your higher guidance (God, the angels and your Higher Self) to give you insights into ways you can help bring about an energy revolution.

Do not ignore your responsibilities, but stop making them bigger than they are. All it takes is five to ten minutes of meditation and research every day to start the ball rolling. Eventually you build up momentum. Your life begins to change in a positive way. It might take quite a bit of effort and persistence. Old beliefs rarely change overnight. Stay open and receptive to what is being said here without blindly believing anything this author or anyone else says. If it feels right, say the following affirmation daily as often as possible: "I am a powerful, creative, spiritual being." It is the truth, no matter what you believe. If you believe you are not powerful, guess what? You will experience being not powerful, which proves that your beliefs are powerful. Today, claim your powerful, creative self.

∞ Myth #11: This All Sounds Too Good to Be True

Yes, it probably does. The idea that life is a struggle, or even worse, that "Life's a bitch and then you die," has been around for a long time. Then there's the idea that the grim reaper stands ready to rob you and cancel all your hard work and struggle. The best you seem to be able to hope for is to leave a legacy for future generations.

Perhaps you believe it's possible to live in a sea of nearly unlimited energy, but you figure it's going to be too far in the future to possibly reap the benefits of these new technologies. If you are a spiritual being, maybe you will be able to witness the changes on Earth from the higher realms. After all, this body you are wearing is likely to wear out (based on "hard" science, thermodynamics and other principles).

Later, we will present a section on immortality — what it is and how to obtain it while living in a physical body. This is not some airy-fairy, pie-in-the-sky fanciful thinking. We will examine the real science of what is required to stop the aging process and stay in a state of perfect health for as long as you choose to remain on this planet.

It is not easy to attain the goals of this book. If it were easy, there would be no need for this book at all. Perhaps you have figured out by now that most of the things worth having in life are not readily attainable without effort. They might already be yours as gifts given by God, but you still must awaken to your talents and abilities and put them to use. This is why we have included a psychology section wherein we detail what is necessary regarding inner work. After all, it's not just about fabricating some machines and getting them out to the world. That's certainly part of it, but as the saying goes, "You must first seek the Kingdom of Heaven within and then all things shall be added unto thee." We seek in this material to demonstrate the truth of the above Biblical scripture.

Now that we have discussed some myths about energy, let's get into dispelling the myths through the science of unlimited energy.

PART 1
THE SCIENCE SECTION

CHAPTER 1

An Energy Primer

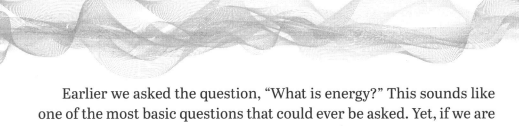

Earlier we asked the question, "What is energy?" This sounds like one of the most basic questions that could ever be asked. Yet, if we are to understand and utilize energy in ways that are far more enlightened than most of those currently being practiced on Earth, we must go back to basics. In fact, we must question the basic assumptions of virtually every field of study, including science, spirituality, metaphysics, psychology and philosophy.

Science has some very strict definitions of energy involving work, force, mass, acceleration, torque, momentum, voltage, current and such. In its simplest technical definition, energy consists of a potential to do work ("potential energy") and actual work (motion or "kinetic energy"). If a human being is resting (regenerating), they are storing up energy (potential). Then, when they awake and begin moving around, they are expressing their stored-up energy (kinetic). The word "kinetic" essentially means movement, action or work performed.

Using extremely simple mathematics, we could say that the total energy in a system (such as the physical body) is the sum of both potential and kinetic energy. The Law of Conservation of Energy states that the total potential and kinetic energy within a closed system remains constant.

Let's over-simplify. A very tired human being lies down in bed to go to sleep. This soul has expended a lot of kinetic energy (worked hard all day) and has very little energy stored up (potential). After a good night's sleep, the soul awakes full of energy and ready to start the new day. Now he (or she) has done very little work (has low kinetic energy) but has been storing up energy all night (has a high potential energy).

We can arbitrarily assign values to the potential and kinetic energy in a system (the physical body in this case). For example, at night this human being has a potential energy of 20 and a kinetic energy (work expended) of 80. Upon awaking, he has a potential energy of 80 and a kinetic energy of 20. The kinetic energy will not be zero, as it does require some energy to stay alive while sleeping. The heart is still beating, the respiratory system is still functioning, etc., which are forms of kinetic energy.

This brings us to an important question: Why do human beings grow old and die? Or, to be more technical, how does the Second Law of Thermodynamics (entropy) affect the well-being of people? This law essentially states that energy within a closed system tends to become more disorderly or chaotic over time. Scientists have observed that the universe seems to eventually "run down," which means all its highly ordered forms of energy eventually degrade into chaotic forms. But chaos still involves energy. Only the form has changed.

We will discover together that entropy is only part of the equation. There is another law that counteracts and counterbalances the law of entropy. The universe "blinks" on and off once each Planck second. Scientists are measuring the effects of the "blinking on" phase of the universe (defined as the movement from the etheric to the physical planes). They have failed to measure the "blinking off" phase, where the universe moves from the physical to the etheric planes. Tapping the energy of the universe during this "centropic" phase yields quantum coherence, or Zero-Point Energy, which reorders and revitalizes the field of entropic disorder. This is because the supposedly closed system of the physical universe is being regenerated by the "open" system of the etheric planes. In reality, each lower level or dimension is an open system because it is being fed by energy from the higher dimensions.

In other words, entropy is the result of going from the etheric to the physical state, and centropy is the result of going from the physical to the etheric state. Each state "flips" once every Planck second (about 10 to 44 seconds).

What about aging and death? If the Law of Conservation of Energy is the most basic, unalterable law in the universe (which it appears to be), then what happens to the energy of a human being when the body ceases to function? Has all the kinetic energy been "consumed" through years of work (physical activity)? At the time of death, is the (arbitrary) measurement the following:

Potential Energy = 0 and Kinetic Energy = 100?

A related question might be: When the body grows cold, where does the heat (the byproduct of entropy) go? Does it all dissipate into the air, or does some of it leave with the soul? Eventually it will be possible to measure the total energy within the human body and to document how much leaves with the soul and how much is dissipated into the surroundings when the physical body dies. No matter how much energy is dissipated into the surroundings (entropy), the total amount of energy will be constant. During physical death, you could say that some of the energy goes back into the etheric state. If you could measure that energy, the equations of conservation would be satisfied.

Here is a problem for scientists: If all the available potential energy in a system has been converted into kinetic energy, does the energy remain in that state forever? Will the universe eventually have no stored energy because all potential has been converted to kinetic and that kinetic energy has been "used up?" Is there a way to convert kinetic energy back into potential energy? Is it really a one-way path? We have begun to answer this question above by indicating that energy moves in a two-way pattern — from physical to etheric and from etheric to physical.

(Note: Mechanical generators appear to convert kinetic energy to potential energy but none of them are 100% efficient, so entropy is still increasing in conventional generators. Later, we will explore the idea of "over-unity," which means generating more energy than is being consumed — only possible in an open system.)

As scientists learn how to measure the movement of the "blinking off" phase of the universe, they will see that the Second Law of Thermodynamics has a counterpart that moves from disorder into a greater order. We are calling this "quantum coherence," or "centropy."

This relates to another age-old question: "Is time a one-way arrow, or can it be reversed?" It seems not only is energy a two-way street, but time is as well. In the laboratory it appears the arrow of time has been successfully reversed (in subatomic particles for extremely tiny time increments). Could not the arrow of energy (entropy) also be reversed? According to this book and the work of some inventors, there has been demonstrated "negative entropy," "negentropy" or "centropy," which are different names for the opposite of entropy. Arranging and rearranging circuitry has enabled researchers and inventors to tap the Zero-Point field (the point where the universe is moving from the physical to the etheric state). It is strongly suggested you do as much research as you can into the idea of quantum coherence.

Reversing the order of energy conversion in no way violates the Law of Conservation of Energy. After all, a + b = b + a. As long as the basic equivalency is maintained, it matters not whether time and energy move forward or backward. In our world, time seems to go from past to present to future, while energy seems to go from more ordered to less ordered. If it is possible to send a particle back in time (as demonstrated on a limited scale), wouldn't that particle experience negative entropy (if the Second Law of Thermodynamics is always valid)?

A few of you engineers and physicists are squirming in your seats as you read this, but where is the proof that energy must flow from potential to kinetic? As you will see, tapping the energy of the "blinking off" phase of the universe preserves the perfect equilibrium of the Law of Conservation.

Summarizing, the universe goes into and out of "existence" once every Planck second. Mathematically we can depict this very simply: During the "blinking on" phase, universal energy moves from potential to kinetic, and during the "blinking off" phase, universal energy moves from kinetic to potential. (P —> K = K —> P)

Another potential problem exists in the concept of "singularities."

What happens to energy in black holes? It appears more energy is being "sucked in" to the singularity than is being emitted as gamma radiation near the event horizon of the black hole. If this is the case (and it certainly appears to be), then where is the energy going? Shortly, we will introduce the topic of our "sister" universe that mirrors our own and has opposite polarities.

Singularities seem to have infinite mass and zero space. How is this possible? Einstein's famous equation $E = mc^2$ implies that there is infinite energy in the singularity of a black hole. This would imply infinite potential energy and zero kinetic energy since no work can be performed if there is no space. Would not this infinite supply of potential energy then be available to be converted into kinetic energy at some future time?

The above seems to indicate that the "Big Bang" involved the partial conversion of this infinite potential energy into kinetic energy (expanding forever if the supply of potential energy in the singularity is truly infinite). It's actually more complicated than this, because there is evidence that at some point in the future, there may come a "Big Crunch." This is based on gravitational observations and applications of Einstein's General Theory of Relativity.

What happened before the Big Bang? There was a tremendous amount of potential energy represented largely by these etheric components. Because it appears there was infinite mass, no volume and no temperature (zero degrees Kelvin) before the Big Bang, scientists cannot fathom how the universe suddenly seemed to appear out of nowhere. But if there was a tremendous amount of energy stored as consciousness, dark matter, dark energy and Zero-Point fluctuations, then it makes sense that something could trigger conversion from potential to kinetic energy (resulting in the movement and evolution of the universe).

In other words, these more subtle (and tremendously significant) sources of energy were already in existence before the Big Bang, thereby validating the Law of Conservation of Energy.

∞ Our Universe Has a Twin Flame

We are going to put forth a theory here that the problem of black holes and singularities is solved by the existence of a sister universe that is a mirror opposite of our universe. While our universe is mostly electrons with a few positrons, this mirror universe would be mostly positrons with a few electrons. The black hole at the center of our universe would be a white hole at the center of our sister universe. The white hole would be mostly emitting energy (kinetic) and only absorbing a tiny fraction (potential). This is the opposite of a black hole. The binary universe concept is consistent with the duality model of observable phenomena. In other words, nearly everything exists as a duality within time and space (positive and negative charges, light and dark, expansion and contraction, etc.). Hence, a mirrored opposite sister universe explains where the energy goes that seems to disappear into a black hole.

As stated above, our universe has a "sister" universe of opposite polarity. The two universes are connected through a black hole/white hole combination. The phenomenon connecting the black and white holes is known as a wormhole. The major energy systems of each universe are balanced. In addition to the electrons and positrons balancing out in each universe, matter and anti-matter are balanced as well, meaning that if our universe is mostly matter with very little anti-matter, our sister universe is the other way around.

In essence there is no such thing as "anti-matter," but if we use this term and include the subtle components of energy detailed above, we will see that there are equal quantities of matter and anti-matter existing in our universe and our mirror-opposite (sister) universe. Therefore, the largest closed system energy model available to us would be that of our universe and our sister universe connected by a black hole/white hole combination. If you add up all the potential and kinetic energy on both sides of the equation (including all the components listed above), you will observe complete balance. Another way of saying this is that if you add and subtract all energy sources in both universes, the net result will be zero, thus preserving the Law of Conservation of Energy.

Note: The easiest way out of the matter/anti-matter conundrum is to simply think of matter as being polarized into two forms, positive and negative. You can assign the positive charge to regular matter and the negative charge to anti-matter or vice versa.

We apologize for not being more accurate with our technical

definitions and explanations of natural phenomena, but this is not a scientific abstract. We are only delving into science temporarily in order to explain how we live in a sea of nearly infinite energy and how the only real question is how to tap into (harness) that energy. Never again should any serious student of spirituality, metaphysics, or physics ever take as credulous the dire warnings from so-called "experts" that we are running out of usable energy on our planet.

Another Note: You have by now realized that we keep repeating ourselves using slightly different explanations and terms for the same concepts. This is intentional (no, it's not bad editing) because most of the ideas in this book involve leading-edge physics and metaphysics. Therefore, a lot of readers will be confused at first and need to view the ideas from several different angles in order to fully comprehend the path we are on.

∞ Energy Is Unlimited in Higher Dimensions

The reason reverse entropy can and has been detected is because there is an infinite field of energy existing in what can be rightfully called the "higher dimensions." If you are scientifically oriented, you might recall the story of the "Flatlanders," a society existing on a two-dimensional plane. When three-dimensional objects interacted with their world, they could see the evidence, but they were unable to perceive the actual objects. For example, a car might leave tire tracks on their reality. After much research, the Flatlanders concluded that something existing outside of their domain made the tracks, but unless and until they managed to develop instruments capable of measuring interactions beyond the second dimension, they would likely resort to various conjectures and imaginings as to the nature of the third dimension.

There is a dimension beyond the four we know (line, plane, depth and time) that exerts influence upon our perceived universe. We see evidence in the Nonlocality Principle of quantum physics. To review basic quantum mechanics, the Nonlocality Principle (directly related to the idea of Entanglement) suggests that everything is connected no matter how far apart individual elements of everything appear to be.

If particles that have been separated by great distances can register changes in each other simultaneously, this implies they are not really separated. In fact, they are connected through a higher dimension that permeates all time and space. This higher dimension connects everyone and everything that seems to reside in the lower four dimensions. It shows that we are truly One Being expressing as billions of life forms.

It is difficult to use an analogy, but let us try. Suppose your human life is like a leaf on a tree. All you can see and feel is the leaf. You know it is connected to something, but you have no idea what that is. Nutrients are "fed" to you through the stems and branches of the tree, so you know there is a "source" of seemingly unlimited sustenance just outside your level of perception. Only if it becomes possible to somehow journey along the stems and branches can you discover the vast network of roots reaching deep into the Earth. At that point, you realize that the tree is sustained by the Earth, which in turn is sustained by the sun, etc.

Of course, we could also use the tree analogy when discussing the idea of reincarnation. Think of each leaf on a deciduous tree (one that drops its leaves in the fall) as a human incarnation. The tree represents the Creator and the individual branch (twig) that holds your leaf is the soul. Every season the twig generates a new leaf (incarnation).

Because we have not learned how to measure the soul or the dimensions from which it arises, we have religions and all sorts of philosophical ideas and scientific theories. This book, even though it contains some hard, verifiable science, relies heavily on information received from the higher dimensions through what is commonly called "telepathic transmission" or "conscious channeling." Many of the more "outrageous" ideas presented herein will eventually be proven using laboratory methods and logical reasoning. Some already have, but the results have been suppressed.

However, the purpose of this material is not to argue the validity of the points being made herein, but rather to direct the attention of scientists, inventors and engineers in such a way that the unlimited energy of the universe can be brought into tangible applications and manifestations on the Earth. Let us now consider how to access this vast source of energy which we are calling Zero Point.

CHAPTER 2

Practical Ways to Tap the Zero-Point Field

∞ How Do We Obtain Energy from the Vacuum of Space (Quantum Fluctuations Known as Zero-Point Energy)?

Scientists disagree regarding how much available energy there is in the vacuum of space. We are referring to the quantum fluctuations that occur at absolute zero temperature (Zero-Point Energy or ZPE). Those who subscribe to the macro point of view (Einstein's relativity and Newtonian mechanics) are fairly certain that the density of the vacuum is so low (approximately 10^{-27} joules per cm³) that any attempts to extract this energy in usable quantities is futile. Yet quantum physicists, using Planck wavelengths and observable oscillations in the quantum field (the micro level), have calculated the density of the vacuum to be around 10^{93} joules per cm³.

This is a huge discrepancy and underscores the need to adopt a series of Unified Field equations that can be used across all of science. In fact, this is the biggest project in physics. Several scientists have presented convincing theories that resolve the differences between the micro and macro views, but they are mostly considered "fringe" researchers. One of these scientists is Nassim Haramein. We have featured his theories in various places throughout this book.

Below, we are taking the liberty of combining the micro and macro calculations, assuming both measurements to be roughly accurate, in an attempt to demonstrate mathematically that, despite the differences between micro and macro, one thing can be made certain: *There is a nearly infinite amount of energy in the vacuum of space that, if extracted and harnessed effectively, would solve all of the world's energy problems forever.*

∞ The Over-Simplified Calculation of the Amount of Energy in the Vacuum of Space and Its Correspondence to the Observable Energy of the Universe

The quantum fluctuations in the vacuum of space have been calculated to be on the order of 10^{93} joules per cm^3. The energy density of the vacuum of space outside the atomic structure has been calculated at around 10^{-27} joules per cm^3. The net available energy, therefore, disregarding all external influences on a given cm^3 (cubic centimeter) of vacuum, would be $10^{93}/10^{27}$ (ten to the 93rd power divided by ten to the minus 27th power) or about 10^{66} joules per cm^3. This is more than the totality of all potential and kinetic energy in the known universe that can be observed within the four major and minor forces of Newtonian mechanics.

What does this mean? Essentially, it states that the potential energy in just one cubic centimeter of the vacuum of space contains more energy than all physical structures in the known universe. This explains how the Big Bang could happen and still preserve the Law of Conservation of Energy. It also explains how black holes and their corresponding singularities can exist in the fabric of time/space. Put another way, there is more than enough potential energy in the vacuum of space to convert it into kinetic energy in the form of Big Bangs, black holes and singularities.

Scientists are discovering that the universe is filled with mini-black holes, each containing a singularity. Not only is the macro universe blinking on and off continuously (about one cycle every 100 billion years), but each subatomic particle is doing likewise (one cycle every 10^{-44} seconds). The mini-black holes in the subatomic realms are behaving similarly to the massive black holes at the center of galaxies.

There is a relationship between the energy available in the vacuum of space, and the concepts of dark energy and dark matter. There is also a correlation between dark energy/matter and the aether. Finally, there is a direct connection between what we are calling the "etheric planes," the existence of dark energy/matter and the available energy in the vacuum of space.

Although it could be argued that there are additional constants and variables needed to exactly correlate dark energy, dark matter and the aether, for our purposes we will over-simplify and consider the aether to be the same as dark matter and dark energy. For our simplistic mathematics, this will suffice, and we will still be quite accurate in our descriptions.

One of the purposes of this book is to build a bridge between the metaphysical and physical realms. This is the ultimate key to resolving the Unified Field Theory. The missing ingredient in all these endeavors is consciousness. The power and energy of consciousness originates outside the realms of time/space, but it precipitates down into the planes of time/space. This is evidenced by the emergence of physical reality from the highly energetic etheric reality, as described above.

∞ Consciousness — The Missing Ingredient in the Unified Field Theory

In an earlier book, we looked at the idea that consciousness can be expressed in energy units. We called them "consciousness units" (CU). Although the brain emits electricity, we cannot accurately say that the energy of consciousness can be expressed as discrete packets or quanta, nor can this energy be calculated using common parameters such as joules, watts, microvolts, etc.

There is a quantifiable unit for consciousness, however, and it is directly proportionate to the level of awareness of an entity. In other words, a soul with a consciousness vibration of 6.0 on the author's density calibration scale would have a greater consciousness quotient than a soul with a vibration of 3.0. Although the exact calculations are not available, in our examples given herein, we use a logarithmic scale when evaluating the potential energy of consciousness.

Since the mathematics of consciousness cannot be accurately determined at this time, we can state a few broad equations using a common variable, which we will call CU for now. We can arbitrarily assign a power of ten (simple logarithmic formula) to the CU of a given soul. For example, a soul with vibration 3.0 would have a CU of one, a soul with vibration 4.0 would have a CU of ten, a 5.0 vibration would have a CU of one hundred, and a soul with 6.0 vibration a CU of one thousand, etc. Using a simple logarithmic equation, you can calculate the CU for any soul with a vibration between these limits.

(In this author's system, a soul's consciousness vibration can reach as high as 12.0. Such a soul in this simple arbitrary example would have one billion times as much power as a soul with a level 3 vibration.)

Since we have no way of measuring the magnitude of consciousness with present equipment, this convention serves only to give you an idea of how consciousness contributes to the overall energy of a system. Assuming the Law of Conservation of Energy is the most basic law of the universe, we must factor in CU when balancing energy equations. The simplest way to express this is as follows: The potential energy of a closed system at time A plus the kinetic energy of the system at time A equals the potential energy of the system at time B plus the kinetic energy of the system at time B. $(PT_A + KT_A = PT_B + KT_B)$

Contained within the overall potential and kinetic energy is the level of consciousness, or amount of consciousness units (CU). Therefore, we can state the equation above like this:

$$CU_1(PT_A + KT_A) = CU_2(PT_B + KT_B)$$

Since not all readers are mathematically inclined, let us say the above equation in plain English. The energy present during the current vibrational state of consciousness times the potential and kinetic energy of the closed system at the present time, equals the future vibrational state of consciousness times the potential and kinetic energy at a given point in time. It makes no difference how great the difference is between Time A and Time B. If Time B is far in the future, the value of CU might be far greater than at present, which implies that other sources of energy (besides consciousness) would not need to be as high in order to balance the equation.

This has enormous implications. At lower levels of consciousness (smaller CU values), souls are much more dependent on "outer" factors regarding energy (such as extracting it from the environment). At higher levels of consciousness, there is less need for external sources of energy. This explains why some yogis seem to violate the laws of physics (through levitation, for example). No laws are being violated in this case, but the value of CU in the yogi is much higher than in an average human being and so the force inherent in consciousness is sufficient to overcome the force of gravity (in levitation).

Consciousness units are not the only factor to consider when tapping into the field of nearly unlimited energy. Below is a list of other factors to consider when calculating fluctuations in potential and kinetic energy.

∞ The Components of Energy

What are the components that make up energy? The incomplete list is as follows:

1. Consciousness
2. Singularities/Black Holes
3. Singularities/White Holes
4. Wormholes
5. Dark Energy (a form of aether)
6. Dark Matter (another form of aether)
7. Zero-Point Energy (vacuum fluctuations at zero degrees Kelvin)
8. Energy of subatomic particles and waves (photons, muons, quarks, neutrinos, etc.)
9. Electrons and positrons
10. Atomic nuclei (strong and weak nuclear forces)
11. Other aspects of strong and weak nuclear forces not confined to nuclei
12. Other aspects of electromagnetism (radionics, Radiant Energy)
13. Gravity
14. Laws of vibration, or "strings" (superstring theory)
15. Normal matter, as $E=mc^2$ equivalents
16. Laws of force, motion, mass, thermodynamics, etc.

Obviously, these components are inter-related and, with the exception of consciousness, are easily convertible from one form to another, such as the relationship between energy and matter (as a function of the velocity of light squared).

To sum up this extremely basic physics lesson, in any exchange of energy observed in the universe, you simply plug in the components to the equation $PT_A + KT_A = PT_B + KT_B$, where A is the total energy at one point in time, and B is the total energy at another point in time. The total potential and kinetic energy at point A in time *must* be equivalent to the total potential and kinetic energy at point B in time.

So-called "over-unity" devices might appear to involve perpetual motion, but of course the reason such devices seem to violate the laws of physics is because not all the components listed above are considered when calculating the energy conservation of such a system. In this case, the "over-unity" result comes from what is thought to be a closed system, but which is, in fact, an open system due to the influence of the aether.

In spirituality and metaphysics, there is a dimension called the "etheric plane." This level of reality contains a very high amount of energy (nearly infinite depending on how it is measured). The energy is a function of the first few components listed above, which are either impossible to measure using today's instrumentation or have simply not been factored into the calculations. As you know, most scientists refuse to acknowledge the existence of the aether. Therefore, we can substitute consciousness units, along with dark energy, dark matter and Zero-Point Energy in place of "etheric" energy.

∞ Nearly Infinite or Truly Infinite?

Before we continue our explanation for the differences between the macro and micro calculations of Zero-Point Energy, let us attempt to illustrate the difference between the nearly infinite and truly infinite aspects of our universe.

Part of the measurement problem involves what is called "Planck units." This is thought to be the smallest possible measurement in the subatomic world, but is it really? The observable quanta (discrete energy packets) may appear to have this "lower" limit imposed by the fabric of space itself, but since there are many aspects of the universe we are not yet able to measure accurately (such as consciousness, dark energy and dark matter), it is certainly possible that there are other limits (or lack thereof) besides Planck's constant. While dark energy and dark matter appear to account for about 96% of all the energy in the universe, consciousness itself seems to be omnipresent, meaning it exists in 100% of the fabric of space/time.

Perhaps we should think of consciousness as another dimension, similar to the way we think of time. If time is the fourth dimension, perhaps consciousness can be thought of as the fifth dimension.

However, this author has a more comprehensive system of densities and dimensions and, in his models, consciousness permeates all the levels simultaneously. If consciousness is omnipresent, perhaps it is not constrained by Planck's constant or any other limit to measurement. After all, from a theoretical point of view, space is infinite. No matter how small a particle or wave might appear to be, you can conceive of the space between such particles and waves. The infinite space between any two points is best illustrated using asymptotes.

To use the idea of asymptotes, imagine an American football game. In American football, there is a peculiar rule that states, "When the offensive team is near the goal line and the defensive team commits a foul, the penalty imposed is half the distance to the goal line." Normally, the defensive team will not commit more than three or four fouls (at most) during this situation, and probably only one or two. Yet what if the defensive team committed thousands of fouls? At first, the football would be moved several inches closer to the goal line, but eventually, the referees would need to get out their magnifiers or microscopes and start measuring in millimeters, or even micrometers. In this case, the sheer size of the football acts as a "Planck's constant," because the football's forward progress cannot be readily adjusted once you get down into micrometers.

Yet, in theory, the defensive team could commit fouls from now until the third millennium and the offense still would not score a touchdown.

Infinity, properly defined in mathematics, states that no matter how large or small a number becomes, you can always add to (or subtract from) that number. It is certainly possible that one might measure an amount of space so small that no significant change of energy will occur. Nevertheless, even the most conservative estimate of the energy in the vacuum of space (10^{36} joules) is still, for all practical purposes, a nearly infinite amount.

It is not necessary to have a truly infinite level of energy in the universe in order for humanity to have a comfortable, high-standard lifestyle for the foreseeable future. Just harnessing a tiny fraction of the available energy, such as 10^{20} joules, would mean nearly unlimited travel, clean industry and modern luxuries for millions of years.

Let us now explain the difference between the micro and macro levels of energy.

CHAPTER 3

The Radiant
Energy Field

∞ An Explanation of the Differences Between
the Micro and Macro Models

We will now go into more detail on the energy calculations. We are going to give out a few numbers below. The conventional macro view of Zero-Point Energy (based on the laws of gravitation and electromagnetics) states that there are approximately 10^{-27} joules per cm^3 of energy in the vacuum of space. However, the micro (quantum) view states there is approximately 10^{93} joules per cm^3. If you factor in how many cubic centimeters of "empty" space there is in the observable universe, you will conclude that we live in a vast sea of energy. The contrasting numbers include about 10^{36} joules in the conventional macro version and 10^{156} joules in the quantum version, assuming an estimated 10^{63} cubic centimeters of space in the known universe.

Let us once again ask the question, "Why is there such a great discrepancy between the macro and micro version of total available energy?" The simplest explanation is that one or both of the accepted models of reality is flawed. Either there is far more or far less energy in the vacuum than has been calculated. Yet some scientists have pointed out an obvious thing apparent to even a kindergarten child: Big things are made up of small things. Therefore, it would make sense that the quantum model is the more accurate one.

If the quantum model is the accurate one, then how do you explain the much smaller macro version of energy in the vacuum? It's really very simple. In a few moments, we will introduce the idea of Radiant Energy. This is energy that "leaks" out from the interior of the atomic structure into the surrounding space between atoms. The measurements we get on the macro level represent the amount of energy radiating out from the atomic structures.

∞ More Detailed Calculations of the Energy Available in the Vacuum of Space

Before we adequately explain Radiant Energy, let us define a term. Planck density is officially described as the density of the universe at one Planck unit of time after the Big Bang. This number is approximately 5.1×10^{93} gm/cm³. Despite the fact that the universe has expanded considerably since one Planck unit of time elapsed (an understatement), the Law of Conservation of Energy states that only the ratio of potential to kinetic energy has changed (energy can neither be created nor destroyed). Therefore, the Planck density of the universe must still be around 5.1×10^{93} gm/cm³ (the total of all potential and kinetic energy at any point in time since the Big Bang).

The energy of the universe, in joules, of a given mass can be calculated using Einstein's equation $E=mc^2$. Therefore, E (joules) = $5.1 \times 10^{93} \times (10^{17}$ cm/s$)^2$ = 5.1×10^{127} joules/cm³. (Since a joule is defined as one Newton-meter per second, the meters and seconds cancel out.)

There are two types of vacuum energy. (1) the energy contained in the vacuum of empty space between atomic structures, as defined by Einstein's General Theory of Relativity; and (2) the quantum field fluctuations that exist within the atomic and subatomic structures of the microcosm (as calculated in quantum experiments). For the sake of simplicity, imagine all the atoms of the universe like floating bubbles in a sea of space. Not only is there space between each bubble, but the vast majority of what is inside each bubble is space.

The total Planck density must equal the sum of the densities of the macrocosm and microcosm. The best estimate we have of the density of the macrocosm is around 1×10^{-27} gm/cm³. Using $E=mc^2$, we see that the total energy of the macrocosm is (Joules = 1×10^{-27} gm/cm³ x (10^{17} cm/s)² which comes to around 1×10^7 joules/cm³. If we subtract this number from the Planck density, we see that over 99.99999% of all energy in the universe exists at the microcosmic level (as quantum-field fluctuations within the atomic structure).

The holy grail of physics involves how to bring together these two realms: the gravitational fields of the macrocosm and the electromagnetic fields of the microcosm (the quantum field). Below we have detailed a "bridge factor" between the two realms.

∞ Radiant Energy

We believe a key component to resolving the discrepancies between the microcosm and macrocosm lies in a phenomenon known as "Radiant Energy." This term was used by physicists in the 19th and early 20th centuries, including Nikola Tesla, who presented numerous demonstrations of this form of energy. Currently, the term "radiant energy" is used generically to describe the entropy (heat) inherent within electromagnetic systems (in other words, the energy radiating from a working electrical circuit). However, let us explore a specific constituent of this energy.

Here is our idea: What if the energy of the macrocosm (around 10^7 joules/cm³) is simply the result of energy "bleeding through" or leaking out from the atomic structures of the quantum field? This Radiant Energy, or "scalar electromagnetic energy" consists of "scalar waves" or longitudinal waves being produced within an electromagnetic system. Electromagnetism involves the potential difference between polarized fields, composed of electrons flowing in a circuit. Radiant Energy is composed of quantum fluctuations that have "bled-through" to the region of the vacuum that is between atomic structures. Since all atomic structures are part of the quantum field, Radiant Energy will be present regardless of the power (voltage and current) flowing through a circuit. Nevertheless, if one is to capture this Radiant Energy and put it to use, it will typically be through some form of electrical circuit.

Remember that Radiant Energy is inherent to the quantum field, not a by-product of polarized systems. It may be magnified and directed in a useful way through a polarized circuit, however. Radiant Energy is properly categorized as a side-effect of Zero-Point Energy, another name for quantum fluctuations occurring at zero degrees Kelvin.

Radiant Energy increases as the EM field becomes polarized (heated). Heat, which is the measurement of the movement of sub-atomic particles, while entropic in nature (more chaotic than ordered in electromagnetic fields), nevertheless magnifies Radiant Energy and increases the overall output (work) of a system. Obvious examples include the ability of heat to boil water, turning it to steam to drive turbines.

Here is the proper depiction of Radiant Energy:

Quantum fluctuations within the atomic structure → Radiant Energy → Quantum fluctuations outside the atomic structure.

This starts as 5.1×10^{127} joules/cm³ total energy available minus Radiant Energy of about 10^7 joules/cm³ reaching outside the atomic structure. This outside radiation can be tapped directly with electrical circuits (and has been done so successfully by many inventors). As you can see, ten million joules per cubic centimeter is a significant amount of energy and that's just background levels. It does not include whatever is tapped from within the atomic structure.

We will return to the subject of Radiant Energy a bit later, but for now, let's go back to refining the definitions of the terms we have already introduced.

∞ More on Aether, Dark Energy and Dark Matter

Let's talk once again about the multidimensional nature of the universe. Going back to the example of the "Flatlanders," a mythical race of beings that live in only two dimensions, you will note that the Flatlanders cannot see or experience directly anything taking place in the third dimension; they can only see the effects of the third dimension on their two-dimensional world. For example, a three-dimensional car would leave two-dimensional tire tracks on their flat surfaces.

Scientists cannot see dark matter and dark energy directly. They only postulate the existence of these realms because of the effects they have on that which can be observed or measured.

Another example of indirect observation would be determining the size and location of exoplanets (planets revolving around other star systems). Telescopes are not yet powerful enough to directly observe exoplanets, but we know they exist by the effect they have on the light emanating from their stars.

In this author's earlier books, he describes the fifth dimension as the etheric realm, so we could say that the aether originates in this dimension, and we observe its effects in quantum fluctuations. Earlier we equated dark matter and dark energy with the etheric realm, but this is not entirely correct.

This is because, according to guidance received by this author, there are 12 dimensions in our universe. Let us define dark matter and dark energy as the cumulative (total and composite) effects of these higher dimensions on the lower ones we can measure. So, in other words, dimensions 6 through 12 are also exerting an influence on the measurements attributed to dark matter and dark energy.

We will now more accurately define dark matter and dark energy as the influences of the etheric realm and higher dimensions on the lower four dimensions of the universe. This includes, of course, quantum fluctuations (Zero-Point Energy). It is still permissible to equate Zero-Point Energy with the aether as well as dark energy and dark matter, but the most accurate way of stating this is to say that the quantum fluctuations are the "evidence" of the existence of the etheric and higher realms. (We could debate how much of the 96% belongs to the etheric planes and how much belongs to the dimensions above the etheric planes, but that is beyond the scope of this book.)

We saw earlier that the total available energy in the vacuum of space is approximately 5.1×10^{127} joules/cm^3. If 96% of the universe consists of dark matter and dark energy, then the energy originating from the higher dimensions accounts for about 4.9×10^{127} joules/cm^3. The remaining energy (about 2.0×10^{126} joules/cm^3) consists of observable Zero-Point fluctuations, Radiant Energy and the total energy of the manifest universe occurring in its varying forms. Of course, 2.0×10^{126} is still an incredible amount of energy (more than humans will ever need in a million lifetimes). This number (4% of the total available energy in the universe) represents the observable Zero-Point Energy and other measurable energy sources available within and outside the atomic structure. The smaller number, 10^7 joules/cm^3, represents the portion that radiates out from atomic structure into the surrounding vacuum.

To summarize, we are proposing that the energy of the quantum field is the total of the aether and emanations from higher dimensions (dark matter plus dark energy), about 4% of which percolates down into the lower dimensions as observable quantum fluctuations and existing energy structures. This includes the Radiant Energy consisting of the 10^7 joules/cm^3 ambient amount outside the atomic field that is the result of etheric (and higher dimensional) energy "bleeding through" from the microcosm into the macrocosm.

CHAPTER 4

The Electromagnetic Null Zone

The following chapters of the science section are directed toward inventors and electrical engineers who are seeking to build electrical circuits capable of tapping Zero-Point Energy. It is not practical to attempt to tap the ZPE field directly since it exists at zero degrees Kelvin. However, as you will see below, there is a way to tap the energy at normal temperatures.

∞ Principles of the Electromagnetic Null Zone

Closely related to the idea of Zero-Point Energy (quantum fluctuations in the vacuum of space at zero degrees Kelvin), is the idea of the EM null zone. The null zone refers to that region of space where the positive and negative polarities effectively cancel each other out, or where there is no polarity. The null zone exists where the positive and negative poles of a magnetic system are arranged in such a way that the electrons enter a stasis or null state (a state of zero polarity).

Imagine you are an electron being pulled (or pushed) to the positive pole. But what if the negative or positive poles in a complex system are pulling you in opposing directions at once, effectively canceling each other out?

In a null zone, a resonant field is created, also known as a scalar field. There is energy, but it is not polarized. This resonant scalar field has properties similar to that of a tunnel diode. In this case, the resonant field acts like a superconductor, with ultra-low resistance between the electrons, thereby causing energy from the etheric realms (dark energy and dark matter) to flow unimpeded through such a configuration of electrons. This resonant field contains a lot of energy. The electrons essentially enter a super-excited state, charged with this scalar EM energy. The energy can then be tapped through the right combination of coils and magnets. When super-excited electrons begin flowing in a coherent manner, a lot of current is produced.

An overly simplified explanation of a superconductor circuit involves Ohm's Law. As resistance approaches zero, the current in a system will approach infinity (at constant voltage). Potential energy (voltage) is supplied by a simple battery to get the system started, and then the quantum fluctuations (Zero-Point Energy) that are always present throughout any closed system, are captured in the form of Radiant Energy, which then feeds back into the circuit, essentially replacing the battery. Assuming, for the moment, that this potential energy has a nearly constant value, the energy of scalar-catalyzed electrons (current) will increase dramatically.

In a properly designed circuit, you do not need high voltage to obtain large amounts of kinetic energy. If the resistance drops to micro-ohms due to a superconducting resonant field, you will produce mega-amps at low voltage. This can be accomplished by placing components along with precision magnets and coils in a configuration that "captures" the quantum fluctuations. Engineers are learning to build circuitry that creates superconductivity by rotating and/or placing still magnets in the proper configuration. There are examples of rotating and still magnets in the Appendix (such as Bearden's motionless electromagnetic generator [MEG]).

∞ Mechanical and Engineering Issues

Various devices have been created and demonstrated over the years, effectively proving that over-unity is possible. The mathematics are rather rigorous because we are dealing with multiple components of energy all interacting throughout a closed system. First, we have the Zero-Point Energy (quantum fluctuations), then the etheric tunneling effect caused by the electromagnetic null zone.

Proper positioning of magnets and coils "concentrates" the energy, which can then be put through a feedback loop in a normal electrical circuit.

As stated above, such a device is started with a simple DC battery. Electrons then "pile up" at designated spots, become "excited" and then are fed back into the circuit. Although this appears to be perpetual motion, in reality, the energy is simply being converted from Zero-Point (etheric) sources into usable physical forms, measured as wattage or joules. Based on the rather large reservoir of potential energy in the vacuum (etheric) levels of the universe, the conversion into kinetic energy will involve a relatively small amount of the etheric reservoir, and so even millions of years of use will not significantly upset the balance of the etheric realms.

In other words, the energy extracted from the vacuum and the dark energy/matter matrix will lower the overall reservoir of available energy by an insignificant amount. Even powering the entire Earth for a million years will only use a tiny fraction of this potential energy. Taking into account the effects of the Second Law of Thermodynamics, it would take billions of years for such a system to "run down" appreciably. In actuality, the dimensions beyond the etheric plane maintain an infinite, timeless, eternal field of intelligence that replenishes any energy siphoned off through electrical circuits. Recall the mathematics of infinity: An infinite amount of something minus a finite amount of it still equals infinity.

Why is negentropy (centropy) not acknowledged by mainstream scientists? Because it is extremely difficult to measure. The Zero-Point field has a natural re-ordering quality, or what engineers and scientists call quantum coherence. A few inventors have coined the term "negative resistance" to deal with this re-ordering tendency of Zero-Point systems. A simple but not entirely accurate analogy would be that of cooling water down until it freezes. Steam is highly chaotic, while liquid water is somewhat more stable. But ice has a nice, neat, orderly arrangement of molecules.

It seems to take a lot of energy to lower the temperature of something to near absolute zero, which offers a convincing argument in favor of entropy. Yet the Bose-Einstein Condensate (the static state of the universe at absolute zero) is omnipresent and contains the nearly infinite Zero-Point Energy. The movement of the condensate toward positive temperatures is entropy, and the natural re-balancing of the condensate is negentropy (or centropy). How is the condensate re-balanced? Through interaction with the etheric realms (dark energy and dark matter).

In the higher dimensions of the universe, negentropy (centropy) is the dominant force, while in the lower dimensions, entropy is dominant. Although this will eventually be proven, for now we must take it on faith, based on the observations and teachings of many higher-dimensional beings who have learned how to harness the Zero-Point/etheric fields.

Although the above dissertation goes into a fair amount of complexity and leaves out a lot of electrical-engineering concepts, it is the best we can do for now. Suffice to say that the Zero-Point/etheric fields (dark energy and dark matter representing about 96% of the energy in the universe) are constantly impinging upon the so-called finite energy systems of this world.

∞ Recycling Energy Dissipated as Heat

According to the inventors referenced in the Appendix, and based on their abstracts, in particular two physicists/engineers named Poynting and Heaviside, today's electrical engineers have ignored the vast amount of energy dissipated in electrical circuits, erroneously assuming this energy to be insignificant or too difficult to harness. Yet this dissipation is part of the Radiant Energy that explains the background levels of vacuum flux occurring between atoms in space.

The abstracts of the physicists, inventors and engineers are, as you would imagine, rather technical, so we have included a couple of links in the Appendix, realizing that most of our readers are not electrical engineers or physicists. For those of you who are theoretical physicists, we are sure you will find some inaccuracies and omissions in this dissertation, and we apologize for that. The author is not an expert in the field of quantum mechanics and receives most of his information from "higher-dimensional beings," so his attempt to explain higher principles in ordinary human terminology is tentative at best.

∞ Summarization of the Theoretical Physics Discussed in this Section

Let us now summarize what we have discussed so far:

1. Matter is neither created nor destroyed — it only changes forms.

2. There exists a tremendous reservoir of potential energy in the vacuum of space (supplied by the etheric dimension).

3. The amount of available energy seems to depend on which method of calculation is used, micro or macro.

4. The discrepancies can be resolved between the micro and macro states of the universe by postulating the existence of Radiant Energy.

5. It is possible to create electrical circuits that tap into the nearly limitless energy of the vacuum.

6. EM Null zones are areas of space where electrons are non-polarized and form resonant fields at normal temperatures.

7. Non-polarized fields are called scalar energy.

8. Resonant fields have extremely low resistance, making them superconductors.

9. Tapping the energy of a superconductor generates high current at constant voltage.

10. Proper placement of magnets and coils results in a fully functional over-unity device without violating the Law of Conservation of Energy.

CHAPTER 5

Another Look at Zero-Point Energy

Although we have introduced the idea of Zero-Point Energy in the preceding chapters, we are going to summarize once again how this type of energy really works. Allow us to also present some additional perspectives on the dynamics of this technology.

∞ Quantum Fluctuations and Quantum Coherence

Quantum fluctuations hold the key to regeneration (negentropy, centropy, reverse entropy). Essentially, the fluctuations involve rapid appearance and disappearance of particle/wave energy quanta (formerly called virtual particles). The universe does not really disappear but rather oscillates between the physical and etheric states. Here is the profound part of this: When the quanta are emerging into our observable universe, they are forming an entropic field. On the macro scale, this correlates with the Big Bang as an entropic expansion of energy.

But what about the "blinking off" phase of the fluctuation — the point where the quanta seemingly disappear into the void? To preserve the Law of Conservation of Energy, the void state consists of an opposite process to that of entropy (technically from light to dark energy, or from kinetic to Zero-Point potential energy if you consider dark energy and Zero-Point to be roughly equivalent). If the energy is truly conserved, then the "blinking off" phase of the quantum fluctuations involves negentropy (centropy or reverse entropy), also known as quantum coherence. Mathematically, you would invert the entropic formula to calculate how much energy is being converted from kinetic energy into potential (dark energy). The universe therefore oscillates between entropic "blinking on" and negentropic "blinking off." The energy must go somewhere. It does not simply disappear into nothingness every time it blinks off. That would violate most every law of physics.

Just because we cannot see and easily measure the energy of the "blinked off" phase of the fluctuation does not mean there is no energy. In fact, energy is required to "blink on" again. Quantum fluctuations are, therefore, essentially perpetual motion machines. Energy is converted back and forth from light kinetic (measurable) to dark potential or Zero-Point (indirectly measurable). The problem scientists have with so-called perpetual-motion machines is that it appears energy is being created out of nothing, that this "phantom" energy is replenishing the dissipation caused by work or kinetic energy output. They believe the Law of Conservation of Energy is being violated because you are getting "something from nothing." But the "nothing" referenced here is the vast field of Zero-Point Energy in the form of dark energy and dark matter, also known as the aether.

What about the force necessary to "collapse" the quanta back into the aether, or Zero-Point state? Some scientists are calling this "negative work," the result of quantum coherence. To answer this question, we need to think of the aether as part of the initial state of the universe before the Big Bang brought physicality into existence. The energy was already there in the form of a singularity (no space and infinite mass). Infinite mass implies infinite energy, based on Einstein's formula $E=mc^2$, so the "beginning" state of the universe (before the Big Bang) consisted of no space/time and infinite energy. Therefore, you could say that a portion of this infinite energy returns to a more primordial state once every Planck second (during the "blinking off" phase of the micro universe) and once every 100 billion or so years (in the macro universe).

Another way to think of this is that during the "blinking off" phase, temperature is being converted from positive Kelvin to zero Kelvin, a direct "violation" of the Second Law of Thermodynamics. After all, doesn't all energy conversion result in heat dissipation? Isn't heat the end product of chaos theory? Admitting that the universe blinks on and off billions of times per second (changing state every Planck second) means that scientists will have to abandon the idea that the Second Law of Thermodynamics is the supreme law of the land.

The mathematics involved in calculating the total energy transfer of the universe between light and dark energy (or between entropy and negentropy) involves the use of Planck density and Einstein's famous equation, $E=mc^2$. We have calculated the total potential energy in the vacuum of space in previous chapters.

We differentiated between the energy of the vacuum held within the subatomic (quantum) field and the energy of the vacuum held outside atomic structures. This outside vacuum is the region of space that exists between the atoms of light and dark matter. It is a non-zero quantity because energy from within the subatomic structure radiates outward into the space between atoms. Although this non-zero field between atoms represents a much smaller quantity than within the atomic structure, such phenomena, known as Radiant Energy, is nevertheless enough to power devices far and wide. The net resultant kinetic energy due to Radiant Energy conversion is about 10^7 joules/cm^3. Having ten million joules of energy available in every cubic centimeter (about the size of a sugar cube), is more than enough to drive today's modern machinery.

Of course, this is background energy. Tapping the vacuum from within the subatomic structure would provide nearly unlimited energy. The technology to do this is not far in the future. In fact, prototypes are already in design. Nevertheless, tapping the Radiant Energy is far easier and does not require microscopic "surgery" and precision instruments.

∞ The Influence of the Etheric Realms on the Lower Worlds

Although we could write volumes about the celestial and God worlds (and this author has given a considerable amount of information about these realms in previous books), what we are most concerned with here (since this book is about energy) is the relationship between the subtle realms and the lower, or more physical realms.

Specifically, what we are calling the etheric realm, or 5th level of reality, corresponds to what early scientists referred to as the "aether."

There are several laboratory experiments that indicate the presence of an etheric field of immense energy. Whether the reference is to Zero-Point fluctuations in the vacuum of space, dark energy, dark matter, or residual energy in magnets, it is evident that this field of energy actually exists and permeates so-called ordinary matter.

One inventor, Bruce de Palma, invented a machine that appears to "capture" some of this etheric energy. (See the "N-machine" in the Appendix.) Another scientist, a Dr. Aspden, demonstrated that magnetic energy arises out of a "fluidic" substance. If you rotate a magnet once, then bring it to a stop and then rotate it again in the same direction within a short period of time, it takes far less energy to achieve the second rotation. How can this be? It makes sense only if the electromagnetic spectrum behaves as though it is part of a fluid — in this case the elusive "aether" that modern scientists thumb their noses at. The analogy of stirring a glass of water is used. If you swirl water with a straw, then stop for a moment and start stirring again in the same direction, the water is still in motion and requires less additional energy to swirl it again at the same rate.

Thinking of the aether as a fluid makes a lot of sense. So-called "empty" space is more like a vibrating, radiating liquid.

We are referred back to superstring theory, in which everything vibrates. When the vibrations are in harmony, energy is augmented due to the EM null zone, or affinity, created in harmonized systems.

If you pass vibrations generated by an electronic device through a medium such as water, you notice geometric patterns forming in the liquid. When the vibrations have affinity with each other, the patterns are beautiful and symmetrical. When the vibrations are not in harmony, you see a chaotic pattern in the liquid.

Using the expression, "We exist in a sea of energy," is quite correct. Imagine the vacuum to be like a liquid filled with both harmonizing and non-harmonizing vibrations. The key is to generate sound, color and light emanations that create an affinity with the natural "liquid" of the etheric planes.

Proper values and placement of magnets, coils and components of an electrical circuit is the equivalent of setting up an affinity with the existing vibrations in the vacuum. We can calculate specific frequencies of different materials, and we can use Planck's constant to figure out the dimensions, magnitude, resistance, capacitance and inductance of necessary components in a Zero-Point Energy device.

Now it is time to return to the holy grail of physics and present our own ideas regarding the Unified Field Theory.

CHAPTER 6

The Unified Field Theory and the Bridge Between Physics and Metaphysics

∞ Prelude to the Unified Field Theory

We suspect there is only one type of energy permeating the universe (from the aether plus higher dimensions), simply manifesting as two different energy fields (gravitational and quantum, disregarding for the moment the nuclear forces). The relatively small amount of energy existing in-between atomic structures represents the radiance vectors ("bleed-through") emanating out into the macrocosmic vacuum from the quantum field. The strong and weak nuclear forces are merely effects of this Radiant Energy as it interacts with basic subatomic particles. Electromagnetism is the effect of this energy when it becomes polarized (observed as the interaction of positively and negatively-charged particles).

Radiant Energy, the nonpolarized quantum fluctuation "bleed-through" moving from within atomic structures into the vacuum between atoms, is also known as "scalar electromagnetic energy." This is the same energy and should be able to be expressed in terms of universal constants.

The effects of Radiant Energy when it interacts with various particles and waves, and as it enters, exits, and re-enters various atomic structures, gives rise to the strong and weak nuclear forces, so we can essentially eliminate them from the Unified Field equations. Nevertheless, there is a relationship between each force that can be accurately expressed by determining the constants associated with each field equation.

Before we can offer a series of Unified Field equations, we need to review some of the earlier points we have made, including the holographic nature of things, and once again the idea of consciousness units (CU).

∞ The Holographic Nature of the Universe

Dr. Nassim Haramein has calculated, in his paper, "The Schwarzschild Proton," that the mass of one proton is exactly the same as the mass of the entire universe. How is this possible? If Dr. Haramein's calculations are correct, the entire universe exists within every proton. Not only does this essentially prove that we are living in a hologram, but it also suggests that we do not need to go looking into the farthest reaches of intergalactic space to tap into the nearly infinite field of energy. Instead, we only need to look within, literally, as in the trillions of protons that make up our physical beings.

The Bible says, "The Kingdom of God is within." According to the latest scientific discoveries, this statement is literally true.

Considering the mass of the universe within every proton, we can calculate how much potential energy actually exists inside every proton. According to mainstream science, the mass of the universe is about 3.0×10^{55} gm. Using Einstein's equation, the total energy available inside every proton would be 3.0×10^{55}gm $(10^{17}$ cm/s$)^2 = 3.0 \times 10^{89}$ joules.

No matter how you calculate it, the results speak for themselves. We live in a sea of almost unlimited energy.

∞ How Is the Energy of the Quantum Field Extracted?

This is the multi-trillion-dollar question. The gravitational field strength of 10^7 joules/cm^3 is enough to justify attempts to harness energy from gravity. Yet, even if we only extract a tiny part of the energy from the quantum field (estimated at 10^{124} joules/cm^3), we will have enough energy to power every need on Earth for millions of years. The coherence and stability of the quantum field is such that the energy being drawn from it and turned into entropy would only increase slightly if millions of typical loads were placed on this energy stream (industrial and residential power). This is the free renewable energy source the world is waiting for.

To harness the Zero-Point Energy, the easiest way is to tap the radiant field. To properly do this, we must understand how and why energy is already bleeding through from the quantum level to the macrocosmic (gravitational) level. Of course, we need accurate Unified Field Theory equations that explain the relationship between gravity and electromagnetism. The strong and weak nuclear forces will eventually be shown as derivatives of the gravitational and electromagnetic fields, or rather, derivatives of Radiant Energy. For now, we are including these forces within the domain of the quantum field since nuclear forces depend on atomic structures and their decay and orbital rearrangement, which is part of the quantum field.

We are not mathematicians and are merely detailing the theoretical basis for extraction of energy from the vacuum. There are many well-qualified physicists and electrical engineers that are already working on Radiant Energy from the vacuum. In a historical context, the foremost of these is Nikola Tesla. We have included a portal into Tesla's abstracts and essays in the Appendix.

∞ Working with Protons

The simplest and most direct approach (but not necessarily the easiest) is to work directly with individual protons. What are the catalysts required to unleash the potential energy within the proton? Do we work to capture the Radiant Energy bleeding through from the quantum field into the gravitational field, or do we somehow break apart the structure of the proton?

It could be argued that if the universe is a hologram, breaking apart the proton would essentially be equivalent to destroying the universe. Perhaps the quantum field is somehow "protected" to prevent this from happening. Since there is more than enough energy radiating from the quantum field, it is certainly not necessary to tap this field directly, plus, working with Radiant Energy would be a whole lot less dangerous.

If you study Tesla's patents and drawings, or are fortunate enough to come across some of his personal notes, you will likely come to the conclusion that he "discovered" the Radiant Energy and put it to use in his many devices (most of which were disabled or destroyed by the interests of J.P. Morgan and related factions). Proper study of the means by which he successfully extracted the Radiant Energy is being conducted around the world by electrical engineers and inventors. It is only a matter of time before someone successfully creates a consistent output from a Radiant Energy machine. However, there is one major factor we must consider: consciousness.

∞ What About the Power of Belief?

We all know that beliefs are powerful and significantly affect the world in which we live. Metaphysics says that your thoughts create your reality. This is true up to a point, although it might be more accurate to say, "The collective consciousness of humanity determines what humanity experiences in this world." Each individual soul contributes to the consciousness of the whole, obviously, but what is not so obvious is that the quality of consciousness has a great deal to do with the effectiveness of creative thought. A highly enlightened soul has a lot more power than one who is caught up in the business of the day, merely repeating the ideas and behaviors of others who came before him. We went into detail earlier regarding the ability of highly evolved souls to affect the world.

In this science section, we want to examine the mechanics of thought and belief. What actually happens when a belief is projected out into the world? How does such projection take place?

In previous discussions, we introduced the idea of consciousness units (CU). How big is a CU? What is it made of? How does it interact with fundamental particles and waves? Is there a cosmological constant that can be discovered in order to relate consciousness to the existing forces of nature? A related question would be: "Is Planck's constant the smallest unit of measurement possible? Can consciousness be expressed in terms of Planck units?"

Let us return to metaphysics for a moment and look at the axiom given therein: "Everything is consciousness." This pantheistic approach suggests that the 4% of the universe that can be measured directly consists of varying degrees of consciousness.

For a moment, let us discount the idea that consciousness exists within dark matter and dark energy (the source of the quantum fluctuations). We will assume there is no consciousness in the vacuum of macrocosmic space (the area outside of the quantum field and not directly influenced by Radiant Energy). That leaves all observable phenomena in the known universe as the domain of consciousness — in essence, everything that is. It means gamma rays have consciousness. It means quarks have consciousness. It means neutrinos have consciousness.

∞ The Mechanics of Consciousness

If everything has consciousness and the Nonlocality Principle applies to the field of consciousness, then there is no separation between elements within the field of consciousness. Your consciousness is not separate from my consciousness. The neutrino's consciousness is not separate from the electron's consciousness. There is a free-flowing river of information spontaneously and simultaneously connecting all things in the known universe.

In order to experience phenomena in the observable universe, consciousness must direct itself from one part of the field to another. Everything is vibrating within a field of consciousness, but unless that field directs itself to achieve something (work and force), everything remains in a stasis (the Bose-Einstein Condensate). It is consciousness that "directs" the subatomic forces to move in the way they do. The modes of operation of this direction manifest as what scientists call the four major forces: weak and strong nuclear, electromagnetic and gravitational. Attraction and repulsion (the nuclear forces and gravity) begin within the field of consciousness. Polarization (the electromagnetic force) also begins within this field.

What are the steps necessary to prove this? We look no further than to the basic premise of quantum mechanics that states that the observer of an experiment can never be completely independent of the outcome of the experiment. We also refer to the Uncertainty Principle, an example of which is detailed below.

In metaphysics, things remain in a possible or probable "wave state of uncertainty" until consciousness directs itself (through thought and belief) out into the "external" world (the laboratory in this case). At that point the waves collapse into particles (the possible and probable realities collapse into a dominant timeline or observable reality).

A silly example might be pertinent here. In the next moment, I have a nearly infinite list of possible things I could do. If I'm sitting at a computer, I could adjust the screen, move the mouse, open or close an application window, take a drink from a glass sitting on the desk, move the chair, and a thousand other activities. As long as I have not made up my mind what to do, all these possible realities exist as a wave function, but as soon as I make a decision (to drink from the glass, for example), that act becomes part of the dominant timeline. The wave of possibilities has now collapsed into discrete action (drinking from the glass).

What caused the glass to be raised and the liquid to be consumed? It began with the intention and concluded with physical action. In other words, the outcome was determined by consciousness (in the form of decision and action). Of course, the entire activity was much more complex. It began as a thought (I want a drink). Nerve impulses then traveled from the brain into the arm and hand, which reached out and grabbed the glass, etc.

What started as a decision in consciousness was then transformed into a Newtonian process of converting potential energy into kinetic energy (the action performed). In the case of psychokinesis (moving objects with the mind), the effect of consciousness on that which is observed is more direct. Instead of directing one's thoughts through nerve impulses and body movement, the energy emanates directly from the consciousness of the observer, and enough of that observer's intention is converted into kinetic energy to move the object.

Let us illustrate the above scenarios: (1) drinking from the glass; (2) moving the glass with the mind.

CU → neurons → signals to nervous system → movement of hand to glass → drinking from glass

CU → field of consciousness directed toward glass → moving the glass with CU force directly

These are really the same process, except that in most cases there are intermediate steps, such as CU directing certain neurons to fire in the brain, which in turn activate the nervous system that is responsible for moving the arm and hand toward the glass. The point is, regardless of how many intermediate steps are taken, the basic principle is the same. Consciousness directs the process of manifestation in the outer world.

"In the beginning God created the heavens and the earth," it says in the first chapter of the Bible. If God is consciousness, then this statement makes sense from both a physics and metaphysics perspective. The consciousness of God contains an infinite variety of ideas, held in a sort of stasis until they are "activated." When Source puts energy, focus and attention into a particular idea, the consciousness is then directed "outward" into manifestation in the cosmos.

The Vedantic approach to spirituality essentially states that there is only one consciousness (the Mind of God) and all seemingly separate sources are illusions. You could say that human beings are co-creators with God, or rather, extensions of God seeming to take form within the manifest Creation. (Recall the leaves on the tree analogy of the soul given earlier.)

Let us recap what we have said so far in this section: Consciousness is a basic force, which can be expressed as CU (consciousness units). These units may have a relationship to Planck units. CU go out from a directed source (the mind) and affect work on the so-called "outer" reality.

Here are some related ideas: (1) The only thing that actually moves in the universe is consciousness. (2) All work performed anywhere in the universe is directed by consciousness. (3) The four basic forces of physics exist due to this movement in consciousness. (4) Consciousness was the force behind the Big Bang. (5) Energy and matter are derivatives of consciousness. They exist because of consciousness. (6) Energy, work, force and mass are components of consciousness.

Consciousness takes many forms. It can be the obvious desires, will and intention of human beings to perform work, or it can be the desire, will and intention of the universe to evolve, regenerate and order itself. In other words, when a cell divides, it is under the direction of consciousness. All evolution and unfoldment of universal laws and principles are the result of consciousness moving among its various aspects. When consciousness becomes aware of itself and its movement, it evolves into a field of intelligence. This field of intelligence is roughly the same as what people call "spirit."

Essentially, we are saying that consciousness is the most basic principle in the universe, more fundamental than energy itself. The Law of Conservation of Energy is merely another way of saying that consciousness is eternal. Its form can change, but its overall quantity remains the same.

Let's use the analogy of Lego blocks. A child has an extensive collection of Legos. He can make a nearly infinite array of different buildings from these blocks, but the blocks themselves do not change. Consciousness is a constant, but the movement of consciousness is what creates everything that is.

How about an example from mathematics? The Mandelbrot Set is a recursive function that, when plotted using complex numbers, forms a beautiful sacred geometric progression. As it expands, it forms ever more intricate patterns. Although the forms created by the generation of the function are constantly changing, the function itself remains constant.

So how big or small is one consciousness unit? Small enough to pass through any atomic barrier, that's for sure. If you try to separate an experiment by imposing ten-meters-thick lead walls between the observer and the experiment, it makes no difference. No matter now near or how far, no matter how many barriers you put between you and the experiment, you are still affecting the experiment with your thoughts. This is due to the Nonlocality Principle and the fact that consciousness is One. The consciousness of the waves or particles in the chamber is the same as your consciousness. As long as you are uncertain or are not focusing on the experiment, it remains in the wave state of possibilities. As soon as you look (observe), the wave state collapses into a discrete position. The Uncertainty Principle is yet one more way of saying, "Consciousness creates reality."

∞ Movement of Consciousness

Consciousness is the most basic force in the universe. All other forces are derived from consciousness. When consciousness becomes aware of itself, it forms a field of intelligence, also known as spirit. The only thing that actually moves is consciousness. What appears to be movement is not actual particles or waves moving; it is consciousness forming a relationship with objects or patterns from a different point of perspective with respect to time. It is like a reel of film. As long as the reel is stored in the casing, everything exists but nothing is moving (consciousness is "still"). But as soon as you put it in a projector (the mind), you see what appears to be characters moving on a screen (because consciousness is moving). In other words, the mind is the projection mechanism that consciousness uses to perceive itself in different states (movement).

Dr. Julian Barbour introduced the theory that nothing actually moves except consciousness. The world is like a series of stills, or nearly infinite now moments. Things only appear to move because we are constantly shifting our perception. Time itself is an illusion. It appears to exist because consciousness keeps changing its perspective (at a very high rate of speed). Think of a movie projector that can operate at trillions of frames per second — very high resolution.

This again reiterates what we have been saying all along — we live in a holographic 3D movie or virtual reality — a simulation. This idea is now making it into the mainstream and for good reason. Both physics and metaphysics support this perception.

The simulation hypothesis in no way invalidates the idea of the soul or higher dimensions, as some naysayers would argue. The holographic movie set we call "our Earthly life" is merely the way reality is projected from consciousness into the lower four dimensions. There are still higher aspects of Self operating beyond the projection. There is a movie director and producer that exist outside the reel of film that comprises the movie.

∞ The Quantum Factors and Equations of Consciousness

The Unified Field equations must include CU (consciousness units). What is the relationship between CU and the four so-called basic forces of nature? Without going too heavy into mathematics, let us state this using constants:

$$\text{CU(weak nuclear)} = (df)(k_1)(wf)$$
$$\text{CU(strong nuclear)} = (df)(k_2)(sf)$$

$$CU(\text{gravitation}) = (df)(k_3)(gf)$$
$$CU(\text{electromagnetism}) = (df)(k_4)(ef)$$

where CU = consciousness units
where df = the density formula for determining magnitude of CU
where k_1 = a constant that relates the weak nuclear force to the force of consciousness
where wf = the weak nuclear force
where k_2 = a constant that relates the strong nuclear force to the force of consciousness
where sf = the strong nuclear force
where k_3 = a constant that relates the force of gravity to that of consciousness
where gf = gravitational force
where k_4 = a constant that relates the force of electromagnetism to that of consciousness
where ef = electromagnetic force

Within "df" are several factors we talked about earlier, including the vibration level of the being projecting the consciousness and a logarithmic equation determining the amount of energy being directed by the force of consciousness.

Essentially, we are saying that there is one force in the universe and that is the force of consciousness. This can be proven indirectly in the experiments with waves and particles based on the presence or absence of an observer (the Uncertainty Principle). The observer represents the force of consciousness acting on an object (or subatomic particle). We already know that CU have no mass and cannot be stopped by any barriers. Therefore, they are finer than x-rays and gamma-rays and are more basic than all subatomic particles.

The magnitude of CU is determined by level of vibration. In our earlier discussion, we gave a logarithmic value to the composite vibrational level of the consciousness of a given life form. In our overly simplistic equation, a vibration of 3.0 in consciousness would be ten times weaker than a life form with a vibration of 4.0. A being with a consciousness of 6.0 would be 1,000 times stronger than a being with a vibration of 3.0. Of course, the actual formula for calculating the net force of a thought form emanating from a being is far more complex and is denoted by "df." This formula can be calculated by empirical observation of thousands (millions) of souls at various levels of consciousness directing their mental energy toward objects or events in the outside world.

While such research would be lengthy and rigorous, it is within the scope of possibility to determine the actual formula for calculating the amount of force being exerted on "external" people or objects by consciousness. It would also be possible, through multiple variable nonlinear vector differential equations, to determine the actual energy of one CU. We are assuming that higher-vibrational, more focused and determined individuals will emit more CU than someone at a low vibration with very little focus and determination.

When calculating the density force formula (df), some of the variables will include: (1) the overall environment of the thinker; (2) the quality of the thoughts being emanated; (3) the emotional component including desire, will, level of motivation and anticipated outcome; (4) the ability of the soul to visualize the desired outcome; (5) the presence or absence of distracting thoughts; (6) the presence or absence of distractions in the environment; (7) the presence or absence of opposing or countering thoughts and feelings from other souls in the vicinity of the thinker; (8) the presence or absence of supporting thoughts and feelings from others, including beings in other levels and dimensions such as spirit guides; and (9) the level of alignment within the various levels and dimensions of the soul, including the state of the subconscious mind and ego (known as the level of "soul integration").

As stated earlier, this author has devised a consciousness composite density scale ranging from 3.0 to 12.0, representing levels three through twelve of the 12-dimensional model of the universe. The first section of the consciousness equation was given as a simple base-10 logarithmic progression, meaning that each step up in vibration amounts to a ten-fold increase in CU. For the moment, we will define CU in discrete single units, so that the higher the vibration of the soul emitting the thoughts, the higher the actual number of CU. In actuality, there are probably many other factors. If CU are discrete units, they may be "super-charged" in a highly excited and enthusiastic individual or wandering without much force in a lazy or lethargic individual. To keep things as simple as possible, however, we will assume that the excited soul has a higher value of CU than the lazy soul.

Let's give an arbitrary example. Person A is highly motivated, has a strong desire, practices visualization repeatedly, and has a quiet, meditative space from which to send out intentions. Person B is unfocused, tired, lives with negative people, and has no clear picture of what he wants in life. Person A's ability to create could be millions of times stronger once all variables are considered. Person B is still creating (because every soul is creative) but it will seem to such a soul that life is happening to him, that he is a victim of circumstances because the creative force of other souls around him might be much greater than his own.

We can express this in an overly simple formula:

$CU(df)_{total}$ = Level of vibration multiplied by (intention or directed energy + focus or visualization + desire or will + influence of other souls)

In other words, the total energy in consciousness units being emanated by an individual is determined by the intrinsic level of vibration of that soul, as well as his level of intention, ability to concentrate and focus on the desired outcome, plus the intensity of desire or will, along with the influence of souls around him that may or may not be aligned with his vision and desire.

The following information is so important that we are revisiting it using a slightly different approach than what we delineated above.

∞ Another Look at the Holographic Nature of the Universe

As stated earlier, there are some scientists who have calculated and shown mathematically that the universe is a hologram. Using Planck density as a basis for calculating the available energy in the vacuum of space, Dr. Nassim Haramein was able to demonstrate that the mass of the entire universe exists within every proton of every atom.

If you consider the idea that the Big Bang is a holographic projection from a single point, then it follows that every point in the universe is essentially the same point. It is simply experienced as being separated by time and space.

There are several proofs being presented to suggest that time and space are ultimately illusions. We can say with certainty that there is nothing that proves time and space are real. We have been through this before but let us repeat: Show us where yesterday and tomorrow exist. They are ideas within the mind that is thinking right now. It is only now. It is impossible for it to be other than now. When you are thinking about the past and future, you are doing it now.

The central idea here is that the only thing that moves is consciousness. The rate of change of the universe is a function of how quickly consciousness shifts its perception from one part of the hologram to another. It is suggested that the universe "blinks" on and off once every Planck unit of time (about 10^{-44} seconds). That is the rate at which consciousness shifts its perception, giving the illusion of movement and change. However, the universe itself is static — it is not changing position. It is consciousness that is constantly changing its viewpoint of reality. This theory is supported by the work of Dr. Julian Barbour, who likens reality to a high-resolution movie, or advanced simulation. Instead of 24 frames per second, as is the case with traditional movie projectors, consciousness moves through trillions of frames per second.

Think of moving your hand from left to right in front of your body. Is the hand really moving? Or is your consciousness moving trillions of times per second and viewing the hand from a different vantage point every time? The overly simplistic way of thinking this would be, "I want to see what my hand looks like at this position, and now this position, and now this position, etc."

This is no different than thinking about being in a jet airplane traveling at 1,000 km/hr. Is it really the jet that is moving, or is the jet stationary and the ground below you is moving at 1,000 km/hr? The answer is, they are both correct, depending on the vantage point of the observer. All time is a measurement of relative motion. It matters not in calculation whether the hand is moving and consciousness is still or whether consciousness is moving and the hand is still. However, according to quantum experiments, it is only consciousness that actually moves. (Poor Newton must be spinning in his grave.)

∞ The Big Bang Revisited

If we embrace the idea of the nonlocality of time, then it follows that everything is happening at once, even though things appear to be sequential. Therefore, the Big Bang is happening right now as well. In fact, the entire history of the Big Bang is happening now. We can theoretically witness the entire history of the universe unfolding in front of our eyes, and, if we have a powerful enough telescope, we can look back in time and see the history of the universe literally.

We can imagine the Big Bang as a balloon stretched out in front of us. The size and density of the balloon depends upon where in the timeline we are viewing it. The entire history of the universe is contained in the balloon. We can see the origination point where we began blowing up the balloon. As we move out from the origin, we are moving forward in time. Or, we can start at the "end" of the balloon and work our way toward the origin point (going backward in time). Although the future expansion has seemingly not happened yet, we can imagine and extrapolate it. Even though we cannot see it or calculate it precisely (due to the Uncertainty Principle), we can become aware of the entire field of possibilities and probabilities that make up the unmanifested aspect of the universe (the area into which the balloon can be blown up). The space outside the balloon is the void (unmanifested creation), but it exists because you can differentiate between the area contained within the balloon and the area outside it. As the balloon expands, the "outside" space must accommodate it, or rather, the balloon will displace the area outside it.

To preserve the Law of Conservation of Energy, as the balloon expands to fill more of the void, the increasing volume must result in decreasing density. If the density decrease is less than the volume expansion (after calculating using volume equations), then the excess energy must originate in the void. Although there is currently no way to measure this accurately, such an idea is similar to the way scientists discovered dark energy and dark matter (comprising about 96% of the known universe).

∞ Applying the Holographic Principle to Consciousness Units

If the entire universe is contained within its parts, including individual souls, then each individual soul contains trillions of protons that each have the same number of consciousness units as the universe. Whether this number is finite or infinite ultimately does not matter, because the difference between the totality of Creation (God) and the individual soul is that the soul differentiates the God energy by converting a portion of the potential energy into kinetic energy. In other words, the individual soul takes a portion of the universal energy contained within it and directs that energy from the center of being into the "outer" world, thus appearing to have less potential energy than before (keeping with the Law of Conservation of Energy). So essentially the amount of CU directed into the manifest reality by the individual soul is equal to or less than the entire energy of the universe.

In the case of the "average" human being, this amount of kinetic energy (directed from "inner" to "outer" reality) is much, much less than the entire energy of the universe. To determine the amount of potential energy capable of being converted into kinetic energy (the soul's ability to manifest its power), you must insert the magnitude of intention, will, desire, visualization and imagination into the formula given in the previous section, after factoring in the level of vibration of the individual soul. Essentially, every individual soul has the capabilities of creating from the point of view of God since the entire universe exists trillions of times within each soul. This upholds the spiritual axiom that we are co-creators with God.

Actually, there are many constants and variables needed to calculate the energy, in joules, of a particular attempt at manifestation by an individual soul (or collective group of souls). Such a quantity of kinetic energy surely exists, but measuring it is problematic since we do not know the exact value of the variables that factor into the equation. For example, the soul is tired one day and energized the next, had a quarrel with a neighbor just before trying to create something, or contracted a virus, etc. The overall energy level of the soul (the composite vibrational value) can be determined using multiple-variable calculus. In other words, the moment-by-moment creative output (kinetic energy) of a soul can be integrated over a given time period and then averaged accordingly. The longer the period of integration, the more accurate the overall energy picture becomes.

However, the natural evolution of the soul must be considered when estimating the total energy output of a creative individual. Integrating the period of the lifetime of a soul and comparing it to individual decades of human growth would yield a rough approximation of overall energy output.

Individual soul growth is often depicted using a graph of awareness over time. The x-axis is the dominant timeline and the y-axis is the level of awareness. The composite of a soul's growth appears to be a wavy "stairway to heaven" in a soul with ideal growth factors. During periods of planetary acceleration, such as the one we are currently experiencing, the slope of the line increases. In other words, the individual enters a period of rapid soul growth.

We have reproduced the diagram of soul evolution from *The Mystery of Time*, a previous book by this author (see figure 6.1).

It is implied that a soul growing and evolving normally will have greater and greater power over a period of time. There are exceptions, however, if you measure soul growth over a very short period

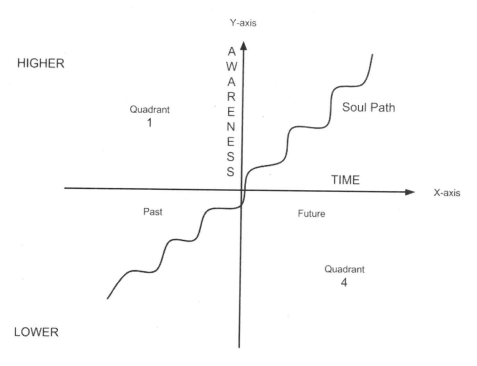

Figure 6.1 — Soul Evolution

of time. Souls can seem to go backward for a while before correcting course and moving forward again. But if you calculate level of vibration over a long enough period, you will see the soul's creative ability increasing.

By comparing the soul growth of individual souls to one another, it can be determined how much relative influence each soul has on the whole of humanity.

Let us keep this information in mind when we re-examine the issue of introducing Zero-Point Energy devices into the mainstream population that heavily believes in scarcity and lack.

If you want to determine the likelihood of a certain device performing adequately in the presence of witnesses, you must calculate the effect of CU emanating from each witness and correlate this with the CU emanating from the inventor or promoters of the device.

We can greatly over-simplify this challenging interaction by saying that those who believe in the success of the device will have a greater magnitude of CU than those who disbelieve. However, if the disbelief is strong enough, it can certainly overcome the confidence and expectancy of the pro-device persons. If you have three inventors who strongly believe in the device (and have formed a positive resonant field of consciousness around the experiment), and you have 100 persons who moderately disbelieve in the principles of Zero-Point Energy, it is possible, but not likely, that the pro-device faction will prevail. In order to predict the success of such an experiment, you must be able to calculate the total positive and negative energy output from the observers. Remember, the object and the observer are one. (The observer is the observed.) Therefore, the Zero-Point Energy device will mirror the composite consciousness of the observers. This is true with any external machine, not just Zero-Point devices. Since almost everyone believes in computers, for example, the energy interacting with a computer is favorable to the continued successful operation of the device.

Inventors using unpopular ideas must have a strong enough belief in their creations to overcome the skepticism and doubt prevalent in the minds of others. Sometimes when a new technology is quickly embraced by society, it is because the human beings have help from extraterrestrial or higher dimensional sources. People are often programmed to believe or disbelieve the various changes being made to the society (consciously or unconsciously).

Subliminal programming, hypnosis, mind control, brainwashing, propaganda, and other such manipulation techniques, can affect the equation in situations such as that discussed above. If you believe "something" strongly at the conscious level, but you have several levels of skepticism at deeper layers of the subconscious, it is doubtful you will be successful at manifesting that "something" quickly.

∞ Other Metaphysical Considerations

You can see by our discussion above that we are blending physics and metaphysics, hopefully in a way that is clear to your understanding. The two fields of study merge at the subatomic level, especially when examining the dynamics of superposition and wave mechanics. By changing the consciousness of the observers, the waveforms and particles change their behavior accordingly. After all, basic metaphysics says, "You see what you expect to see," or "Your thoughts create your reality." Unfortunately, metaphysicians tend to oversimply the dynamics of creation, failing to account for the multidimensional nature of reality and the intricate complexities of group consciousness and mass belief.

It would certainly be much easier if everyone had the same magnitude of kinetic energy. After all, you would just need 51 people that believe in your device and 49 who do not, to be successful. But of course, that is not how it works, as we have demonstrated above. Human beings tend to be very complex, and it is sometimes nearly impossible to tell whether someone is contributing positively or negatively to an outcome.

This discussion merely underscores the need to raise the overall consciousness of the planet and all life forms upon her. Once consciousness reaches a certain level, the supportive aspects of Zero-Point Energy will quickly catalyze the mass production of these devices.

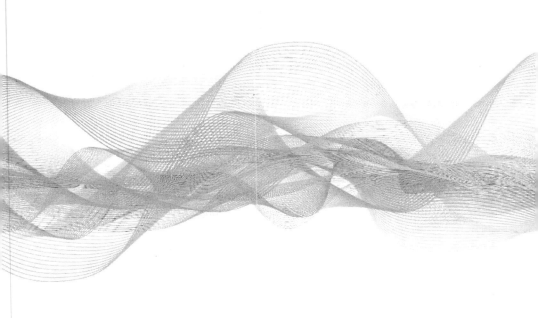

PART 2
THE METAPHYSICAL AND SPIRITUAL SECTION

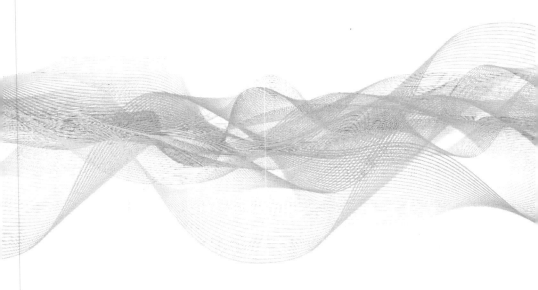

CHAPTER 7

The Nature of God

∞ The Non-Local Field of Intelligence

We ended the science section with a transition into metaphysics. Now we will look at the same issues but from a "higher" perspective.

Let us return to the central question of this book, "How do we tap into the field of nearly unlimited energy that exists everywhere in the universe?" We have looked scientifically at this and we will now attempt to bridge the gap between that understanding and the wisdom of the sages, mystics and teachers of philosophy.

The brain is a receiver/transmitter of the non-local field of intelligence. Imagine the silliness of opening up a radio and looking inside to try and find the musicians that are playing a song. Yet those scientists who believe the brain is the source of intelligence (and psychological experience) are doing just that. The brain simply tunes itself to various frequencies that are continuously broadcasting from the non-local field.

Atheism is the height of ignorance. (Note: Here, we are talking about the belief that God does not exist. We are not including "anti-religiosity," which is a justified response to the dogma of the church.)

It could be argued that the "laws of chance" or "randomness" somehow are responsible for creating basic life forms, even though the "odds" of this happening might be several quintillion to one. Yet there are no odds that can explain the existence of something as vast and complex as the human brain. Those readers who have read the very first book by this author, *Life on the Cutting Edge*, know that there is mathematics that describes the potential capacity of one human brain. The number of possible paths through which information can flow in one human brain is vastly greater than the number of atoms in the known universe: ten log ten to the 98th power or ten to the ten to the 98th power. It is a number so huge it would take 250,000 years to write it out long-hand at normal writing speed. The zeroes after the one would stretch around the Earth several times using a 12pt font.

The most logical question possible, when faced with the magnitude of the brain, would be, "Why?" What is the purpose of this nearly infinite capacity? A reasonably intelligent person would conclude that the brain is a device for receiving and transmitting a large amount of data from the field of infinite intelligence that exists throughout all time and space (one of the definitions of non-locality).

A non-local field, by definition, exists outside of time and space. That means it is everywhere and nowhere at the same time. It exists in the past, present and future, and it exists beyond the past, present and future. It exists within every aspect of space, and it exists beyond space. The idea of non-locality also explains why we live in a holographic universe. Being omnipresent (everywhere present), it exists within everything and outside of everything.

Being omnipresent, this field of intelligence, called God, is capable of transferring the individual experiences of itself from one physical body to another (reincarnation). It is also capable of "trading places" with aspects of itself through the phenomenon known as "walking in." This is when one soul leaves a body and another soul enters it. The soul is an aspect of the non-local field that could be considered to be "semi-local," meaning it can identify with the local aspects of the field (the body/mind personality), or it can identify with the non-local field itself (becoming one with God).

The "mind" is a semi-local aspect of the unlimited field of intelligence, similar to the soul. You could define soul as the higher aspect of mind, but that would be an inaccurate definition. This author defines soul as the seventh level of the human being. In his model system, there are 12 aspects to the Self. Consult the book *Soul Integration* for a detailed analysis of the 12 aspects of Self. Roughly speaking, the six lower aspects refer to the local aspects of the field, and the six higher levels pertain more to the non-local aspects. In other words, the field (God) has gradients or levels of consciousness, ranging from pure non-locality (God consciousness) down to the most local aspect (the physical body/universe).

∞ The Realms of Illusion

Most enlightened teachers refer to this world as part of "maya" or the realms of illusion. Because the non-local field of intelligence (God) exists within everything in its totality (a concept impossible for the lower mind to understand), there is actually nothing except God. Non-locality, by definition, does not have an opposite. An opposite would imply there is something outside the field, which would imply that the field occupies a limited amount of space. Therefore, it would be a localized field, one having discrete boundaries. The brain consists of a localized field because it has actual dimensions and can be turned on and off (destroyed). The field of intelligence continues when an individual brain dies or is destroyed. A brain-dead human being can no longer receive signals from the non-local field, but the non-local field still exists. A broken radio can no longer play music, but the band members still exist independently of the radio.

It is possible to believe that the band members are inside the radio, just as it is possible to believe that the localized field of the human world is God. If only God is real (by definition), then there is really no such thing as a localized field. Yet, it certainly appears that such is so. It would not be useful to ignore the localized field or to pretend it doesn't exist. For all practical purposes, the physical body exists and needs to be taken care of.

A reasonably sane human being will pay attention to the body and attempt to keep it safe. We could say that the physical body and universe of time and space exist as a lower-dimensional vibrational field of localized energy that is, in reality, not separate from the non-local field of intelligence (God). It only appears to be separate. Therein lies the illusion.

Just as a chair or table appears to be solid, the localized field appears to be real. Yet we know the chair and table are mostly "empty" space — not solid at all. Believing that the physical world is all that exists is the essence of maya, or illusion.

An illusion is something that appears real because you believe in it. Truth is that which is so regardless of belief. Although the localized field is, by definition, unreal, it appears real because you believe in it. Withdrawing your belief in the localized field allows it to dissolve into the nothingness and omnipresence of the non-localized field. In other words, the duality of the localized field dissolves into the non-duality or oneness of God.

An enlightened being is one who recognizes that the non-local field is all there is. There is nothing outside of God. One teacher defines God as "That which cannot be differentiated." Another definition of God is "The singularity." Both statements are valid. The universe is a holographic projection of a singularity. Singularities have infinite mass and no space. By definition, they have, therefore, no time. They are everywhere present (omnipresent) and contain all intelligence (awareness). This is also known as omniscience, or the all-knowing aspect of God. Being omnipresent and omniscient, the non-local field must also be omnipotent, meaning all-powerful, since the singularity contains all mass, and mass is energy (recall Einstein's famous equation). Therefore, using logic and deduction, we can prove that God contains infinite, unlimited energy.

Most scientists acknowledge the existence of the singularity, or they believe in multiple singularities. It has been demonstrated in a laboratory that there are millions, or billions, of singularities existing throughout the fabric of time and space. Yet, by definition, there can be only one singularity, since it contains infinite mass (all mass). Therefore, this one singularity manifests itself as multiple images, or instances, of itself, and appears to be in different places within the time/space continuum. This, once again, is consistent with the properties of a hologram. In this case, it is not a two-dimensional plane appearing to be a three-dimensional object, but rather, a zero-dimensional singularity appearing as everything in the universe. The whole is contained within the parts, and the parts are contained within the whole. It works both ways. You are in God, and God is in you. This is what Jesus meant by the expression, "The Kingdom of God is within."

CHAPTER 8

The Consciousness
of Increasing Energy

∞ Clearing the Belief in Separation

The deepest layer of negative programming and conditioning involves the belief system that we are separate from God. This belief arises from being identified with the physical form and the body/mind/personality that arises from such identification. Do not underestimate how deeply entrenched the belief in separation has become. You may intellectually, consciously, realize that you are One with God, but most likely the vast majority of experiences you are having in your life reflect the idea that you are a limited human being, unable to do things like grow new teeth, stop the aging process, or increase your strength significantly.

You probably also believe you are subject to the laws of the lower dimensions, including entropy, gravity, karma, and more. When you are identified with the lower dimensions, you are under the influence of the laws and dimensions of those realms. If a yogi can levitate, it is because he (or she) has raised his (or her) vibration sufficiently to no longer be under such influences.

There are only a few human beings actively demonstrating the reality of living with unlimited energy. Such souls do not sleep, many do not eat, some do not even drink water (they are breatharians), and a few can even go without oxygen. They are literally living in the higher dimensions while still maintaining a body here on

Earth. Of course, because the physical form is subject to the laws of entropy, they must be bringing in enough centropy to continuously regenerate the body.

It is commonly misunderstood by most persons that a yogi or high master is no longer affected by the vibrations of this world. That is simply not true. Unless the high-vibrational being is constantly working to overcome entropy, he or she will fall back into the lower realms. This is why most yogis and high-level beings reside high in the mountains, often in caves, far from the negative vibrations of coastal cities. It is not that they are avoiding or trying to deny that they live in a low-vibrational world. (Perhaps some who are not truly enlightened are in fact simply trying to avoid the responsibilities of the worldly life.) The reality for a truly realized being is that they are far more effective at helping the world if they can remain detached, literally and figuratively, from the daily drama of life. It is difficult to maintain their high state if they come down off the mountain, out of the cave, and into the hustle and bustle of city life.

If a being is so enlightened, why is it difficult for them to mingle with so-called "ordinary" human beings? Remember, the power of belief is very great, and if 99.99% of humanity believes in the reality of the lower dimensions, that belief is almost insurmountable. Getting out of the dense field of vibrations is essential if a soul wants to stay in a non-dual state.

If you have carefully studied the science section, you know that there are many different fields of consciousness associated with humanity. If a group of highly evolved souls come together and focus their consciousness in a certain direction, it has a significant impact on the overall state of humanity. Because we live on a free-will planet, no soul can forcefully change the consciousness of any other soul, yet each soul has some degree of influence on all other souls. If a large group of souls refuses to wake up, the vibration of that group will have a strong impact on other fields of consciousness co-existing on Earth.

The over-simplistic way of saying this is that there are positive and negative fields of consciousness in and around planet Earth. Those souls creating positively will experience positive results, but only within the confines of their resonant field. This is why Zero-Point Energy machines work well within such a group but fail in the presence of large numbers of doubters or those with low energy. Once again, the Law of Attraction overrides the individual wills of souls on Earth. If you are an inventor with a working over-unity device, but you are associated with a lot of negative people, your device will not work properly. It will encounter a negative resonant field that counteracts the effects of your positive field.

As stated before, the level of vibration of an individual soul determines how much power and influence that soul has. The so-called "power elite" appear to have a great deal of power and influence, but that is false power. They are merely hypnotizing members of society and getting them to believe in certain "realities," such as the idea that they are powerless to overcome the effects of the central banking system, secret societies or negative extraterrestrials.

We will continue to revisit the subject of illusions, expressing this in slightly different ways each time, because it is vital that you look, every day, at how the belief in separation is affecting you. Do not become discouraged at the difficulty of overcoming this belief. You chose a difficult assignment when you decided to come to Earth. About 99.99% of humanity still believes in separation, and belief is very powerful because each one of us is a powerful, creative, spiritual being. We are creating all the time. We live in a sea of unlimited energy, and how we utilize and direct that energy determines our personal outcomes.

Most of us are using our creative power to deny the reality of Oneness. We have adopted core negative beliefs, such as "I am powerless to change the world," or "Life is a struggle," or "There's not enough." As powerful creators being guided by these beliefs, we see evidence of our power everywhere we look because our belief in lack and limitation seems to be real. As we truly release these beliefs, we begin to see another reality — one of joy, love, abundance and prosperity. Even if our bank account has not yet reflected our change in consciousness, we begin feeling wealthy and grateful for what we do have — which opens the door for more to come flowing into us and through us.

∞ Building Momentum

In this world, it is necessary to begin where you are and expand the aspects of consciousness you want to see manifest in the world, while simultaneously releasing those aspects you no longer wish to manifest. This is accomplished through reprogramming the subconscious mind, clearing negative emotions, releasing core negative beliefs, and directing your awareness and intention toward that which you truly want to create.

Most change of consciousness does not happen overnight. You might need to do many years of affirmations, creative visualization, meditation, hypnotherapy, timeline healing, holistic healing and other modalities before you see a significant shift in your experience of reality. A lot of souls are impatient and expect immediate results, then get discouraged and give up when things do not instantly set themselves in motion. We live in a quick-fix society. We want instant results. Many young people are growing up in the age of telecommunications and expect to push a few buttons and obtain instant enlightenment. "There's an app for that!" Like the instant enlightenment pill, it will never happen. Even if instant realization were possible, you would not attract that experience to you until you are ready for it, and you are not ready until you do the hard work of reprogramming and healing negative emotions.

So, little by little, you chip away at the beliefs that are holding you back, until there is a shift. The momentum has now built up sufficiently that you start to feel as if the universe is carrying you forward. At that point, you cannot stop your success even if you try.

How long does this take? Obviously, it's different for every person, but a good rule of thumb is that you may be working on yourself daily for 15 to 20 years, and even then there will be times when you seem to fall back into an old state of consciousness. Those who have been working on themselves their entire lives will be a lot more enlightened than the average person but will not necessarily be free of samskaras (negative influences and karma). To review the idea of transcendence, it is not that you become totally free of human follies and negative emotions, but your awareness grows to the point that your little human problems become insignificant compared to the awareness of who you truly are.

∞ Ending Resistance — The Key to Unlimited Energy

Basic electrical theory states that as resistance within a medium approaches zero, current (kinetic energy) approaches infinity, at a constant voltage (potential energy).

Mathematically, Ohm's Law is stated thus: Current (kinetic energy) equals voltage (potential energy) divided by resistance. Put in layman's terms, the less resistance you have to the flow of life (prana), the more usable energy you can generate. This is true physically, psychologically and spiritually.

Total resistance in a human being consists of physical tension and stress plus negative emotional issues plus core negative belief systems and their corollaries and secondary branches. There are also subtle forms of resistance in the astral, etheric and causal bodies (see *Soul Integration*). Resistance at the psychological level is directly proportional to the inability to accept reality as it is. Fighting and refusing to accept "what is" causes resistance. Denial is an unconscious form of resistance. We stick our heads in the sand when we don't want to confront something unpleasant in life. Either we pretend things are different from the way they are, or we push the unpleasant thoughts and feelings deep into the subconscious mind, suppressing and eventually repressing them. Then we wonder why the body gets sick or seeming accidents happen in our lives.

As we have stated numerous times, a certain amount of resistance is necessary, at least physically, lest we spontaneously combust (burst into flames) much like a short circuit. If our wires (level of consciousness) are not configured in a healthy manner, we will be unable to carry the currents of life, and our circuits will burn out. If there were no resistance at all, current would be infinite, and there would be no differentiation whatsoever within the spectrum of life. However, most of us have far too much resistance. This resistance causes heat (entropy), which leads to decay and death.

What is the ideal level of resistance? That which keeps entropy and centropy in balance. When we accept "what is," we not only have the awareness necessary to make changes where it is beneficial to do so, but we lower our resistance to the ideal level — the level necessary for balance and immortality.

Let's review a concept introduced in the science section — that of the electromagnetic null zone. In electrical circuits, the idea is to create what is called a superconducting resonant field, whereby the electrons arrange themselves geometrically in a pattern that liberates tremendous amounts of energy. In modern laboratories, this is typically done at temperatures a fraction of a degree Kelvin (near absolute zero), but it is possible to create superconducting fields without expending the energy necessary to cool the environment to such a great extent.

The best way to do this is by arranging positive and negative polarity magnets such that you create electromagnetic null zones (areas where the positive and negative polarities are exactly balanced). The electrons, therefore, are no longer moving from negative to positive, but are in a null state where there is no polarity (or rather, the polarities cancel each other out). At that point, the electrons form a resonant field (an affinity). The balanced state causes a lowering of resistance, which leads to superconductivity.

Returning to the psychological and spiritual focus, a balanced state of consciousness is one in which there is no longer the constant tension and stress of striving to become something. This is not a lazy or lethargic state, but rather, an ecstatic state of complete acceptance of "what is." The awareness is totally in the moment, but not in a passive way. This is an active state, with complete attention. You are sensitive to every detail of what is taking place within you and outside. Resistance drops to the optimum point for healthy physical functioning. Disease is quickly eradicated if this state is present for any extended period of time.

All physical disease involves an imbalance on some level. Imbalances are caused by either too much resistance or not enough. Too little resistance in the body can lead to invasion of negative viruses and bacteria. The immune system acts as a regulator for resistance. It keeps the bad stuff out and lets the good stuff in. Like beating the heart or expanding the lungs, you do not need to consciously "try" to find the perfect balance. But you do need to get out of the way and allow the natural process of the body to do its job.

Forcing the body to endure unnatural conditions, such as stress at work, obsessive exercise or inharmonious environments, makes it nearly impossible for the body to do its job.

Your first task, when attempting to heal resistance and increase overall energy, is to ask yourself, "In what ways am I in resistance?

What am I not accepting about my current situation? How am I trying to force things to be different than the way they are?" Maybe you are expressing yourself in passive-aggressive ways, projecting a pleasant exterior while being secretive and manipulative. Or you have strong feelings about something but are in denial, trying to convince yourself that everything is fine. Start by being honest. Stop lying to yourself. Face your innermost feelings. You don't need to judge those feelings. Simply acknowledge them.

If necessary, seek therapy or healing. There is nothing shameful about asking for help. You still must do the work on yourself, but often it helps to have someone who understands and can be present with you. Probably your therapist has gone through similar humiliating circumstances at some point in the past and has compassion for what you are experiencing. Be humble. Admit your mistakes. Then remember that you are a powerful, creative, spiritual being having a human experience of guilt and shame (or whatever the negative feelings are).

By entering into loving acceptance of "what is," you immediately lower resistance and open up to the boundless field of unlimited energy that is your birthright. You are a part of this infinite field, whether or not you believe in it. Learn how to lower your resistance by working through your uncomfortable feelings and negative thoughts. Take your time, but recognize procrastination and make a commitment to move beyond it.

∞ Overcoming Ennui (Lethargy)

Often the first step in breaking out of limitation, whether physical or emotional, is to take action — any action that is not destructive. Lack of motivation to get out of your rut, or a feeling of insurmountable obstacles, is common at one time or another to most human beings.

For whatever reason, many of us find ourselves deeply mired in situations that seem to distract us from discovering our powerful, creative, spiritual selves. Maybe it's working two jobs in order to pay the bills, taking care of a sick parent, surviving a dysfunctional marriage, or daily enduring a tyrannical boss. You will not be able to magically exit your situation instantly, but you can do something every day to build momentum toward a more positive outcome. Even if it is meditating for five minutes before the kids wake up or taking the last ten minutes of the day to reflect after everyone else is asleep, the main thing is to begin.

The little seed you plant toward a different future by taking five or ten minutes per day will slowly grow into an unstoppable force if you keep feeding and watering your visions and higher ideas. This is not new information. Teachers throughout the ages have extolled the virtues of persistence and commitment. However, if you feel unable to do anything some days, at least forgive yourself. Ask your Higher Self to take over. Ask to live life through the Higher Self, even if you feel your Higher Self has abandoned you or doesn't listen.

Deep breathing is necessary to overcome physical lethargy, possibly along with increasing your intake of multivitamins and minerals. Learn which herbs and formulas promote clear thinking and which raise serotonin. Read the list of ways to increase your vibration found in *Soul Integration*. Go online and find inspiring videos.

∞ Overcoming Distractions

Since over 99% of humanity is dominated by entropic energies, it is logical to expect that more than 99% of all activities and events on Earth result in more entropy. In other words, almost everything is a distraction to your path of centropy (awakening to higher dimensions of consciousness). We are not suggesting you must meditate in a cave like some yogis. No matter where you live or how peaceful your lifestyle, there will be distractions, and you must simply accept this. Rigorously holding onto ideals and being too strict with your lifestyle may create a lot of tension and stress, which dissipates energy. If you are constantly worried about every little thing you put into your body or are having a hissy fit because you walk past a television broadcasting fake news (spoiler alert: it's all fake news), then you are over-reacting to the illusions of this world. Fighting against the darkness you see all around you is the fastest way to get sucked into it.

Go back to basics. Ask yourself, "What am I resisting?" The number one trap that spiritually oriented people fall into is getting frustrated and impatient that more people are not waking up quickly. "Why is the world like this? It should be like that. Why are people cruel and indifferent to suffering? They should be sending love and compassion and resources."

Our examples are obvious illustrations of the conflict between "what is" and "what should be." Start with total and complete acceptance that "it is the way it is." Make that your mantra: "It is the way it is." Yes, it's extremely basic and almost silly, but it's the truth. It is the way it is. That doesn't mean it will stay that way forever. That doesn't mean it cannot change. But stop fighting what is. Be present in this moment, with all the suffering and misery contained in this moment.

Planet Earth is a difficult place for most people. There are multiple layers of negative conditioning. One layer involves people covering over their suffering and misery with all manner of pleasure-seeking. Their lives are one big distraction from morning till night. Look at the preoccupation with video games, texting on the telephone, sporting events, nightclubs and bars, game shows on television, fashion and modeling, Hollywood, etc. None of these activities in and of themselves are necessarily harmful, but usually they have become addictions designed to cover up a deep feeling of inadequacy, loneliness, or fear of looking within.

Perhaps you have put away these obvious forms of distraction for ones that are more subtle. Maybe you pride yourself on only watching "alternative" media. Certainly, this is preferable to the mainstream news, but it can also be a distraction. Not very many alternative sites are helping you wake up and move away from distraction. Most have a distinct bias, even if they claim to be "fair and impartial." It is important to stay aware of what is taking place around you and in the world but use the Internet as the tool it was designed to be, not as a distraction.

Again, we are not saying be overly strict with yourself. Sometimes, down time is the best remedy, especially if you work at a stressful job and need to unwind. A high-quality comedy show or series on Netflix or Amazon might be a wise choice to take your mind off something that has become an obsession. Know that this is an intermediate step and not a solution to the problem.

Carefully observe which activities sharpen your mind and senses and which ones dull them. Also notice what foods seem to expand your consciousness and which ones contract it. What makes you feel heavy and tired? What energizes you? Pay close attention to the signals in your body. Does this person help you feel energized and light? Does that one leave you feeling tired and drained?

The most difficult distractions to overcome are your habitual thoughts. A difficult but enlightening exercise is to keep track of your daily thoughts. How many are positive? How many are negative? Which ones keep repeating or are pushing out the other thoughts? What are your obsessions? Do you wake up in the middle of the night and start worrying about unpaid bills or something you said to a loved one? Are you judging the appearance of your body? Where are you trying to force yourself to be different? "Why did I eat that ice cream cone? What's wrong with me?"

According to some psychologists, we have about 50,000 thoughts per day on average. Maybe a meditator only has 20,000. What is the nature of these thoughts? If you are like most people, about 80% of them are about taking care of the body or placating the ego. "What am I going to eat for dinner? How can I get so-and-so to like me? What am I going to say to the boss next week? How can I make more money at my business? How come I don't seem to be able to lose more weight?" Perhaps 20% of your thoughts are more positive, such as, "Higher Self, show me how I can help my friend with cancer," or "I am ready to find a quiet place and communicate with my ascended master spirit guides."

Being a therapist or healer has multiple benefits. Not only are you helping others, but you are helping yourself stay focused on positive thoughts and feelings. You are continuously reminding yourself of what you need to do to promote healing and well-being. If you have a busy clientele, you don't have time to indulge in negative thinking or self-absorption. You might occasionally use yourself as an example when helping a client, but for the most part, you are not thinking about yourself at all. Your sole mission is to help the person in front of you. This is accomplished by being totally present with full attention on what is happening physically, psychologically and spiritually with the other person. When you are working with someone, you are not prone to distraction (at least not as much).

For those of you in the helping professions, there are some pitfalls and traps. You might become distracted by ideals and visions that say,

"This client should be healed of cancer. Look at all the work I've done on her (or him)." Remember not to have an investment in the outcome of your healing or therapy work. You are not there to save someone. Your purpose is to remind the client of his or her greatness within and to help the person love and accept what is. Getting someone to love the little self might be the greatest step in healing.

Certainly, you can help another soul set goals and stay focused, but you are just a guide, like an athletic coach. A running coach does not run the race for the athlete, but helps him be aware of the dynamics of the art of running, and gathers data on the competitors, track conditions, etc. Your job, if you are a therapist or healer, is to help the client open up to higher perspectives, which includes increasing awareness of blocks and obstacles on the path. A person with barriers who is totally present in the moment will have the strength and awareness to see the solution to overcoming the barriers.

Remember the famous observation credited to Einstein regarding the definition of insanity: Doing the same things over and over but expecting different results.

CHAPTER 9

A Metaphysical Issue — The Law of Attraction

∞ A Deeper Look at the Law of Attraction

In the early 2000s, a movie came out called *The Secret*. This popularized the idea that our thoughts create our reality. The author has refined this statement because "thought creates reality" is a partial truth; it is not the whole picture. A more accurate statement, which he has put forth in most of his books, is the idea that "the quality of your consciousness determines your experience of reality." We will go into depth on the meaning of this statement shortly.

Another idea that is paramount to a higher understanding of *The Secret* is the correlation between individual and collective consciousness. Remember, every soul's beliefs are powerful, even if he/she is using consciousness to maintain beliefs in lack, limitation, scarcity and powerlessness. If 99% of the world believes in limited energy ("I must go to the service station and fill my automobile with refined fossils"), this belief will keep supporting those who want to maintain their illusion of control over humanity by continuing to invest in fossil fuels.

The law of momentum applies here as well. There is a lot of kinetic energy (in the form of momentum) in the status quo because so many people believe in it. This collective belief creates a strong resonant field around the mechanizations of the present society. Yes, a lot of new ideas have entered the mainstream consciousness over the past

50 years. Some of them have been propagated by collective beliefs brought to this planet by other cultures (extraterrestrials such as the Orions and Sirians, for example). One such collective belief system (from the Orions) is that the human form can be improved upon by merging it with artificial intelligence. In other words, they want to make us bionic (a marriage of human and machine).

In order to understand the dynamics of the powerful collective belief systems on Earth, we must comprehend the big picture behind the desire of one or more souls to control the actions and thoughts of another soul or souls. Trying to control reality stems from the same core negative belief that all negativity comes from — the belief in separation from God. Believing we are separate, we imagine all sorts of dangers out there in the world. This gives rise to the idea that we must come up with ever-increasing and more elaborate ways to defend ourselves. Therefore, a huge amount of existing resources on Earth is devoted to militaries, weapons, and overt and covert organizations designed to exact ever more control over so-called "enemies."

Imagine if your middle finger and ring finger were at war with each other. They are always trying to bend and twist each other's joints in the hope that one of them will be the victor. Sounds pretty silly, right? It's no sillier than some aspects of God's body (humanity and other races) being at war among themselves. Just because one cannot see the interconnectedness of all life forms does not mean it is not there. We cannot see individual atoms with our unaided eyes, yet we know they are there.

To sum up our discussion of collective conscious and unconscious beliefs, most of society's ills are due to various forms of the belief in separation, which afflicts over 99% of humanity. This is the core belief behind the idea of scarcity. Scarce resources are the basis of the modern economy. In fact, most dictionaries define "economy" as "the study of the allocation of scarce resources," i.e., supply and demand. That which is seen as scarce will command a much higher price than that which is termed abundant.

As most every reader is aware, if Zero-Point Energy were to become distributed worldwide, it would be nearly impossible to make money from it since everyone would have an abundance of energy. Accepting that we live in a sea of infinite energy and intelligence would mean the necessity of radically changing the present economic system. As this author has pointed out numerous times, the present economic system on Earth is almost the exact opposite of higher spiritual principles.

Understanding the problem is essential if we wish to find a solution. The belief in scarcity, like *The Secret*, does not tell the whole story. Yes, it is a cornerstone of the problem, but unless you discover the reason a building is falling apart, patching it up will offer only temporarily relief. So reprogramming the negative core beliefs is one essential step in moving forward with unlimited energy.

Let us now return to the earlier statement, "The quality of your consciousness determines your experience of reality." In addition to the state of your beliefs and programs about reality, there is another enormous aspect to creating fulfillment and joy in your life, and that is acceptance. Many people, upon discovering the principles laid forth in *The Secret*, go about creating heaps of affirmations, plastering them on mirrors, doors, bedposts and the like. They listen to self-improvement audio programs that serve as cheerleaders for acquiring wealth, success and happiness. The author likens this to digging a tunnel with a spoon. You might eventually reach your goals, but various parts of you may be at war with each other, working at cross-purposes, because you have not really started at the beginning of the creative process.

Earlier we mentioned that you must first come to complete acceptance of where you are before you can get where you are going. A simple physical example of this involves geography. London is somewhat north of Madrid, and Moscow is somewhat north of Istanbul. Suppose you want to get to London and you think you are in Madrid (meaning that you must head north), but you are really in Istanbul. Where will you end up? In Moscow.

Many souls learn a bit of metaphysics and spirituality and then think they are ready to be powerful creators. You are always a powerful creator, whether you believe you are or not. Having the belief that you are not powerful will, of course, create an experience of powerlessness (thereby proving that beliefs are powerful).

Learning about the power of creative thought and doing some affirmations might convince you that you are ready to conquer the world (metaphorically speaking). However, recall that the mind is like an iceberg. About 90% of it is submerged in what is called, appropriately, the subconscious. There are likely many layers of negativity that must be cleared and reprogrammed before you are truly manifesting your creative potential. Generally, it takes most souls 20 to 30 years of working on themselves before they make significant progress at reprogramming their negative core beliefs. Nevertheless, there are things you can do to speed up the healing and cleansing process.

Accepting "what is" becomes the powerful starting point for creating the reality you desire. In the recovery movements, people often repeat the "serenity prayer." (Lord, help us accept the things we cannot change; give us the courage to change the things we can; and the wisdom to know the difference.) You cannot change "what is" until you first accept that things are the way they are. This brings you into the present moment. You are aware of exactly what is taking place within you and around you. It is a place of power because there is no resistance to what is. As resistance lowers, you get more and more in touch with your creative faculties, and you become open to new ideas and strategies that might be necessary to move in the desired direction.

This is what we mean by "the quality of your consciousness." Are you fighting and resisting reality? Do you have a vendetta or an "axe to grind?" Do you hate the government? Are you constantly putting down people who are not "woke?" These are all forms of ego resistance that are sapping your energy and clouding your mind to the real solutions to your problems (and the problems of humanity).

Again, we are not saying you should accept bad behavior or turn a blind eye to the suffering of others. Part of your acceptance includes the fact that these things are taking place. You look directly at the suffering, the injustice, the war, poverty and misery. You then ask your Higher Self to guide you in the highest possible path regarding your response to these things. You respond rather than react.

As you raise your consciousness, you remove judgment from your mind. Being free of judgment, you can then see the highest and best path for you and humanity. You know that your personal energy blends with the collective energy of those around you. Your state of vibration affects those around you and vice versa. You carefully choose the people in your personal life, and where you seem to have no choice in the matter (blood family, etc.), you practice acceptance. But that does not mean you feel obligated to spend all your time with people you dislike.

We realize it is not that easy. Suppose you are the only one taking care of a sick parent. The rest of your siblings are dead or simply refuse to help. Once again, you start by accepting the reality of the situation and then asking your Higher Self for assistance. At first it might seem impossible to improve your conditions, but as you release the resistance (and clear the negative emotions around your predicament), seemingly new energies become available. You receive insights. Even if you are already engaged in the highest possible path regarding caring for your sick parent, you still have the ability to come to greater acceptance and appreciation for the difficult lesson you have chosen. You enter a space of gratitude for the opportunity to experience this challenge. Easy? Definitely not. But essential to taking the next step on your spiritual path.

When you stop seeing the world as a battlefield, something to be overcome or conquered, you begin attracting experiences that support your life of love and acceptance. More and more loving and accepting people begin showing up and supporting your vision and purpose. You see everything and everyone as part of your support system, even those with negative intentions. They are there to help you discern right from wrong behavior. They motivate you to work on yourself and find love and compassion. It is a wonderful challenge to contemplate loving the murderer, rapist, terrorist or pedophile. Of course, the behavior is awful and might require disciplinary action, but you can still love the lost souls who have chosen to behave badly.

∞ What Is True Power?

In electronics, one of the equations used to define power is voltage times current, or watts times amperes. In physics, this is translated as potential energy times kinetic energy. In metaphysics, it means taking your creative abilities (potential energy) and converting them into usable skills (kinetic energy). The combination of your potential and the work you perform equals your overall power. In business, power typically means the ability to get things done — or to win friends and influence people, as Dale Carnegie would say. Notice there is nowhere in this statement where it is implied that we seek to control and dominate others. We influence, yes. We are all powerful influences on each other, whether we are aware of this or not. Our energy interacts with that of others in many seen and unseen ways.

Tony Robbins, a well-known motivational speaker, packs an auditorium or hotel convention center with people who pay top price to listen to him speak for a couple of hours. Why is he so popular? Of course, the immediate answer is charisma, which means essentially that he has a giant aura of self-confidence (power). He is projecting that power into the audience (empowering people). By sharing his ability to win friends and influence people, he makes his audience feel like a million bucks (probably about how much he makes leading a weekend workshop).

The ego has an insatiable lust for power because it is the belief in lack and scarcity made manifest. True power is replaced by false power when put in the hands of the ego. We are not sure if there is an analogy in physics, but in metaphysics, we must return to the power of belief. If lots of human egos gather together behind a common belief system, a semblance of power results. However, this "power" may not be in alignment with natural cosmic forces (universal law). It is what many mystics call "misqualified energy." Since this is the spiritual section of the book, we should define misqualified energy, or false power, as that force which, when directed outward, causes harm or disharmony to others.

One spiritual teacher says the whole purpose of the soul's journey is to learn the true, natural, cosmic laws and to align with them. He states that the central cosmic principal is to refrain from doing harm to others. If your actions uplift and liberate the consciousness of humanity, you are aligned with true power. If you are oppressing, controlling, or limiting the expression of consciousness in others, you are aligned with false power.

Perhaps an adequate analogy in physics would be a circuit that explodes or shorts out due to improper construction. Yes, there is still power present, but it is not made to perform useful tasks and, in fact, will likely start a fire if not immediately suppressed. Virtually all the wars fought in the world throughout history (analogous to a short-circuit) involve the misuse of power. Because of the belief in separation, souls think they must forcefully take power from others in order to survive or defend themselves. Trying to limit something that is unlimited (false versus true power) results in an exploding circuit (failure of the energy systems in the body or society). This brings a surge in entropy. An explosion is an example of a very quick conversion from more ordered energy patterns into more chaotic and disordered patterns.

The result of misqualified energy (misuse of power) is chaos and confusion in the world, and this is what we see around us every day. Any time a soul or group of souls feels they must violate the free will of others by imposing mandatory laws and regulations designed to serve themselves at the expense of others, the result will inevitably be chaos (entropy). The result might be quick, in the case of war, or happen more slowly, in the case of gradual extraction of material wealth from the citizens to the "power elite" at the top of the pyramid, something that can be observed in today's economics.

The simplest way to tell if you are misqualifying energy is to ask, "What is the motivation behind this activity, desire or goal?" If you are sensitive to energy patterns, you might be able to discern when there is a harmonious flow of potential to kinetic energy or whether there is excessive resistance (or not enough) to create a viable circuit. The body will tell you when you are out of balance. Illness is either too much or too little resistance, depending on the particular malady. Usually it is too much, but not always. A lack of healthy boundaries (too little ego) can result in a soul taking on the energy of others in an unhealthy way.

To sum up, properly qualified energy is present when the conversion of potential energy into kinetic energy results in greater order (centropy). Misqualified energy is the result of a conversion process that increases chaos (entropy). Of course, some entropy is necessary. If you burn fuel, you create a more disordered form of energy (heat). Although there are alternatives to the burning of various substances to produce a temporary benefit, such as heating a home or business, it is unlikely that this form of energy conversion will become obsolete right away. We have given several reasons why in our discussion above. Nevertheless, the main topic of this book is how to harness

Zero-Point Energy, and properly harnessed, we achieve a balance between entropy and centropy.

The truth is, we are all powerful beings, created in the image and likeness of our Creator. However, by believing we are powerless or have extremely limited power, we misqualify our God-given energy by channeling it in destructive ways. The starting point for healing is to recognize that we have all the power we could ever need or desire within us. We learn to live life from the inside out. This means radiating and generating energy and information, sending it out into the world with the intent to share, energize, uplift and enlighten, instead of trying to grab things from outside ourselves in order to fill a bottomless pit of desire. The Law of Attraction figures prominently here. The more we give love and compassion (qualified energy), the more it is returned to us, thereby completing the circuit.

The false power being demonstrated by those souls who believe they are in control of this world, and the beliefs of the dominions upon which they supposedly rule (the collective consciousness that thinks the false power overlords are really in control) will be transformed as we recognize the difference between true and false power and start aligning with the right use of power. False, or illusory, power, depends on belief and loyalty to that belief. True power needs no belief at all, for it is inherent within the structure of the universe.

False power is the result of putting the ego on the throne instead of God. Although everything is God, you will not realize this if you have loyalties to the ego's demands for domination and control, borne out of its deep fear of inadequacy. The ego *is* the fear of inadequacy based on the belief in separation. Recognize this and you are well on your way to freedom from tyranny, oppression and control.

Although you might need to temporarily abide by many of the rules and regulations put forth by those with false power that are designed to enslave you and keep you from awakening, the trick is to stop identifying with that false reality. For a while, you might choose to pay your taxes and use fiat currency when trading goods and services, knowing that these instruments of commerce are based upon the false beliefs of those loyal to separation. Yet, energetically, you can remain free from the constant worry, anxiety, fear and depression that loyalty to false power generates.

The system is designed to enslave you. Let's be very direct and to the point. There's no need to hide behind euphemisms and false platitudes. Recognize the problem. Wake up from your denial. Accept what is. Then you have the ability to change it. When you release your loyalty to false power (including the belief that someone or something outside of yourself can bring you salvation), you open the door to recognizing and remembering what true power is. You become the light of the world. You become a catalyst for genuine positive change.

∞ More on the Law of Attraction

Although the universe is infinitely abundant in every conceivable way, souls evolving on Earth (and many other planets) will not experience this state of infinity unless they have the consciousness necessary to perceive it.

Lack and scarcity are illusions, but as long as you believe in them, they will seem real to you. Therefore, even if someone were to demonstrate a working Zero-Point device, you would not see the results. In fact, you would not even attract someone like that into your space unless a part of you was ready to have your belief system challenged. Instead, you would be aligned with a resonant field of other individuals who also disbelieve the idea of unlimited energy.

Like attracts like applies to energy (and everything else). There are actually three states that exist within humanity regarding the Law of Attraction. The first, we have just stated above. Those who believe in unlimited energy will tend to attract others who believe likewise and, therefore, will be privy to successful demonstrations of Zero-Point Energy. Those who believe in lack and scarcity will not experience abundant unlimited energy.

The other two aspects of the Law of Attraction are what this author calls "teacher-student" and "student-teacher" relationships. When a soul has not yet given up his/her negative beliefs (such as the belief in lack), but is ready to begin the process of making a fundamental shift in consciousness toward abundance, such a soul will tend to attract a teacher (or group of teachers) who can assist him/her in making the shift in perspective.

Likewise, if you are already aware of the unlimited nature of the universe, you may be called upon to work with souls who are just beginning to wake up to the larger reality and, therefore, you will be in the teacher role.

Remember that the Law of Attraction applies to the entire state of a soul's consciousness, not just the conscious mind. You might have been using affirmations and gone to a few workshops in living abundantly, but you still have many deep layers of disbelief lodged in your subconscious mind. At such a point you are not ready to experience Zero-Point Energy. However, if you are drawn to this book and similar studies, it is an indication that you are at least at the student phase of the process and are rapidly releasing all limited beliefs regarding the nature of the universe.

Earlier we looked at the complicated mathematics of determining what this author calls the composite level of vibration of a soul's consciousness. Since there are almost 8 billion souls on planet Earth, many living in crowded cities, the field of consciousness of humanity (if you could see it clairvoyantly) would look a lot like layers of fog and smog. There might be a few pockets of brightly colored, harmonious layers where a group of souls have predominantly positive thoughts, but over three-fourths of the fog would be of the negative variety. A few positively-oriented souls might be sprinkled among the gray, dull, heavy layers of disbelief.

There are only a few places on the Earth where the level of consciousness is higher than 4.0 on this author's density scale. According to higher teachings, for Zero-Point Energy devices to flourish, the consciousness of a given area must be above 4.5. Therefore, this technology is "waiting" for humanity to awaken sufficiently to be able to use it responsibly. It is not that beings in the higher realms are intentionally withholding information. They do not need to do this. We, as a whole, have been doing a good job of withholding our own good for millennia.

Most of the books in this author's collection are designed to help you raise your consciousness vibration. This is the most important ingredient in the formula for harnessing Zero-Point Energy. As long as humanity's vibration is less than this 4.5 threshold, there will continue to be various ways new technologies will be held back, including outright suppression by the so-called "powers that be."

The first step is education. People need to know that they have been lied to about the nature of the universe. You do not live in a dog-eat-dog, survival-of-the-fittest Darwinian universe (with Newtonian overtones). Although both Darwin and Newton contributed greatly to our understanding of everyday life on Earth, their theories were seriously flawed. Human beings are not animals even though they occupy bodies that are somewhat animalistic in nature. Identifying with the human form is the problem. You begin to believe you are the body and that the spirit is just a fantasy. This belief lowers your vibration until you begin experiencing an identification with the animal realms.

Imagine if you were to believe you were an automobile. That would be considered a form of insanity. Yet this biological vehicle you are wearing is a lot like an automobile. It is a vehicle for experiencing the lower dimensions. Believing you are a body is no more or less insane than proudly declaring you are a Mercedes Benz.

CHAPTER 10

Levels of Consciousness Vibration Required for Zero-Point Energy Fields

Although detailed information can be found in *Soul Integration*, we will give a somewhat modified summary of the way this author defines the levels and degrees of consciousness pertinent to our metaphysical/spiritual discussion of unlimited energy.

The author has two model systems worth mentioning at this point. One involves singularities plus 12 dimensions, labeled as follows:

(0) Existence, location (point, singularity)
(1) Magnitude, quantity (line)
(2) Planar, area (flat plane)
(3) Depth, volume (3D objects, physical reality)
(4) Linear time (sequence of events, includes astral planes)
(5) Aether (etheric planes)
(6) Causality (causal planes)
(7) Soul (lower celestial planes, angelic realms)
(8) Oversoul (middle celestial planes, ascended masters)
(9) Monad (upper celestial planes, atmic realms, avatars)
(10) Christic/Buddhic planes (lower God planes, great central sun, intergalactic realms)
(11) Individual God Self (middle God planes, great great central sun)
(12) Universal God Self (upper God planes, Creator Gods, other universes)

In addition, this system has a level 13, which is the unknowable Source beyond all levels and dimensions, often called the Tao or Great Mystery. Being unknowable, it is always beyond whatever level or dimension you happen to be vibrating at.

The systems used by the author include "aspects of Self" which are labeled as follows:

1. Mineral plane
2. Plant kingdom
3. Animal and lower human domain
4. Higher human domain, higher mind, astral body
5. Crystal light body, etheric body
6. Causal body, Merkabah vehicle of light
7. Soul (the "home" level)
8. Oversoul (ascended masters)
9. Monad (avatars)
10. Christic/Buddhic Planes (lower God planes, great central sun, intergalactic realms)
11. Individual God Self (middle God planes, great central sun)
12. Universal God Self (upper God planes, Creator Gods, other universes)

In this model system, the first six aspects are called the "lower" bodies and the second six aspects are called the "higher" bodies or "Higher Self."

It is obvious that the two systems are not entirely compatible. In the first system, the lower four dimensions are essentially the realms of entropy, while the upper eight levels fall into the category of centropy or regeneration. In the second system, centropy does not become entirely dominant until the vibration reaches level 7, that of the pure soul essence. The etheric and causal bodies are still corruptible if they are not perfectly balanced with the other lower bodies.

In some discussions, levels 4, 5 and 6 (astral, etheric and causal) are called the "subtle planes" or "intermediate realms." Shamans and mystics are taught to master these levels before proceeding into the higher dimensions. A lot of souls get "caught" in these intermediate planes, mistaking them for the celestial heavens (levels 7, 8 and 9).

You will also note that the descriptions of the upper levels are almost identical no matter what model system is being used. That is because once you reach beyond level 7, there are almost no words that can describe what exists there.

Probably the closest to a synthesis of the two levels we can come to at this point is to relate to them in terms of how much entropy and centropy is present. Let's break the models into four categories:

Level	Degree of Entropy/Centropy
1, 2 and 3	Almost entirely entropic (lower levels)
4, 5 and 6	A mix of entropic and centropic (intermediate levels)
7, 8 and 9	Almost entirely centropic (higher dimensions)
10, 11 and 12	Irrelevant to our discussion (beyond entropy and centropy)

Based on the above, a soul who reaches level 4 (the astral planes) has the ability to bring some centropic energy into the Self, meaning there can be partial regeneration (perhaps a slowing down of the aging process in the human body, for example). At level 5, the physical body begins to undergo a fundamental change into what has been termed "ascension into the crystal light body." Here the centropic realms begin to significantly affect the lower self, and it is possible to stop the aging process entirely in the human body. At level 6 (the causal body), either entropy or centropy can dominate, depending on the focus of the soul vibrating at level 6. Such a person can choose to leave the body and go into higher dimensions of spirit or may stay on the Earth in a state of immortality for as long as desired.

Souls who reach a state of consciousness beyond the lower six levels are living almost exclusively in the realms of centropy. You could say their ability to merge with the Godhead makes them powerful centers of regenerative energies. Once a soul reaches level 9 (the avatar), they completely transcend the so-called "laws" of the lower dimensions. Teachers such as Babaji and Krishna (vibrating at levels 9 and 10 respectively) are essentially unlimited from the perspective of those seemingly trapped in the lower dimensions. These avatars can materialize and dematerialize bodies, bilocate (create multiple versions of themselves simultaneously in different places) and travel anywhere in the universe at the speed of thought.

Is it not obvious at this point that level of vibration of consciousness is the determining factor in how much energy you are able to move or direct through your being? It has been said by this author's spirit guides that the love and compassion of great beings in the higher realms is the reason humanity still exists on this planet. Originally, such enlightened souls were not allowed to intervene in the affairs of humanity, but that was changed once the militaries of the world got their hands-on nuclear weapons.

Extraterrestrials from Andromeda, Pleiades, Sirius and many other star systems (including Arcturus) began coming to Earth right after the first atomic tests in the 1940s. After bombs were dropped on Japan, it was determined that future warfare with nuclear weapons would not be allowed over highly populated areas.

The reader might be saying at this point, "If intervention is allowed regarding the nuclear situation, why can't beings from higher dimensions help bring Zero-Point Energy devices into the world?"

Actually, intervention is only allowed in situations where the entire Earth would be rendered uninhabitable if humanity were left to their own devices. In other words, if a certain weapon or technological activity leaves no safe places for those who do not wish to be victims of war, then intervention is allowed.

There is also intervention in cases where the grid system of Earth becomes so unstable that massive earthquakes would occur near populated areas. In recent years, some intervention has also been allowed regarding chemical and electromagnetic warfare, geo-engineering (spraying of chemicals into the atmosphere, known as "chemtrails") and, to a lesser extent, regarding the proliferation of genetically modified organisms and other biological agents.

These issues were discussed in depth in previous books, so we will not go further into the subject at this time. The main purpose of this section is to help you realize how important it is to raise your vibration if you want to see the era of unlimited energy birthed onto the planet.

Now let us summarize this chapter by creating a table depicting the levels and dimensions.

Earlier in this chapter, we delineated two sets of planes or dimensions, each with their own principles and consistency. If you have read previous works, you will be familiar with the 12-dimensional model. During an extensive analysis of levels of consciousness given in the work *Soul Integration*, we divided these 12 levels into two categories of six dimensions each. We discussed the aspects of self, including six lower bodies and six higher bodies.

In this book, we have divided these 12 realms into four categories: The Lower Worlds, the Subtle Planes, the Celestial Planes and the God Worlds. This is because the laws of energy, motion, time and space differ significantly in each category. While there are universal laws that apply to all levels and dimensions, certain properties can be ascribed to each of these four categories. They are detailed as follows:

LEVEL OF VIBRATION	APPLICABLE LAWS AND PRINCIPLES
Lower Worlds/Selves	
Physical (Mineral, Plant and Animal)	Newtonian laws, gravity, entropy (thermodynamics), procreation, cellular division, chemical reactions
Emotional (Desire, Will, Sexuality)	Law of Attraction, psychological patterns, needs of the ego
Mental (Ego, Intellect, Conscious mind)	Visualization, intention, goals, planning, ideas, concepts, lower laws of creativity
Subtle Planes/Selves	
Astral (Imaginative, Psychic, Intuitive)	Karma, Cause and Effect, Affinity (the higher aspects of Law of Attraction)
Etheric (Nonlocality, entropy/centropy blend)	Law of Love, higher laws of creativity, Ascension, Regeneration
Causal (Merkabah, Akashic Records)	Aspect of soul that remembers past lifetimes, a crystalline realm of pure light
Celestial Planes	
Soul ("home" level) Lower Celestial Heavens	Angels, Light Beings, first level of Higher Self
Oversoul Middle Celestial Heavens	Archangels, Ascended Masters, Group Soul Complexes
Monad (Atmic Self) Higher Celestial Heavens	Avatars, Central Sun Beings, Celestial Orders, Love, Oneness

God Planes

Christic/Buddhic Self (Lower God Realms)	Great Central Sun Beings, Intergalactic Beings
Individual God Self (Middle God Realms)	Great Great Central Sun Beings, Universal Beings
Universal God Self (Upper God Realms)	Creator Gods, Other Universes, the God-head

As mentioned in the previous chapter, there is a level 13, which is the unknowable Source, Tao, Great Mystery, Void, or whatever name you wish to call it.

CHAPTER 11

Integrating Physics, Metaphysics and Spirituality

∞ A Summary of the Spiritual/Metaphysical Section

Science is playing "catch-up" to the teachings of enlightened masters, yogis, philosophers and sages. For example, the Nonlocality Principle of quantum physics essentially states that all is One. Spirituality states that all is One with God. There is no separation. We are all connected intimately to our Source. In fact, the belief in separation from God is the cause of all misery and suffering. No exceptions.

Everything is God. Everything is contained within the Mind of God. Therefore, it is impossible to actually be separate from God. However, it is certainly possible to believe in separation, and since beliefs are all-powerful, you set up an impossible situation. There appears to be, and you experience, separation, but it is really an illusion.

The above statement offers proof that we are powerful, creative, spiritual beings. In fact, we are so powerful that we can create an entire world based on the idea of separation and then experience it as if it were so.

Some corollaries to this central idea include the belief that there are forces outside of ourselves that can harm us — so-called "enemies" or "dark forces" or "Dark Lords." Believing we are separate from our Creator, we start to imagine all sorts of dangers lurking in the darkness and, as a result, begin defending ourselves from our imagined enemies. Believing they are real, we inevitably create an experience of being attacked, enslaved, oppressed or ruled by so-called dark entities.

Energy is related to power. If we say someone or something is powerful, we mean it has the ability to perform a great deal of work (kinetic energy) or has the potential to create on a large scale (potential energy).

∞ More on the Power of Belief

Belief is a collection of thoughts, ideas and concepts formed in consciousness and then radiated outward into the universe. There is energy in consciousness; therefore, there is energy in belief. The stronger and more tightly held the belief, the more power (energy) is radiated. This is why souls that have a very strong belief in something tend to create it, sometimes against insurmountable odds.

Beliefs give rise to self-fulfilling prophecies. If you believe in death and destruction strongly enough, you will experience it. If others adopt your beliefs, they will experience the results as well.

If you believe there is not enough energy in the world, that it is scarce and expensive, or that you must pollute the Earth in order to extract and burn the raw materials, then you will contribute to the destruction of the environment. If you believe your livelihood depends on oil, gas, coal or nuclear energy, you will likely fight to defend those industries even if it is crystal clear that they are destroying the planet.

If you do not believe in abundant energy, an inventor of a Zero-Point Energy machine could demonstrate his device right in front of you and you might not even see the results. This is similar to the case of the stage hypnotist who can convince you that there is no rope in front of you and you then trip over the rope. He could just as easily have convinced you that there is a rope there when there is none, and you will walk around or jump over the imaginary rope. What most people do not realize is that the world is one giant stage and we are the actors (to paraphrase Shakespeare). Most human beings are so identified with the characters they are playing, that they have forgotten it is only a play (to paraphrase Dan Hicks). They are completely hypnotized by the things of this world. In modern-day language, this is known as being stuck in the matrix. (The matrix refers to the collective beliefs, attitudes and prejudices of humanity.)

Why are we going so deep into metaphysics in a book about energy? Because negatively polarized consciousness is the main barrier (obstacle) to tapping into the nearly unlimited field of Zero-Point. In other words, consciousness units (CU) can be positively or negatively polarized. If negative, they will seem to subtract from the available energy of a closed system (by increasing resistance and entropy).

∞ Another Attempt to Quantify Consciousness Units

In actual mathematical equations, negative beliefs are most probably fractions between zero and one, thereby diminishing the overall available energy in a system. The energy is still preserved in perfect balance, but a negatively polarized soul will be unable to access very much of it. Arbitrarily, if love has a CU of 100, perhaps hatred has a CU of .01 (1/100). At some point in the future, it might be possible to quantify the actual stream of consciousness emanated by an individual soul (or group of souls).

It certainly appears that a person filled with rage has a lot of energy, but it is highly entropic (chaotic) and usually leads to destruction in some form.

For now, the higher dimensional beings are suggesting we use a logarithmic scale for measuring the amount of energy present in consciousness, based on overall (composite) level of vibration. Earlier we used factors of ten (logarithms) related to density level as one possible model (i.e., 3.0 vibration equals 1, 4.0 equals 10, 5.0 equals 100, etc.).

We will suggest a combination of the above two measurement systems, keeping in mind these are very rough approximations. Let's say that a vibration of 3.0 equals a CU value of 1/100, 4.0 equals 1/10, 5.0 equals 1, 6.0 equals 10, 7.0 equals 100, etc. Another way of saying this would be that a highly negative person with a vibration of 3.0 decreases the overall accessible energy of a system by a factor of 100, while a person with a vibration of 7.0 increases the overall accessible energy of the system by a factor of 100. We picked these numbers to illustrate the idea that attaining a level five consciousness means no longer being a significant part of entropy, or dissipation of energy.

Please remember that these are arbitrary models of how to measure the energy of consciousness. They are given here simply to illustrate the idea that the more you raise your consciousness, the more true power you manifest in your life.

What about the so-called leaders of the world? Don't they have a lot of power? No, not really. They have the illusion of power. They appear to be powerful because people believe in them or believe they have the power to control the society and the individuals within it. Essentially, people are feeding them energy through the power of belief, because deep inside, these so-called leaders have forgotten who they are and now must rely on the energy of others in order to sustain their illusion of power and control.

Underneath the bravado, military might and tough words is the belief in separation and the intense fear of being powerless that accompanies that belief. Therefore, they must make up for their sense of inadequacy by rising up in the political or military ranks and becoming one of the world's predominant stage hypnotists (to quote an earlier analogy).

Hitler, for example, was extremely popular at one point in his career. He might not have been particularly likeable, but he was respected by his military officers. Such men were hypnotized into believing that they belonged to a superior race. Despite the horrors of war involving the purging of various ethnic groups (ethnic cleansing), they found this acceptable in order to uphold their collective belief in superiority.

Members of the Israeli military are trained to see Palestinian soldiers as sub-human so that the Israelis will not feel remorse or think about the families of their victims when killing the enemy soldiers.

Americans were hypnotized into believing they were victors in World War II after dropping atomic bombs that killed hundreds of thousands of people in Japan.

Today, in most countries, people are hypnotized into believing that changing political parties will somehow solve their problems. But Einstein said that you cannot solve the problem on the level where it was created. He also said that doing the same thing over and over and expecting different results was a definition of insanity. A reasonably sane person, seeing the same problems occurring over and over again and again in the world, will reach the conclusion: "Clearly we need to change at a fundamental level if we want to see change in the world."

One of the most popular and unanimous teachings within the realm of spirituality and metaphysics is the idea that change begins within. Even Michael Jackson stated that he needed to begin with "The Man in the Mirror." Trying to change the world by forcing people to change is a lot like racing up to the front of a movie theatre and trying to rearrange the characters on the screen.

Above, we have stated the truth from a metaphysical point of view, and we have accurately outlined the problem (negative belief systems and programmed/conditioned responses that are drilled into the subconscious mind over long periods of time — in other words, negative hypnosis).

∞ Integrating Science and Metaphysics

To bring the scientific and metaphysical paths together, we need solutions that work with both fields of study (just as the micro and macro versions of physics need to find a Unified Field Theory that works in both cases). So how do we go about this? First, each "camp" needs to keep an open mind and discover the best that the other has to offer. Science is practical. It seeks to answer the question, "How does the universe work?" Metaphysics comes from the idea that consciousness is the primal force behind Creation. Therefore, we need to add consciousness to the list of ingredients in the cosmic soup, and we need more scientific method applied to the metaphysical path.

Science has proven that we live in a sea of nearly infinite energy. The next step is to get our priorities straight. Our top priority needs to be finding practical, non-polluting ways of harnessing that energy. To do this, we must change our consciousness. We need to stop believing in lack and scarcity, and we need to scrap the present economic system that is based on lack and scarcity. Webster's Dictionary defines "economics" as "the study of the allocation of scarce resources." Our present economic system is almost the exact opposite of higher spiritual principles. How can we possibly move forward with harnessing the nearly infinite supply of energy if we are bound to a system that depends on never harnessing it?

If the metaphysical truth, "Our beliefs create our reality" is to be addressed, we need to ask ourselves, "If almost everyone in the world believes in scarcity, what are they going to experience?" If Zero-Point Energy represents the end of scarcity, how are Zero-Point devices going to be implemented in a world that believes otherwise?

(Note: If it looks as though we are repeating ourselves yet again, you are correct. This idea holds the solution to the world's energy problems, and we cannot repeat it often enough.)

The world we see is the collective creation of the states of consciousness of the souls living here. If you want to know what people are thinking and believing, just take a look at the world. Because a small percentage of humanity believes in abundance and prosperity, Zero-Point devices can be built and demonstrated on a small scale (as they have been for over 50 years). Yet as soon as the inventor makes it to the commercial development phase of the project, endless problems tend to surface. The reason should be obvious. The positive energy of the inventor and a few forward-thinking individuals are no match for the millions who believe it cannot be done.

Remember the story of the explorers who landed in Central America in their huge sailing ships, parked them in the harbor, and began interacting with the natives? The native peoples had never seen anything larger than a canoe and had no frame of reference for huge ships. Therefore, they could not even see the ships that were right there in plain view.

One of this author's favorite adages is "We are like fish looking for water." This is true regarding the energy situation, just as it is true regarding spirituality. For thousands of years, humankind has been looking for God, yet God is within, closer to us than the heart and mind. Likewise, the abundance of God is here, right in front of our faces.

Now, scientists are beginning to demonstrate that this is the case. Nassim Haramein, as we detailed earlier, recently produced a paper called "The Schwarzschild Proton," which shows that the entire universe exists within every proton of every atom. This essentially states that we live in a hologram. One of the properties of holograms is that the whole exists within the parts. Dr. Haramein goes on to indicate that there are trillions of black holes, white holes and wormholes existing within the fabric of space itself. If the macro phenomena exist within the tiniest of subatomic particles, isn't this akin to saying,

"The Kingdom of Heaven is within?" Not only are we inside the Creation, but the Creation is inside us.

J. Krishnamurti, the great philosopher, said, "The observer is the observed." What does this actually mean? Along with Dr. David Bohm, the renowned physicist, these gentlemen concluded that there is no actual observer of reality. The observer is part of the observation. There is no "me" in here and no "you" out there. In fact, there is no "out there" out there, as another researcher put it. *A Course in Miracles* states that "Everything exists within the Mind of God."

Can we see that scientists and philosophers are saying the same thing in different words?

∞ Practical Considerations Regarding Resonant Fields

Let us assume, for a moment, that what is said above is entirely true — that physics and metaphysics are saying the same thing. Then how does this affect us in our daily lives on Earth? What can we really do about it? What are the practical steps required to bring about an energy renaissance? The answer lies in a concept we introduced earlier — resonant fields.

In electrical theory, a resonant field consists of a group of electrons that have "scalar potential," meaning they have become non-polarized. In other words, they are not seeking a positive pole but have achieved a stasis, or balance. Such a resonant field has extremely low resistance and hence becomes a superconductor.

This idea can be applied in a macro sense as well. Human beings are capable of forming symbiotic relationships (mutually beneficial arrangements). In business, this is called a "win-win relationship." When a group of souls comes together and shares a common purpose, it creates, to some extent, a resonant field. For example, a group of transcendental meditators that radiates a unified purpose becomes quite powerful. In fact, this has been documented in various research projects.

It is this author's belief that human groups forming resonant fields are what has so far prevented World War III. The energy of the group accumulates exponentially, meaning the power of two souls gathered may have the power of four individuals who are not gathered, and the power of ten souls in a resonant field might have the power of 100 individuals who are not in the field. It could take only a few million souls in resonance to affect every other soul on Earth.

If you observe the phenomenon of "going viral" that exists in modern culture, you will see that ideas are presented over the Internet (using Facebook, YouTube, etc.) that, within weeks, get millions of viewers. Obviously, not all viewers of media are going to be in resonance, and some will be in opposition, but the idea is valid. Imagine a resonant field of enlightened souls whose teachings "go viral" within a matter of weeks. Can it happen? Absolutely.

A large group of inventors and forward-thinking individuals can form a resonant field. This field then interacts with the Zero-Point field (that exists everywhere in space/time), amplifying and magnifying the effects of the Zero-Point devices being created by the group.

Someone once said that it only takes 1.8% of souls focusing in a particular direction to change the world. Imagine what would happen if that number of souls embraced the Zero-Point projects of reputable inventors and scientists.

The first step, as always, is education. People need to understand that they are brainwashed. They are hypnotized by the "matrix." Ever since the *Matrix* movie came out, a lot of people are now saying that they have become "redpilled." This is a new mainstream word for "awakened." Sure, the level of awakening might be quite small relative to enlightened spiritual masters, but it is a start.

Regardless of President Donald Trump's many faults and often bad behavior, he represented a small but significant awakening in the people of the United States. He was elected primarily because people were tired of the status quo. Although he did little to change the status quo, the very fact that he was elected attested to the willingness of people to begin waking up.

There are, of course, other examples. Over half of the planet now has access to telecommunications and global media. Since the rise of the Internet, it is now impossible to "put the genie back into the bottle." There are inventors who have published their schematics and theories, which are being read by millions of engineers and scientists. While funding is difficult (for the reasons given earlier), more and more people are discovering just how much we have been lied to by the mainstream media regarding the supposed "scarcity" of energy.

You can create a resonant field of souls simply by sharing this information in study groups. If mediocre singers and artists can gather 1.5 billion "hits" on YouTube, then it follows that you are capable of bringing the ideas in this book to a lot of people in a quick period of time.

A hundred years ago, the idea of speaking and looking at someone thousands of miles away through a hand-held device was pure science fiction, yet today most young people cannot imagine being without their devices. If mobile-phone video can emerge in such a short period of time, then Zero-Point devices are not far behind. Of course, the existing corporate monopolies will only back it if they can profit significantly, and so far, they are too afraid of losing their hold on the populace.

Addiction to oil, for example, is a hard habit to break. Naturally, the oil companies are going to "cry wolf" and pontify end-of-the-world doomsday scenarios if we were to adopt Zero-Point Energy. Yes, it would be the end of the world — for them. Unless they find a way to meter it, tax it and regulate it.

So, the first step is education. Let people know that these are not pie-in-the-sky, perpetual-motion dreams of some madman, but solid, tangible science that agrees with the best and brightest metaphysicians and enlightened teachers.

We have purposely kept the mathematics in this book either nonexistent or extremely simple so as not to scare away too many people. You don't have to be a technical nerd to understand the theory presented here. Do some research. Read books and articles on the subject. Go to symposiums and conferences on alternative energy. Above all, keep an open mind.

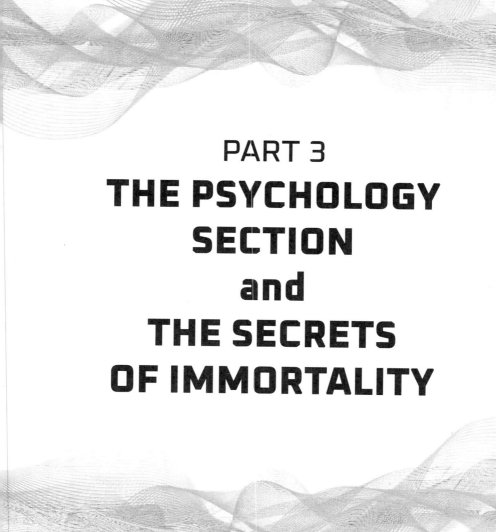

PART 3

THE PSYCHOLOGY SECTION
and
THE SECRETS
OF IMMORTALITY

CHAPTER 12

Unlimited Energy and the Physical Body — An Introduction to Immortality

∞ The Short Version of Immortality Science

No book on the truth about energy would be complete without an investigation into the science of immortality. You will note that we are putting this section in the psychological part, for although there is extremely basic physics involved, the key to immortality is in the spiritual and psychological understanding of the Law of Conservation of Energy. This is the most basic law in the universe. It has been stated in countless ways. You are probably most familiar with, "Energy can neither be created nor destroyed."

To truly understand this law, it is important to know the difference between an "open" system and a "closed" system. Our definition is a bit different than that proffered by mainstream science. An open system is one in which energy sources outside the system are periodically or continuously replenishing the natural entropy of the system. Or you could say energy is being downloaded from the higher realms.

A closed system is one in which equilibrium has been attained. In such a system, energy is not entering or exiting, but simply changing form within the confines of the system.

In theory, the universe is both open and closed, depending on how it is perceived. If the universe is infinite, it is, by definition, an open system, since there will always be something beyond what can be perceived. Yet, if you can conceive of the idea of wholeness, this implies that there is nothing outside of the whole, again by definition, so in that sense the universe is a closed system.

We are maintaining a definition of God that includes all internal and external reality (as a partial perception), meaning that there is nothing outside of God. Therefore, the whole is contained within the body of God, making this a system of perfect equilibrium. Such a system is eternal, meaning it has no beginning nor end and has a constancy (the static state, or Bose-Einstein Condensate). Like a fractal, the results of the generated function are infinite, unfolding in ever more intricate spirals and patterns, while the function itself is eternal and unchanging.

As we continue to fully investigate the question posed at the beginning of this book, "How do we harness the unlimited field of energy that is everywhere present in the universe?" we must examine the personal experience human beings have had regarding the expression, utilization, release, and storing of energy in the human body and so-called "subtle bodies" associated with each human soul.

Scientifically, we can create electrical circuits and assemble magnets, coils and various conductors and storage devices. Spiritually, we can recognize that the Kingdom of God is within each and every one of us. But what about psychologically? What is the state of consciousness necessary to tap into the unlimited field of energy? How can we realize centropy (reverse entropy) in our daily lives? How does it translate into practical activities and experiences of everyday life?

Let us review a basic equation that has been given in previous books. This equation is the one that determines physical immortality. It's extremely simple: *Energy in equals energy out.*

What are the ways that energy enters the physical body? There are several. The most obvious would be food and water. Next, would be oxygen and other components of the air we breathe. Not as obvious would be cosmic radiation. Far from obvious would be etheric energy, or what ancient cultures call "prana" or life force energy. It can also be assumed that there are other forms of energy that exist in dimensions beyond the etheric that might be contributing to the overall level of energy in the physical body. Let's make a simple equation:

Energy In = food + water + oxygen + other chemical catalysts + cosmic radiation + prana + higher dimensions

What are the ways the energy is dissipated or lost in the human body? The most obvious is physical exercise (work). Not so obvious is the activity of thinking (mental exercise). The expression of emotions also uses energy. Then there are the subtle ways that entropy acts on the physical body — cells decaying and possibly not being entirely replaced by new cells. There are the effects of stress, whether internal or external. Then there are chemical contaminants, which are part of the external stressors. Negative belief systems dissipate energy (part of mental exercise). Especially draining are worry, anxiety, conflict, fear, guilt, anger and such. Although it is not always easy to measure the effects of these emotions scientifically, it is obvious from a subjective point of view that they are energy dissipators. One who worries excessively is constantly tired and exhausted. So, let's formulate the other equation:

Energy Out = work (physical activity) + mental/emotional activity + stress + environmental + entropic factors

If Energy Out is greater than Energy In, you have a net entropic system where the body is decaying faster than it is regenerating. Such a human soul is aging.

If Energy In is greater than Energy Out, you have a centropic system where the body is renewing itself faster than it is decaying. Such a human soul is "youthing" or getting younger, or, in the case of a very young human being, is simply getting stronger and more vital.

Since almost everyone in the human race is aging, we can assume that Energy Out is greater than Energy In for almost all souls. But there is evidence that a few human beings are no longer aging and might even be youthing. We know that in order to attain physical immortality, Energy In must equal or exceed Energy Out.

In our examples, we are operating within an open system where "new" energy comes in from the etheric planes and "old" energy returns to the etheric planes. This is over-simplified but is sufficient for our purposes here.

Let's look again at the above statements and form an exact equation for immortality from them:

Food + water + oxygen + other chemical catalysts + cosmic radiation + prana + higher dimensions = work (physical activity) + mental/emotional activity + stress + entropic factors

Since the above statement for most human beings has a "less than" symbol instead of an "equals" symbol, what are the contributing factors to increasing the Energy In and decreasing the Energy Out?

Let's start with ways to increase the Energy In: The quality of food and water make a great deal of difference regarding how much of this form of energy is utilized by the physical body. High-quality food will be easily digested, with the nutrients released quickly and efficiently into the bloodstream. High-quality water contains the proper electrolytes to work with the ions and molecules of the body.

We are not going to go extensively into nutrition in this book. There are a lot of materials available regarding which foods are highest in nutrition (energy). For the most part, a raw vegan diet probably has the highest energetic content, but there might be exceptions, especially if certain foods are easier to digest when they are cooked. Nutrient-dense plants, such as spirulina and chlorella, are obvious examples of foods that convert to higher energy states.

Water would seem to be a simple factor, but this is not the case since different formulations of water convert differently regarding electrolytes and assimilation. You have spring water, mineral water, well water, RO water, filtered tap water, distilled water, high pH water, nano-ionized water, heavy water (deuterium oxide) and several more forms available today. You also have drinks composed primarily of water but with added chemicals and compounds.

Again, we are not going to debate specifics regarding each form of water. You can do that research on your own. However, water that promotes proper electrolyte action and that has a favorable result on ions and the molecular structures of the body would convert to the highest amount of usable energy.

It is generally true that the more oxygen you put into the body, the more energy you will have. Obviously, there are limits, but most human beings are oxygen deficient or even oxygen deprived. There are two main ways to increase oxygen in the blood. First is by increasing the rate and depth of breathing. Second is by ingesting chemical compounds that are rich in available oxygen, such as hydrogen peroxide (H_2O_2) or organic germanium (Ge_3O_7). Not all oxygen-rich compounds are beneficial to the body. For example, ClO_2 (chlorites) are heavily promoted as elixirs of life due to their ability to kill cancer cells and harmful bacteria and viruses, but too much chlorine can be detrimental to the body. One such chemical you might have heard of is called "MMS."

The best way to increase oxygen is through proper breathing. There are several breathing yogas, including Rebirthing, Primal Therapy, Holotropic Breathwork, Breath of Fire, Kundalini Yoga, Kriya Yoga, etc. These techniques have different effects on emotions and overall well-being and may vary in effectiveness from person to person. Rebirthing might be the best technique for one person and primal therapy for another, depending on their psychological makeup. One thing they all have in common is increasing the oxygen flow to the brain (and circulatory system). It is possible to temporarily overdose on oxygen, making the person light-headed, dizzy, or hyperventilated. However, there does not appear to be any lasting harm from over-oxygenation.

What about chemical catalysts? Certain chemicals cause digestion and assimilation to become more efficient. Others may catalyze the rate of oxygen absorption. Vitamins and minerals are obvious examples. Certain herbs or medicinal plants can also promote increased energy, such as tonics (ginseng, maca, etc.). A balanced, intelligent approach to nutritional supplements is highly recommended.

Cosmic radiation is acknowledged by mainstream science as a factor in the energy quotient of human beings but is not readily understood, even by genetic biologists. Closely related is etheric energy, or "prana." Some of the breathing techniques may trigger increased prana, but it is possible to get cosmic radiation and prana without actually doing anything except being open and receptive. Meditation both increases energy and decreases the rate of dissipation of energy. It opens the body to prana by releasing the resistance inherent in stress.

It is possible to invoke the power and presence of beings living in the higher dimensions and to ask them to "download" higher frequencies into the physical body. This amounts to becoming a direct receptacle to higher dimensional energies. Meditating on higher beings or higher dimensions can be a powerful way of increasing the overall energy of the physical body.

Now, let's look at ways to decrease the Energy Out: Here it gets a little bit complicated since staying at rest constantly would certainly decrease the work (exercise) but would not be beneficial to the body at a certain point. So, regarding exercise, it should be done in such a way as to maximize utilization of other forms of Energy In. Exercise should feel good. If it feels like a struggle or severely depletes your overall energy, you are not doing beneficial exercise. Some activity actually seems to increase your vitality and well-being. Pay attention to the way you feel with each form of exercise. If it helps you gain mental clarity or peace of mind, it might be worth the temporary drain on the body.

Repetitive physical activity may have some benefit at first, but quickly becomes a degenerative factor. Do your best to avoid long periods of repetitive exercise or work. Sweating is another complex issue. It is good to sweat to release toxins that have built up in the lymphatic system, but beyond a certain point, sweating can deplete overall energy. If you have a lot of built-up toxins, the benefits of sweating will outweigh the detriment.

Regular, intelligent, light to moderate amounts of exercise are probably best and will contribute to the least amount of overall decrease in the body's available energy. You might even be able to cut total energy expenditures in half just by finding the proper balance between a sedentary lifestyle and an overly active one.

For some, a half hour of yoga and a light workout at the gym might be perfect, while for others, it might involve a greater commitment to exercise. Remember, if your exercise regimen feels like a struggle, it is probably not good for you.

Another *huge* factor in depletion of energy is negative thinking and emotions. Mental activity rarely increases the overall energy of the body. Therefore, it is important to conserve thinking. Worrying constantly about things you can do nothing about is a huge waste of energy. This author frequently uses the example of a friend from years ago. He would spend the weekend with this person, and she would be unable to enjoy her time with him because she was constantly thinking about what she needed to do the following week. It was Saturday afternoon. "Monday morning, I need to go the Post Office, make a transaction at the bank, go and see a business associate, etc." This author kindly pointed out that all these places were closed until Monday morning and no amount of thinking about them would be of help right now. "Put a note on your front door, or on your refrigerator, or on your pillow, if you are afraid you will forget a Monday morning task, but right now it's Saturday afternoon. You already know how to do your tasks, so thinking about them right now accomplishes nothing useful and merely wastes mental energy," was his reply.

Mental discipline is not easy but is vitally necessary if you want to balance your energy quotient. Negative core beliefs are tremendously costly in terms of dissipated energy. This is especially true of the belief that there is a limited amount of energy available. If you behave according to this belief system, you will be unavailable to higher forms of energy that are streaming into the Earth plane.

Stress is caused by many factors, including the pollution on Earth (especially noise and electromagnetic radiation), work pressures, economic uncertainties, political oppression, propaganda (in almost every country), societal demands, family expectations, childhood programming and conditioning, and inner conflict between parts of the self, to name a few. It is not possible to completely eliminate stress, but it is imperative to manage it.

Most of the above factors are exacerbated by excessive mental exercise (unnecessary thinking), but stress tends to dissipate energy at nearly every level of being, including the six lower bodies (detailed in previous works).

The last form of Energy Out involves what we are calling entropic factors. In the lower dimensions, entropy is dominant over centropy (while in the higher dimensions, it is the opposite). Identification with material form and material things causes one's consciousness to become more entropic and less centropic. Refusing to believe that the universe is only entropic is the first step to undoing this. The latest advances in quantum physics suggest that the universe is equally centropic (as detailed earlier).

As stated in the science section of this book, the universe is continually vacillating between the physical and etheric realms. The "blinking on" phase of the universe is essentially a movement from the etheric to the physical realm, which produces entropy. The "blinking off" phase of the universe involves a movement from the physical to the etheric levels, which produces centropy. Because we are aligned primarily with the physical levels of consciousness here on Earth, we see mostly entropy. You could say that the etheric planes are continuously regenerating the physical plane once every Planck second, yet this is difficult to conceptualize.

Nevertheless, it is possible to "capture" the centropic phase using proper circuitry and devices, as discussed earlier.

Let us summarize the short version of immortality science and psychology: To achieve physical immortality, or the ability to regenerate the body as fast as it is degenerating, it is necessary to balance the Energy In with the Energy Out. By practicing the techniques and entering the states of consciousness described above, we can greatly increase the energy coming into the body. By changing our thoughts, healing negative emotions, reducing stress and meditating, we can drastically reduce the outflow of energy from the body. At some point, the equation becomes balanced. If we are in an older body, we might intend to create a temporary imbalance in favor of "youthing" until our body reaches the ideal biological age, at which time we then plan to create perfect balance, hence neither aging nor youthing.

CHAPTER 13

The Secrets of Immortality — the Longer Version

∞ A More Detailed Look at the Topics Discussed in Chapter 12

We feel it is not enough to simply give the basics as we did in the last chapter, so in the following chapters we are going into great depth on the subject of how to balance entropy and centropy in the physical body, thereby achieving immortality.

The secret of immortality is extremely simple. The physical body, the most basic level upon which immortality can be applied, is an open system. Energy is constantly entering and exiting the system. A simple outline is given in the following pages, detailing the entropic and centropic factors that determine the state of health in the physical body and the six lower bodies in general.

The key to immortality in the physical body is to balance the centropic side of the equation (incoming energy) with the entropic side (outgoing energy). Once equilibrium is achieved, the system maintains a perfect balance, and the system enters the static or unchanging state. Here, we refer only to the amount of energy contained in the system as being constant, not the idea that the life of the immortal being is stagnant or nothing is moving.

Why are almost all people aging? The obvious answer is that the entropic factors are greater than the centropic ones in such souls. To attain a state of equilibrium (immortality), the centropic factors must be increased and the entropic factors decreased until they are balanced.

A key factor here is resistance. In order to maintain a physical body on Earth, a certain amount of resistance is necessary. Otherwise, the body could spontaneously combust, similar to the way a circuit burns out (or even explodes) when there is a short (breakdown of resistance due to the wrong wires touching or a surge in current from an unreliable source).

When attaining immortality, it might at first be necessary to temporarily unbalance the equation in favor of centropy, in effect causing a "youthing" to occur in the body, until you have reached the highest possible state of health and vitality, at which point you then bring both sides of the equation into balance. Some souls attempt to keep the centropic side greater than the entropic, in which case the body will eventually burn out due to excess energy. Yoga practitioners sometimes make this mistake. More energy is flowing into the body than is being dissipated, causing all manner of imbalances, including restlessness, inability to sleep, nervous energy, and eventually the failure of the physical subsystems.

It is important to note that fear of death does *not* increase your likelihood of attaining immortality and, in fact, will quickly raise the entropy in the system because fear is the most dominant form of resistance. If your motivation for doing Kriya Yoga and other life-enhancement techniques is to overcome death, you are not doing these things for the right reason.

It is also unlikely you will attain immortality if you are constantly fighting with the way things are on Earth. Remember that the opposite of acceptance is resistance. Become aware of all the subtle ways you are resisting what is.

It might be helpful to attempt to quantize each centropic and entropic factor, although this is arduous at best and impossible at worst. The most any reasonable person can do is attempt to minimize the entropic factors by living a virtuous and peaceful life while increasing activities that lower resistance and bring more beneficial energies into the body.

Many souls do some of the activities and attempt to attain some of the necessary mental and emotional states necessary to increase the inflow of centropic energy, while simultaneously trying to decrease the negative factors, but usually there remain some unresolved blockages, especially in the psychological makeup of most human beings.

Negative thoughts, emotions and beliefs are a huge determining factor in the overall energy level of the body. Identification with the material realm, a corollary to the belief in separation from God, is perhaps the single greatest contributor to excess entropy in the system. When the physical realm is perceived as the prime level of existence, one's vibration is lowered to match that realm, automatically increasing the entropy.

Most of the work human beings perform on Earth (kinetic energy expended) comes in the form of trying to preserve, protect or enhance the physical body. Excessive dissipation occurs because of the work ethic. In times past (before modern technology), physical labor was required to keep food on the table and wood in the shed. A lot of energy was expended simply taking care of the physical form. From a higher perspective, this occurred because human beings forgot their true origins, thereby seeming to cut themselves off from higher sources of energy, such as prana and Zero-Point.

As stated in numerous prior publications, civilizations have risen and fallen repeatedly on Earth. In each case, a level of imbalance existed in the natural flow of energy of each society until the imbalance became so great as to cause sudden changes in equilibrium-seeking mechanisms. In other words, it was like a rubber band being stretched to the breaking point. After each release of energy caused by the "break," a period of low centropy ensued. This manifested as a condition of "starting over" with basic implements and farming methods, etc., after the higher technologies were destroyed through warfare or natural disasters.

The latest surge of entropy occurred after the most recent ice age (about 12,000 years ago), where in many parts of the world, the "caveman" mentality reigned supreme. Modern scholars who have not learned to think for themselves believe this was the first civilization and that it evolved from the primates. It is not difficult to disprove this ridiculous idea, and in fact many archeologists are doing just that. We will not go into the easy proof that the modern mainstream theory of evolution is false because that has been done in prior publications. In addition to this author's work, you can consult materials like Cremo's *Forbidden Archeology.*

Below, you will find a detailed outline depicting the various ingredients for mortality and immortality. First, we will list the degenerative factors (things that contribute to aging, disease and death). Then we will go into depth on each item. After examining some additional subtle negative factors, we will then list the regenerative factors that increase vitality, youth and health.

∞ Degenerative Factors

1. Second Law of Thermodynamics (Natural Entropy)
2. Physical Body Influences from Lower Dimensions
   a. The Realm of Maya and Attachment to Form
   b. Bad Habits/Addictions
   c. Bad Diet (Processed Foods and Refined Sugar)
   d. Improper or Unconscious Breathing
3. Negative Emotions
4. Negative Energy in the Mental Body
   a. Negative Thoughts
   b. Core Negative Beliefs
   c. Negative Programming and Conditioning
   d. Thinking
5. Stress, Worry and Anxiety
6. Negative Astral Influences
   a. Negative Astral Implants
   b. Other Negative Astral Influences
   c. Invocations to Dispel Negative Entities
   d. Interference from Negative Extraterrestrials
7. Negative Etheric Influences
   a. Dirty Aura and Chakras
   b. Negative Etheric Imprints
   c. Negative Imprints from Present/Past Life Trauma
8. Negativity in the Causal Body
   a. Samskaras (Negative Karma)
   b. Ending Karmic Contracts and Agreements
9. Work, Activity (Kinetic Energy Expended)
10. Negative Environmental Factors

  a. Lack of Sufficient Sunlight
  b. Circadian Rhythm Imbalance
  c. Discordant Sounds and Frequencies
  d. Toxic Radiation and Electromagnetic Pollution
  e. Food, Water, Air and Soil Pollution
11. DNA Death Sequence Program
12. The Frequency Barrier/Fence
13. Negative People and Situations
14. Service to Self (Karma)
15. Darkness, Ignorance and Denial
16. Chaos
17. Resistance
18. More on the Belief in Separation

∞ ∞ ∞

Let us detail each of the centropic and entropic factors displayed in the outline above to assist the reader in reaching energy equilibrium within the physical body. It makes sense to start with the negatives. As you release negative factors, it becomes easier to open to the inflow of positive energies.

CHAPTER 14

Degenerative Factors Explained in Depth

Second Law of Thermodynamics (Natural Entropy)

In the lower dimensions, entropy is naturally more causative than centropy. In order to create a balance, energy must continuously flow into the lower planes from the higher ones. If you are maintaining a physical body on Earth, you are going to be subject to the natural entropy inherent within this dimension. Even if you could do absolutely nothing, meaning that you are expending zero work (kinetic energy), you would still be losing energy if you are not opening to receive higher energies from the centropic side of the equation.

The Second Law of Thermodynamics manifests as friction, heat dissipation and the wearing down of mechanical devices (and biological entities). In a roundabout way, it is responsible for the simple fact that it takes far less energy to break a glass than to reassemble it.

You might say that in the above example, gravity has a lot to do with the broken glass and certainly that is true on one level. When you counteract gravity, such as by raising a glass, you increase the potential energy in the system (temporarily). A lot of energy is expended when you drop the glass (due to the effects of gravity). In other words, a portion of the potential energy has been converted to kinetic energy (the dropping and breaking of the glass).

We are not going to go into the detailed physics of how gravity interacts with entropy, since this is not a course in Newtonian physics.

In fact, we are in the psychological section of the book and have a lot more topics to look at.

For now, let us simply assume that entropy, like gravity, is a factor on the negative side of the table. To make it easier to grasp this, you can simply include gravity under the Second Law of Thermodynamics (although technically this is incorrect).

Physical Body Influences from Lower Dimensions

The Realm of Maya and Attachment to Form

Earth is electromagnetic in nature, but the magnetic side of the waveform appears dominant over the electric side. In a magnetic system, attraction and repulsion are prolific. You could say that everything is somewhat attractive or repulsive, although you might not notice unless you are holding an actual iron magnet.

Yet, from a psychological viewpoint, the Law of Attraction is roughly equivalent to the law of magnetics in Newtonian physics. If you are vibrating at a low level, you are subject to the highly entropic energies of the lower dimensions. Even if you have largely transcended the consciousness of physical survival and attachment to material form, because you have a human body, you are still subject, to some extent, to the magnetic and entropic nature of the physical Earth.

Your body is being bombarded by the lower frequencies inherent in this domain. Unless you counteract these forces with a lot of centropic levels of consciousness, you will get drawn into the entropic environment, either consciously or unconsciously.

As we have stated numerous times, this world is set up to keep you enslaved to the physical senses, appetites and desires that the so-called "power elite" employ in order to keep a steady stream of consumers buying things they don't need with money they don't have (for the most part).

It might seem unrelated, but simply going into debt from buying lots of things on credit is a great example of how the world "hooks" you into greater and greater expenditures of physical energy (working harder to keep up with mounting debts, etc.).

That is one example of how the lower dimensions tend to "suck" you into their sphere of influence. There are many others, some of which have been detailed in earlier chapters and books.

If you are a high-vibrational being walking among large sea-level cities, you are immersed in a heavy, thick, psychic "soup" of negativity. As we said, about three-fourths of the thought forms in this "soup" are negative. So the default (what happens when you do nothing) is negative, meaning that if you are not constantly working to draw forth the centropic factors into your life, you are becoming subject to increasing entropy just by the background influences of the world. The world's idea of "doing nothing" is, essentially, doing something negative because you are losing energy.

Bad Habits/Addictions

We put this topic near the top of the table because it is one of the most practical and significant factors in the depletion of energy. We hope our dissertation here will help you to free yourself from excessive entropy.

You probably know that there are two types of addictions: process and substance. Process addictions are much harder to break because most souls do not realize they have them.

Here is a table that represents the most common addictions on Earth:

Top Substance Addictions	Top Process Addictions
Sugar (over half the population)	Thinking (almost everyone)
Food in general	Worrying, obsessing
Alcohol	Seeking approval/love
Nicotine (smoking, etc.)	Being "right"
Caffeine (coffee, tea)	Work/making money
Sedatives/barbiturates	Television/pop icons
Pain killers (narcotics)	Shopping/fashion
Sleep aids	Whining, complaining
Psychoactive drugs (SSRIs, etc.)	Sex/sexual pleasure/porn
Other stimulants and depressants	Socializing/partying
Diet and sport drinks	Sporting events/games
Artificial sweeteners/flavor enhancers	Phone/texting/video games
Other drugs	Surfing the Internet

One of the biggest addictions is to thinking, a topic we will cover shortly. Closely related is that of obsessive worry.

Habits are similar to addictions in that you seem to lose control of your behavior if you repeat a negative activity over a prolonged period of time. The analogy of wearing a groove in a record is not too relevant to the younger generation that is growing up with digital applications, but most of you remember vinyl records and how the needle must follow the groove.

When doing tasks automatically, such as walking and talking, the groove that becomes a habit is a good thing. However, the groove becomes a rut when the automated behavior is destructive.

Later we will talk about negative programming and conditioning and how to reprogram the subconscious mind. Now, let's talk about substance addictions. We have listed on the left side of the table the most popular substances that are subject to abuse.

Many substances are both physically and psychologically addicting. You might need to confront the physical addiction first and then work on the underlying psychology that prompted the soul to become addicted in the first place.

There is no such thing as a habit or addiction that cannot be cured. Sure, it may be extremely difficult to let go of some things, but it can be done. The first step is to understand the addictive behavior and its consequences. What is the difference between stepping in front of a speeding train and smoking? The answer is obvious: One kills you quickly, and one kills you slowly. If you are hell-bent on dying, stepping in front of the train should be your choice. It's quick. You don't feel much. You don't put your family and friends through years of lung disease and deteriorating health while they take turns beside your bed, and you don't go through the excruciating pain of trying to breathe with destroyed bronchial tubes. Yet how many people would choose the train? As you reach for the last cigarette in your second pack of the day, you are thinking, "Who in their right mind would step in front of a train? Are they crazy?"

We know that reading the above exercise in logic will not cause many people to stop smoking. Yet the first step in overcoming any addiction is to get out of denial. You need to realize that you would likely be better off stepping in front of the train than to continue smoking. (Of course, we are not advocating suicide by any means, just putting things into perspective, and yes, you might be one of the lucky ones who doesn't get a debilitating disease from smoking.)

You need to become painstakingly aware of the details of your habit or addiction. Start with the craving (if it's a habit like smoking). Notice how and when the urge to smoke arises. What triggers it? Are there thoughts or feelings ahead of the craving? What do you tell yourself before indulging in the habit? How do you feel during the indulgence? Afterwards?

In the case of smoking, notice how you hold the cigarette and how the smoke is drawn into your lungs. How do you exhale? What do you think about as you are smoking? Again, you can substitute holding a bottle, taking a drink, or snorting a line of cocaine. The idea is to pay attention to the details of your state of consciousness before, during and after succumbing to the addiction.

What is the goal of the addiction? Does it seem to reduce stress? Or does it remind you of something pleasant, such as the time you and your friends stood around smoking and talking? Does it make you forget the troubles in the world temporarily? In the case of drink, does it make you feel less self-conscious and more likely to approach strangers and strike up a conversation? Do you "let your hair down" and become temporarily more authentic after a couple of drinks?

Most people go unconscious when satisfying their addictions. They do not realize how much energy is "lost" as a result of this unconsciousness (denial).

The long-term effects of bad habits and addictions on level of energy are obvious. Most addictive activities have a temporary "high" or period of seemingly increased energy, followed by a crash. You might feel worse after the indulgence than before you started it. Yet the craving keeps returning until you do some hard work (therapy and healing) and start crawling out of the groove that has become a rut.

Some people, once they quit a bad habit or addiction, have a lot of energy and don't know what to do with themselves, so they adopt a new habit or addiction to replace the previous one.

Learning to live with the seeming abundance of energy that is released once the habit or addiction is eliminated means focusing and directing your attention to constructive, life-affirming activities. There are a lot of good causes in this world and organizations you can get involved with, especially if you are retired and looking for something to do. Start by refining your spiritual practice and trying new meditation and breathing techniques. Join a yoga class or healing circle. If you have an obsessive personality, become obsessed over healthy food and exercise (but not too obsessed).

As you raise your consciousness, old habitual ways of thinking, feeling and behaving will tend to naturally drop away, since these activities belong to a lower state of consciousness. You will no longer feel you are fighting with your addictive personality. Remember to love the part of yourself that tends to fall back into addiction. Then gently bring that part into the light (with the help of healers and therapists).

Bad Diet (Processed Foods and Refined Sugar)

We will not dwell on this topic since there are countless books and videos on the subject already. Our discussion centers around how and why eating bad food and drink interferes with the centropic forces in your body. The biggest issue involves the difficulty of digesting various chemical additives and bad forms of fat and sugar. Anything that is hard to digest is going to require more energy expenditures. Your liver and kidneys are working harder than they should. Trying to digest food when sleeping is a losing proposition. If you eat something bad, it might take four to six hours to finish digesting.

Certain chemicals are known as endocrine disruptors. They interfere with the glands and hormones, causing insomnia, restlessness, nervousness and degradation of vital organs.

The fertility rate of women and potency (sperm count) in men has been decreasing alarmingly over the past 50 years. This is almost certainly due to GMO foods, additives, preservatives, pesticides, and such. There are some conspiracy theorists who are suggesting this is intentional as a way of culling the population. While the profit motive is a far more likely culprit, it is understandable that people would feel this way.

The simple solution is to prepare as many foods as possible from scratch. Many health food companies are aware of the problem and are capitalizing on the concerns of individuals. In most Western cities, you can now get vegetables from an organic salad bar, adequately washed and prepared, to take home.

The excuses that you don't have time to prepare good food or cannot afford it, are simply not valid. Even if you have health insurance (which is ridiculously expensive in the West), you will still spend a lot more money on co-pays, deductibles and uncovered items going to the doctor frequently if you are not eating the more expensive, high quality foods. Remember the expression, "You cannot put a price on good health."

Most junk-food addicts have emotional issues that are being suppressed by eating. If you cannot resist that pizza, macaroni and cheese or burger, look for the cause of your emotional eating. A few months of healthy food and you will no longer crave junk foods. This author, when he stopped eating beef in the 1970s, felt nauseated at the smell and thought of eating it within six months after he stopped. When he eliminated aspartame in the 1990s, the occasional bite or sip of something containing it tasted awful just three months later.

The body is resilient and quickly adjusts to changes, even though at first it fights to keep the status quo. Don't try going from meat and potatoes to raw vegan overnight. The body will likely get sick. Go in stages. Also, do not assume that the strictest or most fad diet is for you. Raw vegan might not be the best diet for your body. Pay attention to its reaction as you make changes. Give yourself time to adjust.

Start by eating chicken and fish instead of beef, pork and lamb. Then make a vegetarian dinner once or twice a week. Eat about half cooked and half raw.

Start your day with a supergreen smoothie instead of high carb, high sugar cereal. Consume a moderate amount of fruit, early in the day (not after meals). Focus more on vegetables at night. Use the "bell curve modified paleo diet." That's a light breakfast, moderate lunch and light dinner. Resist the temptation to eat a lot of refined grains, especially white bread. Next to sugar, refined flour is the worst thing you can put into your body. Eat dark rye or sprouted bread in small quantities. Use brown rice instead of white. Avoid soy sauce and soy products in general (unless they are fermented such as tempeh or miso and then use only in small quantities). Soy promotes excessive estrogen production and can lead to breast and prostate cancer.

We will spare you the one-millionth lecture about sugar, plus we would probably be preaching to the choir anyway. Just remember that almost everything processed has some amount of sugar in it. Unless you make it yourself, you really do not have much control over how many grams of sugar are in your food. Simple carbs, such as fruit sugar, in the amount of 25 to 30 grams per day, are probably sufficient. A little bit of ultra-dark chocolate (above 70% cacao) might be beneficial in your diet. A general rule: The darker the dessert, the better it is for you. Enough said.

Improper or Unconscious Breathing

If you observe, without changing your breathing rhythm, the nature and structure of your "ordinary" breath, you will find it short, erratic and shallow (unless you have mastered certain breathing exercises).

It is a wonder that your blood manages to get enough oxygen to dispel impurities at all. Pollution and lack of oxygen in the blood are probably responsible for up to 20% of all illnesses.

The obvious consequence of shallow, erratic breathing is less prana entering the system, which means more entropy, aging and death.

It is amazing that nobody teaches young people how to breathe properly. It is just assumed that the body will take care of itself. Okay, it's not too surprising that medical professionals have this attitude since breathing, along with the beating of the heart and regulation of nutrients, is considered part of the autonomic nervous system.

However, short, shallow, erratic breathing stems from something much deeper — stored fear in the cells of the body. When you breathe fully, freely and deeply, fear is dispelled, sometimes slowly and often quickly. This is the principle behind Rebirthing, a conscious breathing yoga introduced by Leonard Orr in the 1970s. Of course, the yoga of breath goes back thousands of years and was popularized by Babaji's Kriya Yoga.

When you become conscious of your breathing, a lot of things happen. You become aware of all the subtle ways fear has been controlling your body temple. Most fear started at birth. In fact, the process of coming out of your mother's womb was likely the closest you ever came to dying. When the cord was cut, you had to start breathing on your own or else. You might have been coaxed by being held upside down and spanked. There is usually a lot of trauma surrounding your first breath.

Being forced to breathe involved a lot of fear, and this fear became stored in the cells. It is natural to hold your breath temporarily when feeling fear directly, but this stored negativity results in the short, erratic breathing that characterizes most human beings.

When we explore the ways to increase centropy, we will have more to say on breathing.

Negative Emotions

Emotions are neutral. However, if they impede your ability to grow and evolve spiritually, then they have become negative. The biggest problem with negative emotions is not the emotions themselves, but how you express them. With proper breathing and awareness, the expression of negativity can be quick, efficient and non-damaging to those around you. Most people get stuck in negative emotions by judging them to be bad and wrong and trying desperately to escape them. This does not work. You must feel them. You must understand them. And, you must go beyond them. True transcendence comes through higher understanding. You are a vast, creative, intelligent spiritual being having a human experience that includes negative emotions. That's all. Stop making so much of it.

Negative emotions are the result of negative thoughts. Fear is almost always the result of the thought, "I'm not safe." Anger comes from the thought that you are in some way violated. Sadness comes from wishing things to be different than the way they are. All other negative emotions are blends of these. Guilt is technically not an emotion but a state of consciousness. However, it produces the emotion of shame. Shame is the lowest of the emotions and comes from the belief that you are not worthy, that something is wrong with you, or that you are inherently bad and undeserving.

When negative emotions are expressed fully in a healthy way, it may or may not look dramatic. As stated countless times in previous books, you need both detachment and healthy expression of emotion in order to heal negative patterns.

During the expression, you are converting potential energy to kinetic (emoting), so there is some dissipation or entropy, but the elimination of the negative emotional pattern opens the self to higher frequencies that were blocked by that pattern.

Negative Energy in the Mental Body

Negative Thoughts

We could write a large book just on this subject. Since there is so much information out there regarding the topic, we will be brief. Some negative thoughts are obvious, but a lot are buried in the subconscious and come out in subtle ways. When you catch yourself thinking negatively, start immediately sending love to your mind and body. Notice the origin of the negative thoughts. The vast majority have to do with the safety and security of the body and/or the ego. Worrying about what others think, seeking approval, becoming attached to pleasurable experiences and seeking to avoid painful ones — those are the majority of negative thoughts. The amount of energy depleted through negative thinking is immense. Seeing this, some teachers mistakenly believe that all you need to do is eliminate negative thoughts in order to attain immortality. Yes, this is a key ingredient, but not the only one. If it were, Pollyanna types would all be immortal. Happy people would not be found in graves.

Understanding negative thoughts and practicing healing and therapy techniques will propel you forward greatly in your quest for immortality.

Recognize that almost all negative thoughts stem from negative belief systems, a topic we will cover next.

Core Negative Beliefs

Beliefs are a collection of thoughts and emotions that create a certain perspective of reality. *Belief systems* are a collection of beliefs.

Core negative beliefs are the deepest and most powerful of the negative beliefs. In previous works, we have gone exhaustively into the subject of core negative beliefs, including "sacred cows," which are belief systems disguised as universal truths (examples are death and taxes). Clearing your core negative beliefs is the single most important task you can take on the spiritual path. Yes, you read that correctly. You will do more to attain immortality, you will do more to help the planet, and you will do more to reach enlightenment, by clearing your core negative beliefs than by anything else.

How do you clear negative beliefs? First you must recognize them and follow the process of how they distort and direct your perception. How do you tell the difference between a belief and a fact? A fact is not subject to change. It is agreed upon by the collective consciousness and stays the same even when individual perception changes. An example is two plus two equals four. You might believe two plus two equals five, but you would not have the agreement of the collective consciousness.

How do you tell the difference between a belief and the truth? This is actually a bit more difficult and involves rigorous investigation and often thorough analysis. A truth is that which is actually so in any given moment, meaning that it transcends specific levels and perceptions. Truth is always true no matter what beliefs are adopted by those attempting to perceive truth.

The truth is all-encompassing. There is nowhere in Creation where it is false. It might be perceived differently in different dimensions, and it might be explained in different ways depending on the perceptions of those attempting to know the truth; however, truth, by its very nature, does not change. The circumstances and qualities of the truth might change. Change itself is a truth. In the lower dimensions, there is constant movement of consciousness. This is a truth.

A negative belief is one that seems to hinder or block the perception of truth. The most relevant truth is that of soul evolution. A negative thought or belief is one that seems to retard, inhibit or interfere with soul evolution (the unfolding of awareness or expansion of consciousness). Negative beliefs, therefore, are entropic, meaning they lead to greater disorder and chaos. Dispelling negative beliefs occurs when the belief is seen for what it is — a faulty perception of truth.

One realizes that the truth that is being veiled by the belief does not change — only the belief can change.

Let us use the analogy of the sun shining. On a cloudy day, or at night, the sun does not appear to be shining. One could form the belief that the sun has ceased to shine, or that God is punishing humanity by taking away the sun. But those beliefs have no bearing whatsoever on the truth that the sun is still shining and is simply being obscured by clouds or the planet itself (in the case of nighttime).

When examining the difference between a potentially negative belief and the truth, ask yourself, "Are there any times or situations in which this condition is not true? Are there exceptions to the rule? Does this seeming truth change with changing perceptions?" Death and taxes, for example, are beliefs, not truths, because there are those who have overcome death and those who legally do not pay taxes. Since there are exceptions to the rule, you can be assured that these are beliefs, not truths.

Once you have determined that something is a negative belief, you merely see through it with awareness, and when you become completely present in the moment with that belief, it will be dispelled because ultimately it is an illusion. Illusions only appear to be true when you believe in them. As soon as you withdraw your belief, they disappear.

Negative Programming and Conditioning

Beliefs are acquired through programming and conditioning. This starts either with past lifetimes or early childhood in this lifetime. The difference between programming and conditioning is that you can change programming, but you cannot change conditioning.

Programming refers to the collection of belief systems, experiences, attitudes, prejudices, evaluations and opinions that you have acquired going through a particular lifetime or during early childhood. For example, you might have been programmed to hate Jews or feel guilty about your "sins."

Conditioning is the environment in which the programming took place. Although you can change certain elements of the past (through techniques such as timeline healing), almost all of the physical details in your environment cannot be changed because it would violate the free will of other souls that are co-creating the reality around you. It would also violate what are known as "time paradoxes."

To keep things simple, think of conditioning as the backdrop or set for the drama that is unfolding called "your life." Perhaps you were born into poverty, for example. Then poverty is part of your conditioning. However, you have choice regarding the programs you form in your subconscious mind regarding poverty. Many souls in poor countries are happier than those in the wealthiest ones because they are running a different set of programs regarding the nature of their conditioning.

Negative programming and conditioning affect your energy level. It might be harder to move into centropy if you have a lot of despair and depression in your family upbringing. Whether you chose your parents because of past life karma or to learn specific lessons, you must accept the conditions of your past and present before you can make meaningful changes. The next step is to unravel the negative programs that you formed in reaction to those conditions. It is the way it is. Remember the mantra. As you remove the resistance and begin accepting that things are the way they are, you are ready to tap into your powerful, creative, spiritual self and bring about desired changes.

There are a lot of reprogramming techniques and meditations you can practice to move core negative beliefs and experiences out of your subconscious mind, including past life regression, timeline healing, hypnotherapy, psychotherapy and other methods. You can find and learn these techniques from many sources, so we will move on to the next topic.

Thinking

We have included "thinking" as a separate category of entropy because even positive thoughts are entropic to some degree. Thought dissipates energy (that can be measured by EEG machines and other devices). When you are thinking, you are expressing kinetic energy and, therefore, you are dissipating your life force to some degree. Yes, negative thoughts are far denser and require greater effort to maintain, so they deplete your life force energy much more quickly than positive thoughts, but all thoughts are on the entropic side of the equation. Meditation is, of course, the solution. You might not succeed in completely stilling your mind, but a significant reduction in thinking will reduce your energy output.

Thinking is necessary in order to function in the modern world, but most thoughts are completely unnecessary. The greatest addiction in the world is to thinking. It is believed that thinking is necessary to solve problems, and in many cases that is true, but the vast majority of problems are caused by thinking in the first place. If human beings only produced thoughts when absolutely necessary, the mind would be still most of the time. Some thoughts would become automatic (programmed into the subconscious), similar to the way the autonomic nervous system operates in the physical body. You do not have to think in order to beat your heart, pump your blood, or use your respiration system (breathing). Similarly, you do not need to produce conscious thoughts to perform many activities in your daily life. Every time you walk, do you think about putting one foot in front of the other, or do you simply walk? Automating the thinking process greatly reduces unnecessary depletion of energy.

Obsessing over possible or probable futures, reminiscing about the past, worrying and fretting over imagined realities — all are significant dissipaters of energy. If you are obsessively thinking because you are afraid you will forget to do something important, write notes to yourself, keep a day planner journal book, put reminders on the front door or on a mirror you look into frequently. Recognize and evaluate the situation: Is this thought necessary at this time? How will thinking about this item make me more secure or increase my well-being?

Earlier we gave an example of a woman who could not enjoy her weekend because she was constantly thinking about what she needed to do the following week.

Thinking is habitual. Like any habit, you must make an effort to break the cycle. Are you committed to reducing unnecessary thoughts? Perhaps you can start catching yourself every time you start thinking about something for which you can do nothing at present. At first this will likely be difficult, but with practice you can stop thinking about these things until the time is appropriate.

Thoughts are generated by feelings, and feelings are generated by thoughts. Both negative thoughts and negative feelings dissipate energy. Stay completely aware of your negative thoughts and feelings. Watch how they arise and what decreases them. Stay present. Breathe. You *can* reduce unnecessary thoughts and feelings.

Stress, Worry and Anxiety

We have covered this topic already in some detail and given specific examples of stressful situations, but let's zoom out and look at the big picture. What actually causes stress? Obviously, from an environmental perspective, it's the constant assault on the physical senses by noise, electromagnetic devices, traffic, air pollution, etc. Also, it's the internal thought process. Specifically, it's the sense of pressure one feels when there are a lot of demands placed on the self from both inside and outside.

It's fine to have personal goals, but when you set them too high, you are going to create unnecessary stress. Most of the time, you are the one driving yourself to improve or perform. Even if there are outer expectations from a boss or spouse, you magnify the problem by going into fear or self-defensive postures. Your fragile little ego is afraid of being hurt or made to look like a fool. Therefore, you strive to impress someone or convince another of your worthiness. The word "stress" essentially means to put a lot of energy and effort into something. The word literally implies a depletion of energy. Even when focusing on something positive, the very word "stress" makes it more difficult. "I want to stress that we are all here to work together, so please cooperate."

That is far different than, "Let's work together and make this project a great success." In this case, the word "stress" is being used to mean "emphasis." "I want to emphasize that we should be working together."

This type of putting attention on something involves an expenditure of energy. There is another way of giving your attention that does not deplete or use up potential energy. Attention for the sake of pure awareness is vastly different than pressurized attention. "You must pay attention and stop your mind from wandering," implies pressure to change, an urgency or emergency. A better way of thinking about this is, "Let's be sensitively aware of the movement of thought."

Many people are constantly operating from a sense of emergency. There is even a hysterical component, as in, "I must work harder. I must make more sales. I must do something about this situation." Your ego is driving you, subtly or overtly pushing you to do more, be more, have more, or experience more. With the ego, it's always, "More, more, more."

The next time you feel stressed about something, ask yourself, "What demands am I placing on myself? What demands are others placing on me? What expectations do I have of myself or others?" This constant push to be doing more than you are doing is a major dissipator of energy because you are not accepting "what is." If it is truly to your advantage to do more, pressurizing yourself is not going to be the best way to proceed. From a calm place within, you assess the situation and then determine what needs to be done. You move past thoughts that it cannot be done or that it is too difficult. You examine, from a place of peace, all the alternatives and methods that are possible. Then you act.

You may want to frequently invoke your Higher Self when making decisions. "Higher Self, show me the best way to perform this job. What are the most realistic goals I can have right now?" Then stop and listen. Ask for input from others. Be willing to ask for help (from humans or spirits). Stop trying to impress people. Others are more likely to enjoy your company if you are not in constant stress.

Human beings were never wired to process the incredible onslaught of data being propagated by our modern society. We are not only talking about the conscious stream of news, opinion and constant pressure to outperform and overproduce, we are also talking about the subtle levels of electromagnetic bombardment from Wi-Fi, mobile telephone towers, radio and TV transmitters and, of course, industrial noise pollution.

The incessant striving for greater profits in the workplace means fewer employees working more hours, with ever-increasing productivity goals.

Many years ago, someone coined the phrase, "Stop the world; I want to get off." The merry-go-round we call modern life on Earth has already taken a huge toll in stress-related illness. The body, becoming overwhelmed with stimuli, either goes into "fight or flight" mode or becomes paralyzed and begins to shut down. Diseases such as autism and paranoid schizophrenia are often triggered by the mind's inability to cope with this barrage of information and expectations.

Approximately 80% of all illness is caused by emotional issues, including suppression of traumatic experiences, buried anger and resentment, and, yes, stress. Even when you are in a so-called "regeneration" phase of the day, such as sleep, your dreams are often filled with unresolved subconscious problems. Tomorrow you have an important meeting across town, so all night you are dreaming about missing the train. In typical exaggeration, you have a dream where your feet turn to lead and you cannot get on the train. Then you cannot find the correct station, then the train stalls, etc. Once you awaken and get to the actual meeting, you are exhausted, and it affects your performance.

Perhaps you have learned to meditate and practice therapeutic techniques on yourself. This certainly helps greatly, but the constant noise of modern society is still flowing in and out of your space.

It is a wonder that relationships can survive in this stress-filled environment. You both work hard all day, and then you both have a headache when it comes time for intimacy.

It's fairly easy to tell whether or not stress is dissipating your life-force energy, but it is far more difficult to reduce stress beyond a certain point.

Putting your spiritual well-being first is essential if you want to keep stress to reasonable levels. It is well known that those who work seven hours per day and meditate one hour per day get more accomplished than those who work eight hours a day and do not meditate.

The biggest factor in stress is worry/anxiety. It bears repeating that unless you have a gun pointed at your head, a truck is about to run over you, or the house is on fire, you are probably not in any real danger. You are worried about something that might happen. Worry dissipates a tremendous amount of energy. There are two possibilities: (1) The thing you are worried about never happens, in which case you wasted a lot of time and effort worrying. (2) The thing you are worried about does happen, in which case you do not have the energy necessary to meet the challenge head-on because you spent all your time worrying. Either way, worry is a losing proposition. It is a bad habit that must be eradicated if you are to tap into the flow of unlimited energy. We have examined obsessive thinking and worrying about the future extensively in prior publications, so we will move on to some more dissipators of energy.

Negative Astral Influences

The astral dimension, as detailed in prior publications, is sort of a parallel reality to our physical world. It contains frequencies that are slightly higher and slightly lower than our physical vibrations but is usually invisible to the body's senses (unless you are clairvoyant or highly sensitive).

There are energies, thought forms and entities that reside in the astral planes. They are continuously influencing human beings, especially if there are frequencies within human souls that resonate with the frequencies of such astral consciousness. By "resonate" we mean radiating harmonic octaves of vibration that either magnify (amplify) existing astral energies, or counteract them, as the case may be.

Negative energies are the remnants of negative emotions that have collected in the astral spaces between human beings and form a negative psychic "soup" around the planet, especially at lower elevations and in crowded cities.

Negative thought forms are negative energies that are directed toward specific individuals or groups. If someone hates you and wishes you were dead, they might send negative thought forms to harm you. To a clairvoyant, these look like dark daggers that move perpendicular to the auric field of the intended target. Voodoo, dark magic and spells often utilize negative thought forms. Only the most experienced dark practitioner actually summons dark entities and sends them to do harm to another.

About 90% of those souls who believe they are being attacked by dark entities are actually being influenced by negative thought forms. Only about 10% are really being influenced by astral entities.

There is a veil between the physical and astral planes. Fortunately, most of the time this veil protects human beings from the relatively chaotic lower levels of the astral, but of course, there are exceptions. The barrier between dimensions is thicker or thinner in certain spots and at certain times. Generally, during the early morning hours (between 2:00 and 4:00) the veil tends to be thinner, and energies from the astral may be amplified somewhat during new and full moons (and possibly during other astrophysical configurations such as equinoxes and solstices). In addition, Christian and pagan holidays may accentuate the effects of the astral planes because of the collective beliefs around these holidays and the focus that is given to them. An obvious example is Halloween.

Energy vampires proliferate in Hollywood and their image is distorted by blending various cultural myths together, such as the glorification of Vlad the Impaler (a Romanian master of torture from the 18th century) into the persona of Dracula. While blood-sucking zombies are mostly conjured up by over-active imaginations, there is some truth to the ideas being presented.

There are beings residing in the astral planes that feed off the energy of human beings. Some of these entities are lusting after power, and so they choose humans who have similar traits. This is why over *half* of all major political and military leaders are being significantly influenced by negative astral energies, thought forms and/or entities. Many are outright possessed, meaning that the consciousness of one or more astral entities is overshadowing (blending with) the consciousness of the indwelling soul.

This is not a book about astral possession. You can read about it in numerous other publications. The only reason we are going here is because, you guessed it, these negative beings are sucking energy out of unsuspecting or fearful human beings.

How do you prevent energy vampires from dissipating your centropic force?

There are three types of negative entities, which this author calls (1) curiosity seekers; (2) negative attractors; and (3) karmic contract entities.

Curiosity seekers are like moths flying around a lamp light in summer. They are attracted to your light and want some of it. They are relatively easy to dispel, simply by using the golden light of God's protection. If you spend time in crowded public places, such as metro stations, airports, concert halls, etc., you might collect a few astral hitchhikers if you are not careful.

After being in festivals, parties and sporting events, remember to do some aura clearing. There are simple techniques for cleaning yourself that are given in other books.

More difficult to dispel are negative attractors. These are beings that are attracted to your negative thoughts and emotions, especially anger, fear and guilt. If you don't want to attract these unsavory characters, you need to clear your negative thoughts, beliefs, attitudes and programs. This group of entities are associated with the Law of Attraction, so if you change your consciousness in such a way that you are no longer in a negative resonant field with their vibration, you will stop attracting them. If you have nothing to "feed" them, they will go on down the road to the neighbor's house, looking for a delicious meal of self-hatred, contempt or vengeance.

The third category of negative astral entities is that of karmic contract beings. If you have a negative past trauma or pact with beings from past lifetimes, it is possible they might follow you into this lifetime and expect some sort of retribution or compensation for what happened back then. The way to dispel karmic entities is by going back in time and healing the original contract or agreement. This is best done through timeline healing or soul-retrieval techniques (provided by this author and others).

If you are eating and exercising correctly and choosing your friends carefully but still feel tired and exhausted much of the time, you might be taking on negative astral energies, thought forms or entities. Go to a psychic or healer if you are unsure. Get several opinions. Do not blindly believe that you are possessed or controlled by negative beings just because one psychic says so. That person could be mistaken. Do some investigation. Learn the various psychic and spiritual protection techniques and apply them often in your life. Do not blame your problems on astral entities. They are a symptom of what is out of balance. Raise your consciousness. Once you reach a certain level, you will no longer be bothered by astral entities.

Negative Astral Implants

It is necessary to remove negative physical or astral implants that might be dissipating your energy. Physical implants come in three flavors: (1) medical; (2) military; and (3) extraterrestrial.

Unless you are connected to souls through medicine or the military or have been abducted by extraterrestrials, you probably do not have physical implants. (By medical implants we are not talking about dental devices, pacemakers, metal in a joint, etc. We are talking about tiny electronic tracking devices implanted under the skin.)

Far more common are astral implants, which were usually inserted in past lifetimes during wartime on other worlds. Many souls have implants from Orion that could be anywhere from 10,000 to 200,000 years old. Even if the implants were removed by healers or others sometime in the past, you might still have residue (some remaining energy blockages). It is a good idea to go to a healer that specializes in astral-implant removal to make sure you are free of this form of energy dissipation.

Concentrated areas of negative astral energy can accumulate in your astral body. Such concentrations typically occur near the meridians and power points of the body, such as the "third eye" or throat chakra. An astral implant is a highly localized focal point of negative energy that is often intentionally placed within the astral body of a soul who is under attack by astral entities or who has undergone an experience of torture, interrogation or punishment by those who know how to implant such a soul.

Astral implants were popular in certain past lifetimes, especially during the Orion wars that occurred between 100,000 and 150,000 years ago. However, you might have received an implant much earlier or later than that.

These devices are created to control and manipulate the soul, as well as for tracking purposes (surveillance). They may originate from military operations, medical procedures or dark spells (although almost nobody currently practicing black magic knows how to implant souls astrally). A popular application of astral implants is to prevent souls from developing their psychic and intuitive abilities.

From an energy perspective, implants tend to suppress the ability of a soul to open up to higher frequencies, especially in the area where the implant is inserted. If the device is in the third eye, it can prevent clairvoyance and generally block the sixth chakra from receiving centropic energies.

There are many techniques for removing astral implants. Again, we suggest you consult with a healing practitioner that specializes in implant removal if you suspect you have one.

A lot of souls have had their astral implants removed already but might still have some residue (leftover energy patterns). It is a good idea to get checked out periodically to make sure you are truly free from such influences.

Other Negative Astral Influences

The Law of Attraction can be applied to planets, life forms and states of consciousness. Up until December of 2012, planet Earth was considered a third-density world. This means that souls vibrating at level-3 consciousness were attracted here and were incarnating in record numbers due to the unique opportunities and experiences that Earth afforded those souls.

As mentioned numerous times, souls vibrating in levels 3 and 4 are dominated by entropic forces since that is the nature of the lower worlds. The lower the vibration, the more entropy and, conversely, the higher the vibration, the less entropy.

If your consciousness vibration is higher than the ambient level of Earth (about 4.4) and the composite level of humanity (about 3.7), then you are at risk of being "dragged down" by the dense consciousness here.

It is well known that if you spend time in the company of low-vibrational souls, you will tend to get tired, or even exhausted, after a short period of time. This is not only due to the increased entropy from the low vibrations, but also because many of these souls are energy vampires who are consciously or unconsciously draining your energy in the hopes of replenishing themselves — at your expense.

Energy vampires come in all shapes and sizes. Unless you are sensitive, psychic, or highly intuitive, you might not realize the presence of an energy vampire until you are already starting to feel drained.

If your consciousness is above a certain threshold, you will not attract energy-snatchers unless they are your students or you have something to learn from them. In that case, they are karmic relationships.

If your consciousness vibration is below 4.25, you are capable of being "hijacked" by negative beings at the time of your death. Instead of going directly into the higher planes and being reunited with your karmic guardians and soul family members, you might be enticed or coerced into a negative part of the astral plane by beings who feed off disembodied souls. Since virtually all of you reading this are above 4.25 in vibration, this does not apply to you, but we mentioned this because you have probably heard about energy hijackers.

It is not possible to live a life on Earth without being influenced to some extent by negative energies, thought forms and entities, but you can certainly minimize such exposure. Living in a cave, high up in the Himalayan mountains, is probably the best way to avoid negative vibrations, but that is certainly not for everyone, nor is it desirable for all but a few.

The best you can do if you live in a heavily populated area, is to not get drawn in emotionally by the drama and trauma of the masses. This means letting go of your attachments and core negative beliefs. If you have cleared your guilt, shame, fear, anger and related emotions, you will no longer attract negative entities because you have nothing they want.

The exception to this is the curiosity seekers that see your light and want some of it. They are easy to get rid of simply by surrounding yourself with God's golden radiant loving light.

Invocations to Dispel Negative Entities

As we said earlier, there are three types of negative entities: (1) curiosity seekers that are like moths around a lamp in summer — they see your light and because they have forgotten how to access their own inner light, want some of yours; (2) negative beings that are attracted to your negative thoughts and feelings through the Law of Attraction; and (3) beings you have karmic contracts with from previous lifetimes (or earlier in this lifetime).

You can easily dispel type (1) by simply protecting yourself and sending them away with a command, such as: "In the name of almighty Father/Mother God, I hereby dispel any and all negative energies, thought forms and entities immediately and completely from my six lower bodies."

For dispelling type (2) entities, healing your negative thoughts, feelings and beliefs is essential. We have already discussed this above.

For removing type (3) entities, you must complete your karma (soul lessons) with such entities. This is best done through timeline healing, hypnotherapy, past life regression and related therapies.

Interference from Negative Extraterrestrials

As mentioned previously, human beings have resembled lab rats in many ways throughout the recent history of Earth (within the last 500,000 years, specifically). Interbreeding between the Pleiadean-oriented Homo sapiens and various Orion and Sirian strains has resulted in altered longevity as well. The Orions from Rigel and Betelgeuse have a strong characteristic of warrior-like and aggressive mentality (compared to the Pleiadeans). This action-oriented stance on life results in a greater expenditure of kinetic energy in the Orions and Sirians than in the more peaceful and contemplative Pleiadeans.

Being a bit more negatively polarized in general, the Orions and some of the Sirians dissipate energy at a greater rate than the Pleiadeans (not only due to their level of activity, but from factors detailed above, such as negative thinking and core negative belief systems). The Reptilians from Rigel (in the Orion system) have a well-developed (you guessed it) reptilian brain, which is the aspect of human beings responsible for the "fight or flight" mechanism. Of course, this attribute of humanity is capable of saving lives when there is true danger, but it produces a lot of adrenaline and other substances that promote faster aging and decay.

Interbreeding during Pangaea was largely responsible for the drop in vibration of the various life forms that inhabited the first major civilization on Earth. Certainly, some extraterrestrial DNA configurations promote longer and healthier life when combined with existing Homo sapiens, but about 80% of the time, interbreeding with extraterrestrials has resulted in a drop in the vibration of humanity on Earth.

Negative Etheric Influences

"Dirty" Aura and Chakras

The aura and chakras belong to the etheric level of the soul, or fifth dimension. They are not the same thing as the astral body.

Negative energies can accumulate in the centers of the etheric body, causing mutations in the electromagnetic blueprint of the physical body. A clairvoyant can read the chakras and aura to see if there are dark colors or asymmetrical patterns that need healing.

There are many healing techniques for balancing and cleaning the etheric body, including chakra balancing, aura clearing, EFT tapping, acupressure, acupuncture, Reconnection and Reiki.

It is a good idea to do clearing on your home and business environment as well as your body. Visualize spirals of golden light going through your space. Descending, clockwise spirals (as viewed from above) infuse an area with positive etheric energy, while ascending, anti-clockwise (counter-clockwise) spirals are used for extracting negative energy from the aura and chakras.

Once the etheric body is clean, centropic energies are able to stream in and regenerate the six lower bodies.

Negative Etheric Imprints

Etheric imprints are similar to astral implants except that they are not as localized to a particular spot on the physical body. Nevertheless, if you received a major trauma to a certain part of the body in a past lifetime, it can show up as an etheric imprint in this lifetime if the issues around the trauma were never completely resolved.

Let's give an example: You were strangled in a past lifetime, and in this lifetime you have throat and respiratory issues.

Any area of the aura, chakras or electromagnetic blueprint (the main components of the etheric body) that contain imprints from earlier in this lifetime or from past lifetimes can act as an energy drain.

The best way to heal etheric imprints is through holistic healing methods and therapies, especially timeline healing, past-life regression, hypnotherapy and psychotherapy.

You might have multiple lifetimes of trauma that correspond to certain chakras. For example, several times you experienced intense grief when you lost loved ones, and now that grief is causing blockages in your heart chakra, including suppressed sadness. Later in this life, such imprints could show up as heart disease, heart attacks or other coronary problems.

If your body is relatively healthy, that does not necessarily mean you do not have etheric imprints. It only means they are not severe enough to precipitate into health concerns.

The mirror called "your life" will generally reflect to you the areas where you might still have unresolved issues in the etheric body. Continued holistic healing and therapy will reduce etheric blockages until they are insignificant regarding your overall energy level.

Negative Imprints from Present- and Past-Life Trauma

Imprints are blockages in the etheric body that arise from traumas. They are typically healed through past-life regression and timeline healing therapies. Usually an imprint corresponds to a specific area of the physical body. For example, if you were hanged in a past lifetime, you might experience frequent issues with your throat in this lifetime. You could say that there is an etheric imprint in the throat chakra.

Negative imprints are like any other type of blockage. They act like resistors in your energy circuit. What do resistors do? That's right, they dissipate energy in the form of heat, which is entropy.

Thinking of the body as being like an electrical circuit is a really good analogy. You have, in a sense, resistors, capacitors, coils and batteries. As you raise the frequency of your body, you raise the overall capacity, or ability to store energy. Trauma from the past acts like an excessive load on the circuit, diminishing your capacity and eventually your battery.

CHAPTER 14 | DEGENERATIVE FACTORS EXPLAINED IN DEPTH **163**

Negativity in the Causal Body

Samskaras (Negative Karma)

The causal body is level six of the six lower bodies. It pertains to karma, soul agreements and contracts, and includes the part of you that is capable of remembering past lifetimes. Samskaras are negative causal patterns that come from unresolved soul lessons or incomplete experiences (karma). The fastest way to heal karma is through forgiveness. You probably know that forgiveness is more than simply letting go of grievances. It involves the recognition that at a higher level, whatever happened is part of the grand illusion of separation and therefore does not really matter.

Fifty years from now, when you look back on your life, what will you remember? The person who called you stupid? The friend who didn't pay back the $10,000 you loaned him?

Forgiveness means you see the God Presence in the person who seemingly did you wrong, instead of focusing on the little self and its hurts. Forgiveness is not the same as pardon. In the example of the friend who didn't pay you back, you might tell that person, "It's okay. You don't need to pay me back." That's pardon. However, if you feel angry inside and are thinking, "How irresponsible of him," you have not truly forgiven. On the other hand, you might encounter a situation where you truly forgive and feel nothing but unconditional love for a person who didn't pay you back, but you also receive guidance to hold him responsible for his bad behavior; you take him to court to recover your money. That's forgiveness without pardon.

Probably the ideal situation is when you have both forgiveness and pardon, but that's not always the easy way out.

Self-acceptance is the key once again. Also, there are techniques for cancelling karmic agreements. The good news is that you can cancel an agreement and erase the karma even if the other person or persons do not forgive you. They still have karma, but you have completed yours. The only real requirement for living a karma-free life is to forgive yourself and others and to complete your agreements to the best of your ability.

Karmic Contracts and Agreements

A karmic contract or agreement is a pact or promise you made to one or more souls at some point in the past (usually in past lifetimes). This can involve a ritual where you pledge your undying love or commitment to a person or institution, explicitly stating that you are forever indebted to that person or entity regardless of time and space. This means, in your belief, you are held to that obligation no matter how many future lifetimes transpire or what world you incarnate upon.

The only conditions necessary to break a karmic agreement or contract are (1) the desire to end the soul lessons involved; and (2) the act of complete forgiveness of yourself and all souls involved in the contract or agreement. If your soul does not feel it has completely learned the lessons inherent within the agreement or contract, it will not prompt you to perform a ritual to end the promise. By ending the contract, you are affirming and knowing that your soul has learned everything it desires to learn about this particular experience or lesson.

The best way to heal a past-lifetime agreement is through timeline healing, where you go back in time and visit your past life self and give a healing to all concerned. It is also powerful to visualize an actual legal agreement. See it floating in the ethers. It has today's date, a judge's signature, and a seal. Across the front of the contract are the words "PAID IN FULL" in bright red letters.

Remember, you must completely forgive everyone associated with the agreement or contract. You do *not* need the agreement of the other people involved. This is good news.

If you have finished the lesson and forgiven everyone, you are free, even if the other soul(s) have not forgiven you and are still stuck in the energies of the original contract.

Clearing old agreements and contracts can free up a lot of energy that was held in limbo by your dedication or commitment to souls from long ago. Once you have energetically removed the karmic obligation, the other souls involved in the contract can no longer influence you (as long as you have cleared any negative emotions or beliefs around those souls). Even if they try to convince you to re-enter the agreement, it will be easy to say no and move on with your life because there is no longer any energetic "charge" associated with the soul lessons involved.

Work, Activity (Kinetic Energy Expended)

This is a dissipating factor that is unavoidable. Sure, you can rest a lot, meditate and sleep, which does help with regeneration, but your autonomic nervous system, heartbeat, respiratory and circulatory systems are constantly moving, processing and distributing energy throughout the body, and this utilizes a lot of your stored energy and life force (prana).

Although work is unavoidable, you can do it smarter, not harder, as the saying goes. Your body is built to move, and if you learn to move in harmony with the natural structure of the body, you will minimize energy depletion. Proper work is enjoyable and inspiring. It feels good to move your body. If you do a workout at the gym, it should not only be enjoyable while you are doing it, but you should feel good afterwards.

So many people who work out are struggling or trying forcefully to change the body to fit some image of what they think it should be. It takes a lot of extra energy to make the body sexy or to shape and contour it to a preferred appearance. This is not to say it is wrong to enhance the natural beauty through makeup and cosmetics. Healthy, organic beauty products can contribute to your overall well-being.

The body has an inherent, built-in intelligence. If you tune in and really listen to what your body wants, you will gravitate toward the right form of exercise and work.

Interaction with other human beings plays a tremendous role in the well-being of the body. What type of people do you work with? Are they taking good care of their bodies, eating and exercising in an intelligent manner? What about their thoughts? Are they predominantly negative, or do they hold a balanced, optimistic viewpoint on life? Optimism without balance does not promote longevity and immortality. It stems from denial, avoidance and escape from looking at the shadow self.

The point is, if you work around negative people, you will feel tired at the end of the day even if the amount of physical energy expended is small. Boring, repetitive tasks are not healthy. Although the body has the capabilities to do repetitive work, this is the proper role of machinery, including computers and artificial intelligence. AI is not supposed to render human beings useless in the workplace or throw millions out of employment. AI and computers are designed to free up your time to be creative and engage in non-repetitive movement and activity.

When you are working (physically and/or mentally), pay attention to what recharges and what tires you. In today's workplace, there will obviously be some tasks that are more exciting and fulfilling than others, but the key is doing everything with awareness. Even the least enjoyable aspect of your work can be improved from an energetic standpoint. Take frequent breaks when engaged in the unpleasant tasks. Put on some beautiful music in the background. Process any negative emotions or beliefs you have about such things as doing taxes, accounting, handling employee conflict, etc. See if you have any subconscious worrying going on regarding company profitability, future economic trends, etc.

Remember that no matter how negative workmates might be, they are all children of God.

If you have a choice in the number of hours and time of day you spend at work, you might want to distribute those hours across the spectrum of the day, doing the hardest work during your natural up cycles and resting during your natural down cycles. Learn to recognize your circadian rhythms. Become familiar with the times you are naturally more energetic (based on biorhythms).

Do your most difficult tasks at least three hours after a meal but before you get hungry. Eat several small meals or snacks on busy days instead of working straight through for eight hours and then eating when you are ravenously hungry. Trying to do anything after overeating is arduous. If you are tired one to two hours after a meal, you have either eaten too much or are not eating the right foods. We will say more about diet shortly.

Bodies do not like extremes or a lot of sudden changes in schedule. Routine is important. It is not the same thing as being boring and repetitive. Incorporate breaks and variety into your routine.

If you are an athlete, you probably know about being "in the zone." This is where you achieve a harmonious balance between expending energy and attuning to the natural frequencies of your body. Essentially, you are tapping into the prana (life force) while engaged in your favorite sport. This is the only way it is possible to run a marathon. Without a harmonious intake of centropy, the body would collapse after a few miles or kilometers. Breathing is important in athletics, as it increases prana when properly executed and maintained. You can also practice breathing exercises in other types of work. We will have more to say about proper breathing in the centropy section.

Negative Environmental Factors

Lack of Sufficient Sunlight

If you live in the far northern or southern hemispheres, you receive less sunlight than near the equator. Some racial mixtures do not do well in intense sunlight and so the body tends to thrive in colder climates, but there are limits. If you go through long, cold, dark winters, such as those in northern Russia and Canada, you need to compensate for the lack of sunlight. This means taking a lot of vitamins C and D, practicing conscious breathing, taking vacations and holidays to sunnier places, etc.

The body has an amazing ability to adapt, but it takes energy to alter the natural rhythms of the body in such a way that you are getting enough phytonutrients. If you live a stressful life in northern climates, this puts added resistance into the system.

It's true that some plants and animals can live with almost no direct sunlight, including organisms in the deep sea and under the frozen tundra of the Arctic. However, human beings were not designed to go without the sun.

If you are unsure about how much sunlight you need to reach optimum health, then experiment. Spend more or less time in the sun than you usually do and observe the effects. Refrain from using sun tanning or blocking lotions and creams. Of course, if you are extremely pale and have not had much direct sunlight for years, you will need to ease into more sun exposure. If you live where the sun almost never shines in the winter, you will obviously need to travel in order to receive more sunlight.

Tanning booths are not an adequate substitute for the sun, no matter what the companies claim. It's not just ultraviolet that affects the body. Sunlight has a complex mixture of frequencies and phyto-nutrients that cannot be adequately mimicked by modern technology.

If you have the financial and familial means to move closer to the equator, it might be a good idea to do so. Avoid tropical cities if you can. Become familiar with climate patterns and local animal life. Choose a place that is well above sea level, but still within a comfortable growing region.

If you travel a lot, you are probably exposed to various types of radiation from aircraft and other sources. Also, your body is constantly adjusting to different time zones and climates. Some travel is probably good. It helps your body become more adaptable and flexible, and it greatly increases your knowledge of different peoples and cultures.

If you travel on business and there is a lot of stress related to meetings, conferences and such, this will take a toll on your immune system and overall well-being. Do your best to take walks in nature between meetings or relax outdoors if the weather is good.

In the centropy section, we will talk briefly about sungazing and its pros and cons.

Circadian Rhythm Imbalances

The body's ability to regenerate itself during sleep is severely disrupted by today's lifestyle. Many people go to sleep with the television on or with their computer and phone plugged in to charging devices. Even if you turn your electronic devices off at night, you are still being bombarded by Wi-Fi signals from all over the neighborhood, as well as mobile-phone transmission towers and radio and television stations. Electrical power lines are emitting various frequencies outside your window and inside your walls. The vibration of internal combustion engines in traffic, even if it is in the distance, adds to the disruption.

Many people have unusual schedules requiring them to work during times when the body is preprogrammed to sleep. Modern stressful lifestyles cause people to have insomnia. You might wake up several times during the night and begin obsessing about your busy work schedule the following day (or week).

The body's natural cycles do not necessarily conform to the schedules of society. Sometimes the body likes to rest during the day or be awake at night, but usually we force the body to adhere to a work schedule. Some souls have a built-in sense of when they should go to sleep and wake up, while others are dependent on alarm clocks or other stimulants. Sleeping pills at night, coffee (caffeine) in the morning, and various additional stimulants during the day can destroy the circadian rhythms of humans (and animals).

Inability to sleep peacefully for a few hours or more every night can certainly lead to problems regenerating after stressful days of energy depletion.

Pay attention to the various ways you interrupt the body's natural rhythms. Avoid caffeine after mid-day. Do not eat within two hours of bedtime. Finish as many tasks as you can before going to sleep. In other words, do not put off doing things until morning if you know you will fret, toss and turn at night thinking about them. Resist the temptation to eat dessert after the evening meal.

Drink healthy fluids moderately. Take a few sips before bedtime, but not so much that you are getting up frequently in the middle of the night to eliminate.

Have a tiny bit of light streaming into your bedroom, but not so much that it disturbs the circadian cycle. Pitch black is not good because if you do need to get up, the need to switch on a light to see where you are going will wake you up to the point you might not get back to sleep easily. On the other hand, turn alarm clock faces and other digital devices away from you if they have bright lights. A small night light is good or an alarm clock with a soft light face. Never use the snooze button more than once.

Discordant Sounds and Frequencies

Many of us are not aware of the more subtle frequencies that are constantly bombarding us day and night. An obvious source is music, whether voluntarily listened to through speakers or headphones, or involuntarily blasted through an intercom system at work or in public places. Does the television set at the airport help anybody stay clear and focused, especially when it's tuned to the latest propaganda (as it always is)?

It has been well researched that certain frequencies promote healing and growth, while others do the opposite. Do whatever you can to eliminate discordant frequencies from your living and workspaces. Put soft classical or New Age music on in the background, preferably without vocals. Nature sounds are also good. If necessary, wear ear plugs at work to blot out the background music if it is not peaceful and harmonious.

You can find music tuned to specific healthy frequencies on YouTube and other places. Play it softly in the background (with the device at least three meters away) during sleep. Make sure there are no vocals. Some files are up to eight hours in duration. See if it helps you sleep. If not, turn it off and try something else.

Some people seem to need a fan or repetitive sound going in the background in order to sleep. It is a good idea to wean yourself of this bad habit, unless you are using nature sounds, such as recordings of the sea or crickets.

Toxic Radiation and Electromagnetic Pollution

There are many forms of toxic radiation in the environment of Earth. Some of it is natural (background), but a lot of it is caused by humankind. If you are reading this book on a computer, you are probably getting radiated right now.

The best way to avoid getting too much toxic radiation is to vary your schedule. Do not spend hours at a time in front of a screen (phone, computer or television). If your work requires this, take frequent breaks. If you have a choice in your schedule, do not place more than three or four clients back-to-back if you are doing sessions online. Get up and walk around between each client or customer. We realize this is not easy in most work environments.

Remember to hydrate yourself, especially when in a high-radiation location. Adequate healthy fluids will help dispel excess radiation.

Find out where nuclear reactors and weapons manufacturers are located. Has there been a war recently where you are living or working? What kind of building construction is practiced? Is there likely to be excess radioactive chemicals in the ground or building materials? What is the cancer rate in your neighborhood or industrial park? We are not suggesting you worry constantly about getting bombarded by radiation. The good and bad news is that yes, you ARE being constantly bombarded. However, unless you have a chronic illness that you suspect is related to radiation, your body has probably adapted for the most part.

Do your best to get outdoors. The toxic radiation in sunlight is far less than from other sources, so you are still better off getting 30 to 60 minutes of sun per day.

If you are living and working in a highly polluted area, sleeping and resting indoors with the windows closed is a good idea, but you are still better off getting outdoors during active physical periods (unless there is a severe temperature inversion and a lot of smog, in which case you won't be getting much beneficial sunlight anyway).

Remember that it takes a lot of energy to transmute the effects of toxic radiation, so you must increase centropy in other ways to counter-balance the effects.

We are addressing the issue of electromagnetic pollution here, rather than in the section on pollution in general, because it has unique attributes related to toxic radiation. The best remedies for overcoming EM noise, interference patterns and discordant frequencies is to practice the art of Feng Shui and/or Vastu. These are ancient practices in the architecture and placement of objects and design of buildings that maximizes the flow of positive energies and minimizes negative influences.

A few common-sense arrangements should be made. Place radiation sources in the home away from sleeping areas. Turn off devices at night or put them at least three meters away from your body. Better yet, keep them in an office or room separate from your sleeping area. Sleep with your head pointing away from Wi-Fi, television and radio, or mobile phone transmitter towers and stations. You can rather easily find out where they are located.

With the recent roll-out of 5G technologies, it is even more crucial to protect yourself from high frequency EM radiation. If you can, install frequency barriers, shields and plating around objects that emit excessive amounts of EM signals.

You cannot entirely avoid EM pollution no matter where you live, but obviously there is less of it away from large cities.

The main problem with EM radiation is that it tends to interfere with your natural body rhythms, a topic we will address next.

Food, Water, Soil and Air Pollution (Harmful Chemicals and Toxins)

We are not going to spend a long time discussing the various poisons in the food, water, soil and air, because most of you reading this are already well aware of this problem. Probably the most significant recent discovery among genetic scientists is how certain chemical combinations affect the production and destruction of telomeres, stem cells, and regenerative tissues and processes.

A small percentage of the chemicals in the environment might actually stimulate regeneration (inadvertently), but the vast majority, as expected, are detrimental to genetic health.

Endocrine-system disrupters and cell-production inhibitors are major factors in carcinogenic compounds. When cells are unable to reproduce in a healthy manner (involving geometric sequences of healthy cell division and multiplication), mutation can occur. Again, some cellular mutations are beneficial and can greatly speed up the evolutionary process of the human being, but the vast majority of mutations are destructive to the individual. Uncontrolled mutation is another name for cancer. Cell reproduction rates become fast and erratic, and the mutant cells begin consuming healthy tissues and fibers, upsetting the delicate balance of the body's various subsystems. Cancer cell production can be triggered by many things besides the environment. Toxic emotions held in place over long periods of time are the biggest single factor. A depleted immune system can also cause cancer. Invading viruses and bacteria, under the right conditions, can trigger cancer.

Some chemicals are toxic even in extremely small quantities, such as dioxins. Radioactivity occurs naturally in the environment, and the body has built-in defenses against background levels, but when the levels exceed a certain threshold, the body's immune system becomes overwhelmed and either shuts down or begins attacking itself. Auto-immune-system disorders are almost always related to toxins in the environment, although sometimes it takes years, or even decades, for the imbalances to show up in the human body.

While toxic chemicals are not, in themselves, a dissipator of energy, they cause disruption in the healthy function of cells and tissues that counteract the aging process. Essentially, they make it harder for the body to overcome entropy.

Because a lot of chemicals stimulate uncontrollable cell growth, they increase the chaos (heat) and, therefore, the dissipation of energy.

There's a lot of talk about genetically modified organisms (GMO). What are the major health concerns here? First, the levels of pesticides are much higher with GMO crops because the crops are engineered to resist toxins that are designed to kill everything else. In GMO corn, the toxins are hybridized right into the corn kernels, so you cannot avoid the toxin no matter how much you wash the food.

GMO chemicals are known to disrupt the endocrine system, including reproductive hormones and organs. The dramatic drop in sperm count in men and fertility in women can be directly correlated with the rise in GMO production. Although the big agribusiness and big pharma companies would like you to believe otherwise, more and more reputable studies are revealing the problems mentioned herein. As stated earlier, it is so bad that some people are suggesting GMO crops are part of a planned depopulation program.

There are a very small number of souls in positions of power that truly do want to reduce human population, and they have already attempted this in various ways, including introducing sterilization serums into vaccines in parts of Africa, so we are certainly not denying that there could be sinister motivation behind the spread of GMO crops. However, the profit motive in agribusiness is the primary driving force behind the use of these agricultural methods. Some companies offer "terminator" seeds, which means farmers must purchase new seeds every planting season. Obviously, this greatly increases profits.

Regardless of the motivation behind GMO and related practices, the impact on human beings includes the hindering of the body's natural immunity and, hence, interference with the body's ability to regenerate itself and reduce entropy.

Another significant factor regarding environmental pollution is the reduced availability of oxygen in the respiratory system of animals. In sparsely populated areas, pollutants are widely dispersed and seem to cause very little interference in the delivery of oxygen to the cells.

However, in big cities, particularly those in basins and valleys where pollutants settle at night and during temperature inversions, oxygen levels can be noticeably lower. Less oxygen in the air and blood means less prana flowing into the body and, thus, lower incoming energy. Pollution therefore acts like a block to the flow of centropy.

It is best to live in a well-ventilated house in an area where the air mixes easily, meaning not in the bottom of a basin or valley. There should be light to moderate winds during most of the year. The ideal altitude is usually 500 to 1,000 meters above sea level, depending on the latitude.

DNA Death-Sequence Program

Believe it or not, there is a death program built in to so-called "normal" human DNA. This program is the result of numerous episodes of tampering by extraterrestrials as well as mutations caused by atmospheric conditions on Earth. It is not a coincidence that Earth has one of the shortest longevity rates of any developed planetary system. For example, in fourth-density Pleiades, there are several inhabited planets where the average life span is between 200 and 300 years. In Arcturus, there are planets where humanoids live over 2,000 years in the same body (on average). Long ago on Earth, life spans were much greater. So why is the current span so short?

The story is long and complicated, but suffice to say that several benevolent and malevolent extraterrestrial civilizations have tampered with human DNA over the millennia. It is easier to control a population if their life spans are kept short. Manipulating telomeres, stem cells and other DNA components is one way to achieve this. Introducing certain chemicals into the food, water, soil and air is another strategy.

The lower the vibration of a life form, the more entropy and less centropy. As souls drop their frequencies through negative thoughts and feelings and interacting with negatively polarized life forms, the more the vibration drops for the entire species. The lowest part of the current cycle occurred during the Dark Ages, when life spans were barely more than 50 years. We are made to believe that evolution has steadily progressed over the last 10,000 years and that today is the height of achievement in human evolution, but that is just plain false.

The real history of Earth involves a series of ups and downs, including the rising and falling of several civilizations, mostly due to outside interference in human affairs combined with periodic natural disasters.

We realize this section implies that human beings have been lab rats for thousands of years but, unfortunately, that is not far from the truth. Eventually the true history of humanity will be revealed to the masses, but for now you must consult someone who has accessed the Akashic Records or is in communication with highly evolved extraterrestrials in order to get accurate information. (You can also read *The Real History of Earth* by this author.)

Some beliefs and theories regarding humanity's evolution on Earth can be dispelled quickly, such as the insane belief that we evolved from the ape. This lie has been exposed in previous publications. We encourage you to do your own research in this area.

How do you overcome the DNA death sequence? You do this by reprogramming your DNA for immortality, which is exactly what we are focusing on in this section of the book. It begins with having the knowledge of what is required to overcome death. Then you must put the principles in this section to work in your daily lives. Eventually, the death program will be eradicated in a genetic laboratory, but for now, you must learn to reprogram your own DNA through the methods taught by this author and others.

Through changing your consciousness, you can not only preserve telomere and stem cell activity, but it is possible to generate new immortal DNA cellular patterns. Until about 30 years ago, scientists thought the brain could not make new neurons, but that has since been proven false. Any type of cell is capable of being reproduced. Consciousness controls DNA. By raising your consciousness, you learn to reprogram your DNA to grow new tissues, limbs, and regenerative bodily subsystems.

The Frequency Barrier/Fence

Earth has been infiltrated over hundreds of thousands of years by beings from several different star systems. The universe is about 80% benevolent and 20% malevolent on average, but due to Earth's relatively low vibration, the percentages are just about reversed here. Almost 80% of the beings from other star systems who have come to Earth have been predominantly negative.

They came to either mine its natural resources, claim the Earth for themselves, enslave its people, or all of the above.

The light and dark beings involved in the Earth drama each erected a barrier around the Earth, but for different reasons. The light beings put their version of a frequency fence around the planet in order to protect it from negative invaders. The dark beings put a barrier up to prevent humanity from communicating with benevolent helpers in other star systems. They also used frequency calibration techniques to interfere with humanity's psychic and intuitive abilities.

Needless to say, the negative beings managed to get by the frequency fence erected by the positive ones. Today, both barriers are still affecting humanity but to a lesser degree than many thousands of years ago.

The frequency fence is one of the reasons the life spans on Earth are so short. Obviously, this barrier is not made of steel or concrete but rather a combination of atmospheric compounds and microwave frequencies. By changing the gaseous composition of Earth's atmosphere and broadcasting life-enhancing frequencies, the life span on Earth can be dramatically extended. The decrease of intensity in the barrier over the past few hundred years is one reason for improved longevity (along with the more obvious causes, such as advances in medicine and sewage disposal and treatment in developed countries).

Negative People and Situations

Three-fourths of the world is negative. This is a fact. It is not an attempt at doom and gloom by this author or anyone else. If you define "negative thoughts" as "activity of consciousness that tends to hold back soul progress, interfere with or hinder it," then about 75% of all thought forms on Earth are negative. In addition, about three out of every four people currently living on Earth have more negative thoughts than positive ones. Take a young man living in the West, for example. He is single and is dating a couple of women, has a job in the computer industry (IT) and lives with a roommate. Some of his first thoughts upon waking up on a weekday morning might include, "What do I need to do today?"

That's a fairly neutral thought, so we will not tally it in the positive or negative column. Then he remembers the report due later this morning at work. "My boss really doesn't like me. He always finds fault with my work. I'm not looking forward to my presentation." Then his mind wanders to his date tonight. "Anna and I are not doing too well. She thinks I'm too obsessed with my job. I seem to have trouble relaxing and enjoying her company. I really did have a good time at the company party last Friday."

So there you have it: Six negative thoughts and one positive thought. We are not saying all thoughts should be positive. It might be necessary to become aware of a situation that needs improving. "I need to improve the quality of the program I wrote," implies that there are bugs in the first draft, but generally this is a positive thought because it's about improving a product.

People who habitually think mostly negative thoughts are transmitting a negative energy, or in keeping with the theme of this section, they are acting as "energy vampires" to some degree, causing those around them to become drained of their energy unless they take steps to minimize the effect.

What is a negative situation? It is one that is composed of negative people or one that is likely to cause undue stress or even harm to those involved. Some negative conditions are obvious, such as places with war, poverty, riots, racial tension, etc. But what about the workplace, especially on Monday morning when you can actually feel the reluctance on the parts of many employees to be there? Contrast that to Friday afternoon, when people are a lot more light-hearted.

You might not be able to do very much about negative environments directly, but you can radiate positive energy into those places, and this will lift them to some degree. But to do that requires that you stay clear of the negativity yourself.

What are some of the things you can do when you are around negative co-workers, employees or employers? First, put a shield of golden light around yourself. Practice turning negative comments into positive suggestions. "The world is so crazy. They keep electing the same corrupt politicians over and over."

How do you turn that statement around? "I think most people want change, but they are afraid to take risks with someone new." Okay, that's not a complete turnaround, but it's a start. How about, "Let's research alternative candidates and find the best one and vote for him (or her)." If the retort is, "What difference does it make? I'm only one person," you could reply with, "Gandhi was only one person. So was Martin Luther King."

We are not expecting miracles from this sort of process, but every little bit helps. You will know when you are making progress because you will not feel as drained at the end of your workday. The exhaustion you feel is a combination of your own negative thinking and the negative energy you have picked up from others. Start catching yourself the minute you begin to spiral down into a negative pattern. Learn to recognize when you are taking on energy from others before you start to get tired. This takes a lot of practice.

Service to Self (Karma)

Karma is associated with entropy because it seems to prevent the soul from opening more fully to the centropic forces that are always available in every Planck second. Service-to-self mentality also seems to contribute to entropy because it is based on the illusion that there is not enough energy for everyone, and therefore what there is must be hoarded, controlled or doled out to the highest bidder.

While karma and service-to-self attitudes are not directly involved in the dissipation of energy, they tend to move the soul into the realms of duality more fully, which, of course, contributes to entropy.

How can you tell the difference between a soul who is predominantly service to self rather than service to others? It's very simple.

You feel a drop in energy when you are around such a soul. Energy vampires are obviously service to self. Even if you transact business in a way that looks fair and balanced (perhaps receiving adequate monetary compensation for something you have given to such a soul) it will not feel like a fair exchange from an energetic viewpoint.

Therapists are well aware of this. Clients that seem to "take" their energy are doing just that. If you feel drained after working with such clients, it is important to protect yourself more fully (using the various techniques given by this author and others).

If you are truly centered, a service-to-self soul cannot take your energy, no matter what type of therapy, healing or counseling you are performing or how long the session is. Once such a soul realizes he/she cannot take your energy, that soul will either move out of the destructive selfish pattern or will no longer be drawn to you as a therapist.

Of course, if you have karma with another soul, it will be difficult to move out of negative patterns in the relationship (whether it is professional or personal). If you have someone in your life who seems to trigger you constantly, even when you work studiously on yourself, it is probably a long-term karmic relationship. The whole purpose of the relationship might be to learn the lessons of service to self and service to others, or it might literally be to learn how to keep your energy intact and stay centered while in the presence of such a soul.

Through timeline healing, past-life regression and other therapies, it is possible to pinpoint the karmic lessons and how they began and evolved. Once you heal the karma, such a soul will no longer be able to drain your energy or divert your attention away from building your immortal light body.

Darkness, Ignorance and Denial

Technically, these are three different ideas, but we are including them in the same subsection. Darkness has a few meanings, including absence of light. From an ultimate viewpoint, there is no such thing as darkness, because the Light of Truth is all-encompassing, meaning it has no opposite. Another absolute truth that has no opposing force or contrast is God's Love. While it is possible to deny (put out of awareness) God's Love by believing in an opposite, it is not actually possible to oppose God's Love. Thinking you can do so puts you in an impossible situation, and you will suffer the consequences of being caught in illusions if you believe there is an opposite to God's Love.

Another definition of darkness is evil, personified as Satan, the Devil, or the Dark Lords. Since everything is God, these archetypes are also part of God even though they are invented to be God's adversaries. Satan is an illusion, but because so many people believe in him, he seems to be real. Souls can impersonate or embody the principles of Satan, including the idea of service to self (disregard for the well-being of others), or deriving some sort of pleasure from seeing others in pain. Believing there is a force opposing God is the ultimate form of entropy because you see God as impermanent, mortal, and assailable. Because belief is so powerful, you will experience the seeming "opposites" of God's eternal, unlimited energy.

The way to overcome evil is to first become aware of all the ways you still believe in separation. The deepest example of this is the belief that some souls are more worthy of God's Love than other souls. In fact, this author's actual definition of evil is as follows:

"A state of consciousness whereby some souls are deemed more worthy of God's Love than other souls."

If you go deeply enough into that perception, you will see that it strengthens the core negative belief in separation from God, which is at the root of all negativity. The belief in separation is also the root cause of all misery and suffering. Needless to say, it is the biggest dissipator of energy.

Ignorance comes in two forms: willful and unintentional. The unintentional variety is easily remedied through education. A person who does not know something and who is eager to learn can be taught and, therefore, brought out of ignorance.

Willful ignorance is far more difficult to overcome because such a soul does not want to wake up. He has become attached to his limited belief systems and sees awakening as too painful and too much a sacrifice. Many willfully ignorant people have been brainwashed to believe that anything beyond their sheltered little lives will jeopardize their safety. Security is more important to them than the freedom to think for themselves and, therefore, they refuse to accept help even when it is offered without obligation of any sort.

Willfully ignorant people make excuses for themselves when their loved ones are urging them to change. They give their power away to beliefs, substances, processes or lifestyles that are clearly depleting their energy and bringing misery and unhappiness, yet they keep going back to destructive behavior time after time. No amount of filling the entire back section of a pack of cigarettes with dire warnings will stop the addict from lighting up another cigarette. No videos of a person hacking and coughing their last breath will get them to stop making excuses.

Habits are hard to break (especially smoking), but the hardest habit of all to break is giving up negative thinking. Human beings become attached to their negative thoughts, and the ego actually fears its death if it gives up the ignorance it has known for so long.

Chaos

Chaos is the end product of entropy. When you see chaos in the world, it means a lot of souls are enmeshed in the process of entropic behaviors, attitudes, beliefs, emotions, ideas, programs and thoughts. Those who believe they are in control of Earth use various strategies for maintaining their seeming authority. This involves getting the masses to remain in their illusion of victimhood. One of the ways this is accomplished is through the "divide and conquer" mentality: Pit one group of souls against another and keep them fighting among themselves so that they never notice who is pulling the strings behind the scenes.

This is not new information. Teachers have been pointing out these strategies for millennia. Yet this type of deception still seems to work because souls have not healed their Original Cause. (Not to be confused with Original Sin, although they are related.) If you have not read this author's previous books, you are probably unfamiliar with his definition of Original Cause. This is the trauma experienced during the first incarnation of your soul, or the first descent into the lower dimensions. For almost all souls, it was the most traumatic event of all. It occurred many tens of millions of years ago for the average soul on Earth.

The reason civilizations come and go over the centuries and never seem to break free of entropy is due to unresolved Original Cause issues in almost every soul. Underneath all the layers of the subconscious mind, the original trauma still lurks. It manifests as fear of the unknown, fear of death and even fear of life. After all, if you live life fully and joyously, something bad might happen to take it all away. The first descent into matter was experienced as a bad event because of the intense pain of contraction. You can read more about the details of this densification of the soul in the book, *Soul Integration*.

If there were no spiritual self, chaos would be the final chapter for humanity. As the physical universe winds down, there would be more and more chaotic forms of energy and less order. Eventually the last gasp of life would be experienced and then only the silence of the void.

But that is not how it works, fortunately. The universe breathes. It expands and contracts once every Planck second and, on a macro level, once approximately every 100 billion years. So even as the physical universe is becoming more chaotic, the higher dimensions are becoming more ordered. At some point, the universe will contract, and centropy will become more dominant than entropy (although on the macro level that is a long way off — perhaps about 35 billion years in the future).

Do not despair. You do not have to wait all those billions of years to begin ordering your life. On the macro level, there is as much order as you can possibly handle right now. On the micro level, movement toward order happens 10^{44} times per second. In a few moments, we will talk about ways you can open to the centropic forces that are constantly streaming into the lower dimensions.

Remember that energy is neither created nor destroyed — only the form changes. And, ultimately, if you consider our sister universe, there is an abundance of the things we find rare in our own universe.

Resistance

We come back to the main characteristic of entropy: resistance.

Electrical science (Ohm's Law) holds the simple key to increasing our energy:

> Voltage (potential energy) divided by resistance equals current (kinetic energy).

What is the answer to life eternal? Just lower your resistance. It's simple, but obviously not easy, or we would not be going into such depth explaining all the ways that resistance increases.

Metaphysically and psychologically, the way to lower resistance is to accept "what is." If you are fighting with the circumstances and conditions in your life, you are giving away your power (potential and kinetic energy). Once your resistance has decreased to a certain level, you can clearly and calmly make any changes that are desired, or rather, such changes will happen through you as a result of your receptivity to higher frequencies that occurs when you stop resisting.

More on the Belief in Separation

The last item in our list of dissipators is the core negative belief that we are separate from God. Having this belief gives rise to "proof" in the form of discrete bodies that seem weak and subject to constant danger from the environment and other human beings.

What would physical life on Earth be like if the belief in separation were absent? Outwardly, we would still have technologies for making the body comfortable, happy and healthy, but we would no longer be emotionally attached to these comforts. We would no longer be living in constant fear of loss and death.

The newest advances in science tell us that we are not separate. Our whole world runs on technologies derived from this same science, and now quantum computing can be added to the list of applications. What more proof do we need that separation is an illusion? Can we truly see how much misery and suffering is contained within that belief? Look at the enormous military expenditures. See the trillions of dollars that could be spent developing Zero-Point devices.

Visualize a world where every soul leads an abundant, happy, healthy life. This is not a fairy tale. It is possible right now, although, as we have stated, there is a necessary period of transition.

Can you live life with the certainty that the limitless nature of the universe is within you? Can you tap the abundance of energy, love, money, time and talent that are already yours?

Before we move to the section on how to increase centropy, let us spend a little time on the more subtle levels of energy dissipation.

CHAPTER 15

More Information on How We Dissipate Energy

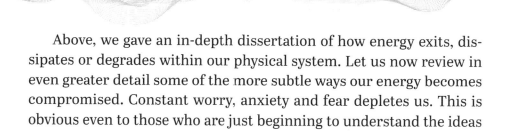

Above, we gave an in-depth dissertation of how energy exits, dissipates or degrades within our physical system. Let us now review in even greater detail some of the more subtle ways our energy becomes compromised. Constant worry, anxiety and fear depletes us. This is obvious even to those who are just beginning to understand the ideas presented in this book. But what about the more subtle ways that we compromise ourselves?

Throughout this book, we have talked about resistance. However, there may be forms of resistance that do not fit neatly into the categories above. Let us list some possible red flags (warnings) that indicate you might be dealing with resistance in yourself or others:

People Pleasing. We mold ourselves according to others' expectations of us. We seek love and approval even if it means doing things that are not in our best interests. By listening to the ego's demands for attention and affection, we seem to lose connection with our Higher Self, the Source of etheric and higher dimensional energy.

Unenlightened Relationships. These can range from outright codependency (a state whereby we put another's needs and problems ahead of our own), to staying in a relationship out of fears for our safety and security. As a therapist, this author has worked with thousands of souls who are in unhappy relationships but are afraid to leave lest their safety and security become threatened.

Unfulfilling Work. The majority of souls in the Western world either hate their jobs or simply put up with them because they do not believe they can succeed doing something they love. We are not going to pretend that changing careers is easy or that there will not be any financial hardships in the beginning if you pursue what you love. Yet by not fulfilling your true desires, you cut yourself off from the unlimited source of energy. You are not listening to the voice of wisdom within out of fear for what might happen if you leave the "safety" and "security" of your present job.

Sacrificing for Family. Another large category of clients this author works with are those who are caretakers for ailing family members. Often a soul will feel drained and tired after spending time with her judgmental and selfish mother who cannot take care of herself. "My brothers and sisters abandoned her, and I'm the only one who can take care of her. We don't have the money to put her in assisted living or have 24-hour care staff, so I'm stuck with her. She yells at me constantly and berates me for every little thing. I can't take it anymore." There's no way around the fact that this is a difficult situation, but there are solutions. There are always solutions. First, if you take care of yourself, you have more energy available to take care of your ailing parent. Feeling guilty about doing something for yourself will end up affecting your loved one. You will resent her, and that resentment will have a negative impact on the relationship. There are books on this subject, so we will not go further here.

Obsessions and Addictions. We talked about this earlier, but let's review. In today's world, it's easy to become hooked on activities or substances that lower your overall energy vibration. The biggest addiction is to thinking. It takes energy to think, as we explained above. Most thinking is a habit. A small percentage of thoughts are necessary to continue functioning in this world.

Here's an exercise (a rather difficult one): For 24 hours, try to document all your thoughts — their purpose, duration, frequency and whether they trigger emotions or actions. If you are like most people, about 80% of your thoughts are about the safety and security of the physical body and meeting the ego's demands for love and approval. Only 20% are necessary or enlightened thoughts. Recall the woman who could not enjoy her time off because she was constantly thinking about her tasks the following week.

Confusion and Chaos. If you live in a populated area, you are constantly taking on the energy of those around you, even if you have a holistic program, do aura cleansing, chakra balancing, yoga and meditation. Of course, you take on far less if you have such a regimen of useful activities, but you cannot stay completely clear in such an environment. This is why a lot of yogis and higher beings live in the mountains or forests. If such souls are genuinely enlightened, they are not doing this to escape the tasks and responsibilities inherent within society, but because they realize they can be of greater service by remaining as detached as possible from the mass consciousness. In today's world of online work, you can be somewhat of a recluse, or even a hermit, and still broadcast your ideas to humanity through the Internet and social media.

Influences from Subtle Realms. Recall the idea that we have six lower bodies. The first three are obvious — physical, emotional and mental — but the next three are often called the subtle bodies — astral, etheric and causal. These subtle realms can and do influence human beings. Not all energies, thought forms and entities in these realms are positive. The negative aspects can affect your energy even if you are not aware of this. In addition to using protection techniques regularly, such as putting golden light around your body and calling in your Higher Self and God Presence, it is essential to heal the negative thoughts and feelings that attract such negative influences. Negative entities feed off guilt, shame, anger and fear.

Practice loving yourself every day to thwart these types of interference. In some cases, negative entities behave like parasites, literally feeding off your personal energy field, leaving you drained and cloudy.

False Detachment or Denial. The ego can try and play the role of the Higher Self and even convince itself that it is the Higher Self. You might decide, "I am beyond this world. Nothing in this world can touch me anymore. It's all illusion." Then your normal human thoughts and feelings go into a state of denial. You are pretending to be elevated above the daily concerns of life, but really all you have done is push your negativity into the subconscious mind. Inevitably, something occurs to take you out of your delusion, such as a major illness, accident, or relationship blow-up. "How could this be happening to me? I meditate, pray and live in the 'bliss' of enlightenment." There are layers and layers in the process of healing. You might clear one layer of negative programming and falsely think you have completed the entire process, but there are deeper layers you have not yet discovered. It's not really possible in this world to be completely free of "samskaras" or negative programming, but you can shrink your problems down while expanding your awareness. True transcendence means "going beyond." It does not mean trying to escape or deny your problems. In transcendence, you realize you are much larger than your human drama, and so you are able to love the little self by seeing the big picture of your life.

Fear of Death. If you have become deeply attached to your human life, a great deal of energy is being spent to protect and guard from the myriad of ways that life could be threatened. Contrary to the belief of most souls, including spiritual teachers, the death of the physical body is NOT inevitable. However, fear of death most certainly keeps you from attaining physical immortality. Every moment, a part of you is dying and another part is being reborn. Being attached to your present physical body is a form of delusion because every moment, cells are dying and new ones are being generated.

Be willing to let go of the past, even if it is extremely pleasurable. As one shaman said, "Live as though death is ever present on your left shoulder." Death is part of life. Every moment someone or something is dying. Attaining immortality is not about trying to postpone the horrors of death. In fact, many enlightened souls and those who have experienced near-death experiences say that death can be the most exhilarating experience possible. A soul without fear of death may choose to remain in an ageless healthy body for a long time in order to more efficiently serve humanity, but if death comes, it is welcomed.

The Effect of Core Negative Beliefs. About 99% of humanity are ruled by deep-seated negative belief systems that are the biggest possible drain on energy. These beliefs have been explored extensively in earlier sections and in previous books, but to summarize, they include:

- "I'm not good enough."
- "Something is wrong with me."
- "I'm not worthy."
- "There's not enough (time, money, love, energy, etc.)."
- "I'm not safe in this world."
- "I cannot have what I truly want in life."
- "Life is a disappointment."
- "Life is a struggle."

There are numerous corollaries to these beliefs, such as:
- "I must work hard in order to succeed."
- "I must protect the ones I love."

While working hard and securing the personal space of your loved ones might be admirable, worrying about safety and security is a big drain on energy. Trying to measure up to unrealistic expectations of yourself and others is a huge issue for many people (based on the belief, "I'm not good enough.") Every day, review the role negative core beliefs are playing in your life and how they are directing your actions. If you have been working on yourself a long time, the effect of negative beliefs may be more subtle and harder to find, but look anyway. You might discover that 90% of the time your life is not ruled by negative thoughts, but that still leaves 10% of your energy draining away. You are like a motor running at 90% efficiency or a car being driven with the emergency brake on.

Most people have a mixture of these ten energy-draining situations in their lives at any one time, and it can often be hard to pinpoint specific issues. There might be a general discontent with life, a sense of uncertainty, or even boredom with things that used to bring joy and vitality. The passion might slowly drain out of your personal relationships, being replaced with dullness. If this is the case, there are layers of subconscious programming that have not been uncovered. An enlightened state involves an alert, attentive mind, one that is not burdened by thoughts of yesterday or tomorrow. The body responds to this quiet mind by feeling renewed and invigorated. Do not attribute your lack of energy to growing old. If your body seems to be running down, look for the reasons (explained above). Then find a tool or technique to help you move blockages and obstacles or go to a trusted therapist or healer. Nobody needs to feel or look old. It's time to revitalize and regenerate. It's time to live more fully.

CHAPTER 16

Even More Subtle Aspects of Energy Dissipation

In Western society, we are conditioned to always be doing something. Even meditation is doing something the way it is most often practiced. There is a goal and a technique or method designed to achieve that goal. Obviously, a certain amount of goal setting and obtaining is necessary in this world, but most of us are unable to slow down and truly enter a state of just being. We are human "doings," and doing anything expends energy.

A related question arises here: "When is physical activity beneficial and when does it dissipate energy?" Excellent inquiry. Let's go into this a bit. Earlier, we stated that working out at a gym, for example, can be a great way to move energy and release blockages, or it can end up hurting the body if it is done improperly. Converting potential energy into kinetic energy is the process of entropy at work.

As stated in the science section, the universe is ultimately balanced between entropic and centropic activity, although we are only able to observe primarily the entropic component. The centropic process (the "blinking off" phase of the universe, or the conversion of energy from the physical to the etheric dimension) can be equated to converting kinetic energy into potential energy. An electric generator, if it is highly efficient, actually moves toward centropy, especially if it captures an already existing entropic force, such as the downhill flow of water (hydroelectricity). There is very little entropy generated by a hydro facility if it is well designed.

Now let's look at a few more subtle ways we dissipate and deplete our energy:

Habitually lying to ourselves about where we are on our soul path. This can go both ways. We can try and convince ourselves that we are farther along on the path than we actually are. Conversely, we can focus too much on our negative qualities and fail to see the immense progress we have made. Like all ego mechanisms, we either succumb to false aggrandizement (grandiosity) or self-debasement (self-judgment). Feeling better than others, or not as good, are signs that we have slipped into ego. Start by acknowledging that you have fallen into a trap, and then ask for help in getting free. Humble yourself, but do not wallow in self-pity.

Outside circumstances are constantly preventing us from working on ourselves. This is a big one in our perpetually busy modern society. Most souls cannot be completely still for even a few moments. If there is downtime, such souls will immediately rush to fill the void with more useless activity. Even if there are a lot of important projects to be done, you will manifest spinning your wheels and not making much real progress. Of course, the most common manifestation of this form of resistance is being the victim. It can be obvious, such as having people in your life who are blatantly trying to take you off your path, perhaps by berating you in front of others for your crazy ideas or guilt-tripping you into spending a lot of time with them. However, it can also be subtle. Something always seems to come up every time you begin your project. It can be a different obstacle every time, not seemingly related to resistance. But the net result is not getting your project or process underway.

"Every time I sign up for a yoga class, I injure myself and am unable to do the asanas." "When I firmly resolve to change my diet, all these important luncheons suddenly manifest themselves in my schedule, and it seems none of the companies inviting me know anything about nutrition." Recognizing this subtle form of resistance is the first step, and then reaffirming your commitment to yourself is next. Finally, you might need to set some boundaries with the people in your life or do something radical like take a year off to work on yourself.

Getting stuck in the head. Energy exists in all our chakras and meridians, including our third eye (the chakra associated with higher mental activity). It's easy to talk about making changes that reduce entropy, and it is even possible to convince ourselves that we are doing the right things to maximize conservation of energy, but unless we are actually feeling the energy coming in and going out of our being, it is all just theory and ideas.

Move your center of focus from your head to your heart and solar plexus — not just your heart. This is incomplete information. You need head, heart and solar plexus (as well as the other chakras). Head represents wisdom, heart represents love, and solar plexus represents power. More power means more energy. Therefore, clearing your solar plexus is vitally important. A lot of emotions can get stuck in your solar plexus, especially related to issues about being powerful and successful.

Learn techniques that harness the power and energy of the third chakra. Make friends with this center. It's where a lot of ego issues are stored. It's the number one chakra that gets blocked in serious students of the spiritual path. Move from your head to your heart and then to your solar plexus. Practice activating all three chakras. Move through the resistance in your solar plexus.

Here are some subtle variations on the "sacred cows" and core negative beliefs. If you have a deep subconscious belief that your body must grow old and die, that belief will continue operating below the surface even if you have convinced the conscious mind that you can attain immortality. Look for subtle indications that you have not yet cleared the belief that entropy is the supreme law of the land and that any attempts to entertain the idea of immortality are crazy. The little voice inside might be saying you should wear a tin-foil hat. You might manifest people in your life who try to talk you out of your "delusions." After all, you have a serious mental problem. You must come to grips with the idea that all things decay and die, and you are just trying to avoid the inevitable. Even many so-called spiritual teachers still believe there is nothing you can do to prevent the decay and death of the physical body.

We are not suggesting you run and hide behind a belief in immortality because you are not willing to look at your fear of death. Healing your fear of death is part of moving toward immortality. All fears dissipate energy, especially the fear of death. The deeper and stronger your fear of death is, the more likely you are to deplete your energy and experience that which you are fearful of. Take time to re-examine all your beliefs. See if you are still getting trapped in the "sacred cows," such as the belief in death and taxes.

Subtle forms of impatience. This is a tricky one. Underneath impatience is a fear that if you don't move fast enough or do enough quickly, something bad is going to happen. On an animal level (the reptilian brain), this is part of the fight and flight mechanism. After all, if a dangerous animal is stalking you and you are unable to run fast enough, you might end up being the evening meal. But we live in a different era. Unless someone is literally chasing you with intent to do bodily harm, you probably don't need to do anything faster. Doing things as fast as possible usually means sacrificing quality. Many companies fall into this trap. They want to make as many products or provide as many services as quickly as possible to maximize profits.

The programming of modern society promotes impatience. Embodying this attitude within a highly competitive workplace might get you temporary rewards, but sooner or later you will find it difficult to get out of the "rat race" even when you are home with loved ones. You see the results of impatience every day on the highways of the world. People drive like maniacs, taking huge risks, only to save a few seconds. If you ask them what could possibly be worth endangering their life and the lives of other drivers, they will not be able to come up with a valid answer.

Impatience is an addiction, similar to instant gratification. Spiritual practices and techniques are essential in moving beyond this energy-depleting attitude and its resultant behavior.

Procrastination. This is the opposite of impatience and is also a manifestation of fear. In this case, the desire for the security of the known ends up controlling the desire to move forward into new experiences.

If you realize you are having resistance to taking action (when action is needed), start by identifying the fear. Go through the possible scenarios. What will happen if you take action? What does success look like? What does it feel like? Perhaps you fear you will lose the love of those close to you if you succeed. Some families have a dynamic of rewarding failure, as strange as that sounds. Oftentimes parents, friends and siblings are jealous of your success. Stepping out of your comfort zone might mean having to make new friends or let go of old ones, and this can be scary. Maybe taking action will put you in the limelight and you will feel exposed and vulnerable.

Notice the subtle ways you fall back into your comfort zone and desire for security. Establish a buddy system to keep you on track if you are addicted to procrastination. Being constantly late to appointments can be a manifestation of this form of resistance. Have your buddy call you 15 minutes before you need to act in order to be somewhere on time. Leave the house sooner than you feel is necessary. Go to bed earlier if waking up on time is an issue. Nobody should ever use the "snooze" button more than once on an alarm clock.

Another Subtle Dissipation: Boredom. What is boredom? This question is not answered sufficiently in modern psychology. One definition is a subconscious conflict between "what is" and "what should be," according to the belief systems of the bored individual. "I want to be skydiving, but I'm stuck at home watching soap operas." Okay, that's a rather extreme example, but you get the idea.

So how does boredom relate to our topic of conserving potential energy and converting it intelligently into kinetic energy?

As we stated above, our society is constantly prodding us to do more, more and more. Make more money, perform more work, reach more people, convince more people to buy our products and services, etc. Then, when we do make money and have a successful business, there is no end to the ways we must spend our money.

What happens when the average person sits down to meditate? They quickly become bored, partly because results in meditation rarely happen instantly, and partly because the subconscious mind is heavily conditioned to be doing something. If meditation does not produce the desired results quickly, we become bored. The body is still, but the mind keeps going. When we stop indulging the mind, as is the case with meditation, the mind rebels. "I must become enlightened," or "I must stop my thoughts," or "I must do a million things after my meditation is finished." This state of unrest, or boredom, dissipates a lot of energy. There is a constant conflict between "what is" (a state of inactivity) and "what should be" (a state of accomplishing something).

What is the solution to this conundrum? Simply, it is awareness. It is attention and presence in the moment regarding the unfoldment of the state of boredom and its related thoughts, such as "I should be doing something productive. I've been sitting for hours and nothing is happening. I don't feel enlightened. I don't feel rested." Awareness begins with noticing and asking, "Who is the observer? What part of the self is demanding results?" It is possible to watch the whole drama as it unfolds, recognizing that the boredom is the result of belief systems about what one should be doing instead of what is currently being done.

We are not suggesting that everyone should do a quiet meditation. Sometimes the highest option is to physically act. But it is wise to ask, "What is the motivation behind this action? What aspect of self is pushing for this action? What is the desired outcome?" It might be a fear that inaction will cause disastrous results. For example, "If I do nothing for a few hours, I will lose money because I am not constantly trying to get new clients."

As we stated earlier when exploring the work ethic (addiction to working hard), it is well known that souls who work seven hours per day and meditate for one hour get more accomplished, on average, than souls who work eight hours per day and do not meditate.

If you are embarking upon a meditation program (an excellent idea for beginners), be reasonable regarding how much time you devote to the practice. This author rarely suggests, even to those who have been on a path of personal growth for a long time, meditating for more than one hour. Often 10 to 20 minutes is sufficient, once or twice a day. Of course, not all meditation involves a still body. There are moving meditations and even dancing meditations. Thirty minutes of style meditation plus 30 minutes of Kundalini Yoga or chaotic meditation, might be the perfect amount. If you seem to have too much energy and cannot sleep at night, you might be doing too much meditation. If you feel exhausted after a long and busy day, you might not be doing enough meditation.

∞ Summarizing the Topic of Resistance

Listen to the body. It has a built-in intelligence. If you feel tired a lot, something is out of balance. Where are you dissipating energy? Is it in negative thinking? Are you worrying about what you are putting off doing while you are meditating? Are subtle energy patterns in the body coming into your awareness and causing some emotional discomfort? Is your body resisting something? A certain amount of resistance is necessary, but too much resistance causes fatigue and even depression.

Once again, let us repeat ourselves: Resistance almost always involves some conflict between "what is" and "what should be." This is even true at a purely physical level. The universe is teeming with energy. As this book's title suggests, there is infinite energy (or nearly infinite, from a quantum perspective). All this energy is streaming into the physical body and all other life forms. Yet the body can only process (hold) a small amount of it in order to operate the heart, lungs and vital organs. The "what is" is the nearly unlimited energy streaming in and the body's management of this energy into a usable, discrete amount. If the soul thinks reality should be different than the way it is, there is a "what should be" scenario that increases the resistance beyond the optimum amount necessary to regulate the body's autonomic functions.

A productive meditation involves noticing the increased resistance due to extraneous thoughts, triggered feelings, or any other form of conflict between "what is" and "what should be," such as, "I am meditating, but I should be taking out the garbage." Often, if the "what should be" involves a useful task, such as taking out the garbage, it might be necessary to implement a priority system. Can the garbage wait, or should it be taken out before the start of meditation?

The quality of meditation is more important than the duration. Five minutes of high-quality attention and awareness might be all that is needed to regenerate the body. Do not become attached to the length of your meditation. Try different formats until you find one that energizes the body and clears the mind. Pay close attention to the form of resistance that comes up (and it will come up, we guarantee). Do not judge yourself if your mind wanders or gets lost in thought. Gently but firmly bring your mind back to the present moment.

Observe what is taking you out of the present moment. Usually it is some form of worrying about the future, which dissipates a tremendous amount of energy. If you can reduce future anxiety by 50%, your energy could possibly triple or quadruple. How many of the things you worry about actually come true? Remember what we said about the uselessness of worry.

Recall earlier how we proved that worry is completely useless. Either the things you worry about do come true, or they do not. If they do not, all your worrying was a waste of time. If they do come true, the worrying has been dissipating your energy — energy that you need to deal with the scenario that is coming true. The bottom line is that there is no time when worry is justified.

Worry is not the same thing as being aware of potential dangers. Your Higher Self is constantly attempting to communicate with your human self and can warn you in advance of any real dangers you are likely to face in the future.

The more you let go of the ego's future concerns and simply listen to the inner voice of the Higher Self, the more you gain confidence that you can meet any challenge that arises. And if you can't, well, you will just have to accept that and do your best.

∞ Prelude to the Section on Regeneration

Getting back to our original inquiry regarding immortality, some energy needs to be converted from potential to kinetic energy in the physical body, but how much? And how efficient is this conversion? Martial arts and certain types of yoga seem to benefit the body, slow the aging process and perhaps even reverse it if practiced in the right way. Yet, obviously, there is kinetic energy involved in these practices.

In Tai Chi and certain martial arts, there is a great deal of emphasis placed on the ki, qi, or chi, depending on how you want to spell it, related to the center just above or below the navel known as the Dantien (aka Dantian — depicted in slightly different locations in different disciplines). This center, roughly equivalent to the solar plexus, is the seat of prana, or life force energy, and serves as the gateway between the physical and etheric planes. A master of Tai Chi or martial arts channels energy into and out of the Dantien, or rather, into and out of the etheric planes through the Dantien. Thus, the master is regulating the constant flow of energy between entropic and centropic configurations. When energy is expressed kinetically, it is done with efficiency and intelligence. Often, when facing an opponent, the master is using very little of his own energy. He is redirecting the energy of the opponent. It is well known in martial arts that you do not resist and fight an opponent. You use the energy of the opponent to defeat him.

A true master retains most of his vital energy (potential) by responding intelligently to the movements and energy expenditures of the opponent. Like the hydroelectric plant, the energy is already in motion and is simply being redirected into a useful purpose.

CHAPTER 17

How to Increase the Flow of Energy into Your Physical Body and Other Levels

Factors that Contribute to Regeneration

Below is an outline depicting the centropic activities and states of consciousness necessary for regeneration, youthing and immortality of the physical body.

1. Quantum Coherence (Zero-Point Energy)
2. Cosmic Radiation
   a. Fasting
   b. Using Invocation
3. Prana (Life Force Energy)
   a. Breathing Methods (intake of prana)
      i. Rebirthing
      ii. Primal Therapy
      iii. Holotropic Breathwork
      iv. Kriya Yoga
      v. Kundalini Yoga
      vi. Breath of Fire
   b. Benefits of Breathing Techniques
4. Positive Thoughts and Feelings (Inspiration)
5. Meditation
6. Positive Environmental Factors
   a. Photosynthesis (Energy from the Sun)
   b. Pure Food and Water (Assimilation)

    c. A Brief Condensed Section on Nutrition and Health
    d. Clean Environment
    e. Alignment with Natural Rhythms
    f. Harmonious Color and Sound Frequencies
    g. High-Vibrational Music

7. DNA Immortality Sequence (Stem Cells)
8. Assistance/Downloads from Higher Beings
9. Understanding/Awareness
10. Enlightened Teachers
11. Dharma (Service to Others)
12. Order
13. Acceptance (Self-Love)
14. Remembering God's Eternal Love

Quantum Coherence (Zero-Point Energy)

We know, from our earlier exploration into this topic, that Zero-Point Energy exists throughout the universe. It is ever-present within the quantum fluctuations (the "blinking on" and "blinking off" phases of time/space). How do we make use of this energy to regenerate the physical body?

In the section on dissipation, we focused primarily on the blocks to the assimilation of coherent energies (centropy). Since energy fluctuates by moving from physical to etheric, and from etheric to physical, the solution is to open the "gateway" between these two realms. How do we do this?

In religion, a popular phrase is "Ask and ye shall receive." Is it really that simple? Well, sort of. The Law of Attraction states that what you focus on, you attract. This author takes it a bit further: "What you focus on, you become." That's true in the lower realms. It's irrelevant in the higher realms because your eternal, real Self does not change based on your beliefs.

When you focus on a particular thing, your energy automatically interacts with that thing (person, place or experience). You become quantum entangled with the reality of that person, place or experience. It's easy to see this in personal relationships. You become involved with someone, and their life becomes part of your life.

To open the channels to quantum coherence, you must focus on it. Specifically, you need to get acquainted with the etheric dimension. Fortunately, there are many holistic techniques designed to increase the flow of prana (life force energy from the etheric state). We will detail some of those methods and processes in the "Prana" section below.

Before we do that, let's get back to the asking and receiving. You can ask your Higher Self to attune you to the etheric frequencies. Imagine a golden light (other colors also work, but gold is preferred because it filters out unwanted frequencies automatically). This light comes from the etheric planes, enters the top of your head (crown chakra), and flows down in a clockwise spiral through your body. You can visualize the spiraling golden light moving through your body and out the bottom of your feet (and base of your spine, if you are sitting).

Calling forth the energies of the etheric planes attunes you to those frequencies. In reality, you have an etheric dimension to your being. All souls are 12-dimensional, but only four or five dimensions are "activated." To activate a level of Self requires that you focus on (direct your attention and awareness to) that level. By moving into resonance with a specific higher frequency, you draw more of that energy into your being, which creates coherence (order).

You can use invocations (Divine decrees), third-eye focus meditations, holistic healing techniques, chanting, toning, mantras, color and light therapy, and many other tools to help you attune to the etheric frequencies. We have included some common methods in the Prana (Life Force) section.

Cosmic Radiation

There are many forms of radiation throughout the light and dark universe. Cosmic radiation is a catch-all term that describes plasma emissions, gamma and x-rays, other ultraviolet and infrared frequencies, as well as energy residues from the movement of subatomic particles. Some of the cosmic rays are attuned to the frequency of the various bodies of the Self. When a cosmic ray resonates with one of the harmonics of the soul, it energizes and regenerates the levels and dimensions of your being.

Most of the time, souls are not aware of the effect of cosmic radiation, but it is there, nonetheless. It is the primary reason some souls can not only go without food and water but can even sustain the body during a prolonged period of not breathing (such as some yogis).

Fasting

A soul who goes without food and water is being sustained by prana, quantum coherence and cosmic rays (for the most part). In this case, it is more than just the etheric realm that is supplying the centropy — there are frequencies from the dimensions above the aether contributing to the negative entropy. Then, if this is true, why do people starve? Why do they seem to die of hunger?

There are two reasons. First, if a soul has a lot of entropy (negativity), they are already rapidly depleting their potential energy. By not consuming food and/or water, the nutrients and electrolytes are unable to stimulate the assimilation process sufficiently to recharge and regenerate the physical matrix. The body is still receiving some prana and cosmic radiation, but not enough to make up the difference.

Second, fasting (going without food and/or water) creates a cycle of purification and cleansing that can be quite intense. Let us explain why.

When you stop eating, all your emotions, thoughts and beliefs about food are going to come to the surface, including memories of past lifetimes where you starved or were malnourished (where you didn't have enough centropy to overcome the deficit created by going without food and water).

As stated earlier, most people are emotional eaters and eat way too much. The best quantity of food is generally about one-fourth of the amount the average person in the West consumes now. Of course, this must be nutritious, high quality and pure. If a person suddenly stops eating, the body needs to quickly adjust and, as you know, bodies do not like sudden change.

If you are fasting because food is not available (famine), there are likely a lot of negative emotions, including fear, coming to the surface from the subconscious, including memories of similar traumas in the past. Probably you had a family. Maybe you were a provider (parent) and unable to fulfill your duties. Possibly you witnessed your children starving.

Another aspect associated with fasting is the energy shift that occurs when the digestive tract is no longer required. Prana and cosmic radiation become unblocked because the subtle (astral, etheric and causal) bodies are better able to attune to the frequencies coming in from the cosmos. Remember, digestion takes a lot of energy and focus for the body. That is why most people feel tired after a big meal.

The proper use of fasting can dramatically increase the overall energy in the body. Once you release all the negative emotions, thoughts and beliefs surrounding the idea of going without food and water, your attention is easily focused on the higher frequencies (cosmic radiation) coming in, and then you are able to more easily "ask and receive."

Using Invocation

When you invoke the power and presence of an angel or ascended master, you are calling forth frequencies from beyond the etheric planes. These energies can be sufficient to supply the needs of the soul normally furnished by food, water or even air. In the prana category below, we include breatharians (those who still breathe the atmosphere of Earth but no longer require any other visible means of sustenance).

You can invoke the cosmic rays directly. Simply state: "I invoke the power and presence of the cosmic rays of light emanating from the heart of God. I ask these rays to fulfill and sustain my six lower bodies. Thank you, God."

Here, we are including the plasma, gamma, x-rays, etc. (even though technically they are part of the physical universe), but only if they contribute positively to regeneration.

Prana (Life-Force Energy)

Prana is the energy of the etheric planes that is assimilated through breathing. Photosynthesis is one form of prana involving the conversion from oxygen to carbon dioxide (in the case of animals) or from carbon dioxide into oxygen (in the case of plants). We include photosynthesis in a separate category.

Is it the oxygen itself that delivers energy into the human being (and other animal life forms)? No. Oxygen is a catalyst for the process of assimilating prana (etheric-life-force energy). Oxygen is carried into the blood stream by prana (through the process of the respiratory system). Interestingly, the word respire comes from "rest in spirit" or "revitalize spirit," depending on your particular linguistic interpretation. With every breath you take, you are re-spiriting (reconnecting to spirit, or in this case returning to the etheric planes). The inbreath (inhale) represents taking in the prana of the etheric plane and the outbreath (exhale) represents distributing the prana to the elements of the physical plane.

Increasing the frequency or volume of the breath delivers more oxygen to the lungs (and bloodstream) which makes the assimilation of prana more efficient. Breathing faster or harder does not necessarily mean you are accessing a greater amount of prana itself. However, drawing in more oxygen dispels impurities or energy patterns that can interfere with the conversion of prana from the etheric planes to the physical plane. Below, we will go into a few details on the different varieties of breathing techniques.

Breathing Methods (Intake of Prana)

As we mentioned above, the primary benefit of conscious breathing techniques is to increase oxygen in the blood and, therefore, make the body more receptive to prana (etheric energy). There are, of course, additional considerations depending on the type of breathing. When the amount of oxygen is increased, the body is more receptive to higher frequencies, and the overall energy is increased, sometimes dramatically, depending on the rapidity and volume of breath.

Hyperventilation occurs when the energy increases so fast that the body does not have time to adjust. The increased prana comes up against long-held resistance in the cells of the body, and the result is bodily sensations. What you are feeling during hyperventilation is the actual resistance itself. You are not feeling the increased energy. The energy is clean, clear, light and full of vitality, but it doesn't create sensations in the body — at least not directly.

There are several popular breathing techniques being practiced by yogis, meditators and other practitioners. A few of them are as follows:

Rebirthing. Also known as conscious breathing, this technique involves what is commonly called "circular breathing." First you pull gently on the inhale until your lungs are about 7/8ths full, then you immediately start exhaling with the smallest possible pause in-between. Gravity forces the exhale while you relax completely until you are about 7/8ths of the way to no air in the lungs, then you immediately begin the next inhale with as small a pause as possible. As stated before, rapid breathing increases overall alertness but may cause a lot of bodily sensations, while slow breathing is more relaxing but does not clear blockages as effectively.

The psychological purpose of Rebirthing is to clear negative emotions from the cells of the body, including stored traumatic imprints. Sometimes this breathing method triggers memories of birth, hence the name. There is usually quite a bit of trauma associated with our first breath. After all, this was when the cord was cut, and you had to breathe by yourself or die. You could no longer rely on your mother's sustenance.

Oftentimes, your physical birth is a re-enactment of Original Cause — the first time you felt separate from God. To an unborn baby, mother is God, the nourishing and sustaining force. Modern birthing methods are often harsh and painful, even with so-called medical advances. Although Freud did not always see the big picture, his assertion that many of us are still trying to crawl back into the womb (metaphorically speaking) is quite accurate. Our outlook on life is heavily influenced by the degree of separation trauma from mother we experienced at the beginning of this life.

We suggest you do some research into additional psychological issues addressed by Rebirthing.

Primal Therapy. This is essentially the opposite of Rebirthing. Instead of emphasizing the inhale, you focus on a forceful exhale. You can imagine that with each pushed exhale you are releasing built-up toxins and negative emotions from the body. Sometimes this is called "cathartic release."

We suggest you experiment with different breathing rates to see the various energetic effects. When Primal Therapy is done extremely fast, it becomes "Breath of Fire."

Holotropic Breathwork. This is the name for a series of breathing techniques that are done consciously and rhythmically. You could say Holotropic Breathwork is sort of a combination of Rebirthing and Primal Therapy, but it also includes an entire philosophy associated with each breathing style. The key is "detailed awareness." You stay completely present with each breath and simply notice the flow of energy in the body. There are rapid and slow forms of Holotropic Breathwork. You sometimes breathe in through the nose and out through the mouth, making a hissing sound with each exhale.

Kriya Yoga. This is a complex series of breathing meditations combined with other yogic techniques, including mantra and cathartic release. In many of the exercises, you count during the breaths. For example, a simple Kriya sequence would be counting from 1 to 4 on the inhale and 1 to 4 on the exhale. You can approximate one second for each number or pick a different pace. Of course, you are counting internally, not speaking the numbers out loud.

A more difficult breathing sequence would be counting from 1 to 7 on the inhale, pausing at the top of the breath and counting from 1 to 7, and then exhaling while counting from 1 to 7.

An even more intense breathing sequence would be inhaling while counting from 1 to 10, pausing at the top of the inhale and counting from 1 to 10, exhaling while counting from 1 to 10, and then pausing at the bottom of the exhale and counting from 1 to 10. Each breathing cycle in this example lasts about 40 seconds. As with every breathing technique, stay in complete awareness during the cycles. Notice the changes in energy and thought process.

More advanced Kriyas include chanting and cathartic release, usually on the exhale. You might breathe in and out through the nose, in and out through the mouth, or in through the nose and out through the mouth.

Kundalini Yoga. Breathing is extremely important during yoga practice, especially in Kundalini Yoga. Often you will exaggerate the breath and the sound made during the exhale. An example would be standing and moving your hands together until they are above your head during the inhale and then lowering your hands while making a hissing sound during the exhale.

There are many variations of the breath during the asanas and body movements commonly associated with Kundalini Yoga.

Breath of Fire. This is an extremely short and rapid breath, emphasizing the exhale, but at this speed you cannot really tell where the emphasis is. The rhythm occurs in small breathing increments due to the rapidity. You might do several inhales and exhales per second. You might do 30 seconds of Breath of Fire, then one slow deep inhale/exhale, then another 30 seconds of short and rapid breath. If you become too light-headed, shorten the duration between each slow deep cycle — perhaps 20 seconds of rapid breathing.

Benefits of Breathing Techniques

Because there is a lot of information online regarding the benefits of these breathing methods, we are not going to go into great detail, except to mention a few things they have in common or that pertain to our discussion of how to increase centropy.

As stated earlier, Rebirthing tends to trigger memories of birth (hence the name), which is when we took our first breath. A regular regimen of this technique can clear emotional patterns from early childhood as well, so it should be considered a form of therapy. Effective therapies reduce resistance, which increases available energy.

Primal Therapy's long-term effects are similar — clearing emotional blockages and freeing up energy.

Holotropic Breathwork is similar to Rebirthing and Primal Therapy in terms of results.

The yogas referenced above include, of course, more than just breathing techniques. Yoga means union of body and mind, and any processes that promote soul integration are going to be centropic.

There does not appear to be a lot of research into the benefits of Breath of Fire, but we suspect it has similar results to that of Rebirthing and Primal Therapy.

Positive Thoughts and Feelings (Inspiration)

Positive thoughts are those that support soul evolution, or more specifically, soul growth, happiness and well-being. A "happy" thought that does not support the growth and well-being of a soul is not really a positive thought. You might feel "happy" at the idea of murdering someone you hate, or you might be gleeful when you see someone punished that you don't like. Of course, this is not true happiness.

Not every thought that promotes soul growth is going to feel good. Some beneficial ideas are a threat to the ego's need for security. If you have such thoughts, they are moving on the right track to becoming positive, but they are not quite there yet. You might need a change in attitude or a movement to reprogram something before you can feel a sense of happiness and well-being from a thought that promotes soul growth. If all you do is ask that your thoughts bring you growth, you might have an unhappy life filled with a sense of obligation. "All work and no play...."

Sometimes your greatest sense of well-being comes from a much-needed rest from constant growth-oriented activities. This is important, but again, unless you have growth and happiness along with your sense of well-being, you are not truly manifesting positive thinking. In other words, you need to feel a deep sense of satisfaction and peace (happiness and well-being) at the thought of taking a break from your daily growth activities. If you feel guilty, restless or bored when you are not constantly doing something, then you are not there yet.

This is why we include three criteria for positive thinking: soul growth, happiness and well-being.

The simplest way to evaluate your thought process is to ask, "Does this thought, idea or belief contribute to my soul growth, happiness and well-being?"

A specific way to move from negative to positive thinking is to take your current thoughts and start observing how they are manifesting the opposite of soul growth, happiness and well-being. Ask yourself, "In what way is this thought working against my soul growth?" An obvious example would be laughing at the misfortune of others. You are not contributing to the soul growth of the person you are laughing at, and in fact, you might be amplifying his or her sense of guilt and shame. If you are not contributing to the growth of others, then you are not contributing to your own soul growth. Therefore, your actions in this case are not born of positive thoughts.

If you are not feeling happy, look at your thoughts. "In what way is this thought contributing to my sense of unhappiness, unease, worry or anxiety?"

If your health and well-being are not good, find out which thoughts are behind your experience of illness, disease or imbalance. In the case of illness, there might be an indirect route to discovering the core thoughts behind the malady. If the illness is environmental, your negative thoughts might be obscuring your need to change your circumstances. If your thoughts are positive and there is a negative environment, you will be alerted as to how to make changes in your life to avoid or neutralize the negative environmental factors.

For example, if you live in a stressful location that is not good for your well-being and you have been unable to overcome the negative environment directly through actual transcendence (putting a powerful field of positive energy around you continuously), then you probably have negative thoughts that are interfering in your subconscious mind. These thoughts might be something like, "I cannot afford to move out of this inner city," or "I must be a failure because I don't have a nice house in the suburbs like the rest of my family." You might have a core negative belief that you don't deserve to have nicer things in life or that you are guilty and deserve to get sick.

When there is a lack of well-being, there are either direct negative thoughts behind it, such as the "I don't deserve ..." self-talk, or it is more indirect, such as thinking you cannot move out of a toxic environment or that you don't have the strength to transcend the negative vibrations of others.

Positive thoughts generate energy. They raise your vibration until you are no longer dominated by entropy. Yes, it takes some energy to think, but in this case the attunement to higher frequencies offsets the kinetic energy it takes to formulate and propagate the thoughts.

Positive thoughts create a force-field of good energy around you that is very difficult to penetrate even if you are surrounded by negative people. Of course, it is not easy to stay positive if you are in a constantly negative environment, but it is not impossible.

Remember the Law of Attraction. If there are negative people around and you are feeling and thinking positive, it is as though you are living in two separate worlds. But if you are feeling and thinking negative and there are a lot of negative people around, you are like magnets attracting each other, and you will likely become further compromised energetically.

Affirmations provide a method whereby you can start gravitating toward positive thoughts. The affirmations by themselves might not be enough to do this, but they move you in the right direction. A proper affirmation is a statement of truth designed to penetrate the subconscious mind that could be filled with untruths. For example, to counteract (reprogram) the subconscious belief, "There's not enough," you can use the affirmation, "I live in an infinitely abundant universe."

Remember that affirmations must be statements of truth. You would not use the following statement when you find yourself around negative people. "I am better than these souls." That is not a statement of truth but rather, a declaration of ego. There are examples of affirmations and autosuggestions in this author's first book, *Life on the Cutting Edge (Second Edition)*.

Meditation

There are two definitions of meditation: (1) A state of stillness in the mind, and (2) A practice for becoming aware of the movement of consciousness. When the mind is still, there is very little energy dissipation. At the same time, this state of receptivity means higher frequencies can enter with little or no resistance. A still mind is free of resistance. There is complete acceptance of "what is."

The practice of meditation seeks to increase overall self-awareness, which leads to insights and wise choices in life. A regular practice tends to create discipline in the mind and body, which in turn leads to activities that promote centropy.

Not all meditation practices involve sitting in lotus posture. You might meditate while walking in the forest or on the beach. Movements can be meditative, especially the ones practiced in Tai Chi or Qi Gong.

A silent mind is in an active state of awareness, or pure observation. If there is no thought, there is no thinker. Therefore, there is only consciousness with its eternal movement, expansion and contraction. If you are thinking, "I am sitting here watching my thoughts," then you are caught in thought because there is an observer separate from what is taking place. It is difficult to put into words the difference between silence and thoughts about silence.

In order to have no observer, there must be no ego. The ego will fight and resist its own demise. You might have a few moments of silence, and then the ego will rush back in and begin filling up the space. The more you resist the ego, the stronger it becomes. Simply notice the movement and absence of ego without responding or reacting.

If you are able to be in true silence, you will realize there are no boundaries. Without an observer, there is the entire universe. That is who you are. There is only God. The "me" is an illusion. There is still a body/mind complex operating and functioning in the world, but the sense of a little self is absent. Spirit is operating the human being and is not confined to the physical senses. You are everywhere and nowhere, because "where" suggests space and time, which are ultimately illusions.

Positive Environmental Factors

Photosynthesis (Energy from the Sun)

It is said that the sun is the origin of all life on Earth. That is true from one point of view. After all, without sunlight, plants would be unable to undergo the process of photosynthesis and so oxygen production would be too low to support human life (and most animals).

Energy from the sun should properly be placed within the category of cosmic radiation. The only difference, of course, is that the radiation emanates from the center of our solar system instead of from distant stars. Some forms of cosmic radiation dissipate over distance (while some do not), so the quality of rays from the sun are going to be significantly different than the quality of rays from distant stars. (To keep things simple we are including quasars, star clusters, black holes, interstellar gas and other galaxies in our category of stars generating cosmic radiation.)

There are many souls who practice sun gazing, a process that involves looking directly into the sun. This can be done safely when the sun is near the horizon but is not recommended during the middle of the day (although some sun gazers will dispute this). There are benefits to looking at the sun, such as helping one attune to cosmic frequencies. As far as absorbing beneficial qualities from sunlight, probably bathing the whole body, and not just the eyes, is the best practice. There is a lot of misinformation regarding how much sunlight you can receive without negative side effects. We do not recommend sunscreen unless you have an entirely natural product such as coconut oil. Depending on your skin pigment and level of predisposition to skin cancer, you might be able to immerse most of your body in sunlight for 30 minutes per day without using any means of sunscreen. Generally, the maximum amount of exposure should not be more than 60 minutes. If you use a natural sunscreen you can increase the duration but probably no more than 60 minutes for sensitive skin and 120 minutes for more seasoned individuals.

Obviously, those from northern climates tend to burn more easily than those from the tropics. If you tune into your body carefully, you will know how much sun to take in. Those who live in places that do not get much sun are definitely at a disadvantage regarding energy assimilation. However, the human body is highly adaptable, and it adjusts itself accordingly. You can thrive in a northern climate, but it is generally a lot more difficult than in a tropical zone.

Pure Food and Water (Assimilation)

As you know, food and water provide the body with nutrients and electrolytes, including enzymes, vitamins, minerals and fiber. These substances generate heat in the form of calories, which drive the various systems of the body — normally. In third and fourth-dimensional humans, the entropy (heat production) is strong. Chemical reactions in the body (metabolizing nutrients) generate enough energy to maintain the autonomic nervous system as well as most conscious bodily functions generally for 70 to 100 years at present.

Put in straight language, until you raise the vibration of your body high enough to tap directly into the centropic realms, you will need food and water in order to maintain your body. Since you will be processing nutrients until you reach a high level of physical vibration, why not put the best-quality, nutrient-dense food and purest water possible into your body? It certainly makes sense. Yet, for various reasons, including political and economic, most food is not high quality and is devoid of proper nutrients.

The biggest problem with low-quality food (aside from additives that produce toxic reactions) is that the body must work harder to extract the small amount of nutrition available in such junk food. Most processed food is hard to digest, and so the digestion system must work overtime to break down the ingredients. Any time part of the body works hard, guess what? That's right, you are expending energy. The increase in energy supplied by the nutrients is offset by the extra work required to digest, assimilate and distribute the nutrients to the places that need them.

What is the best diet? That is a loaded question for most nutritionists. This author often recommends a modified "bell-curve" paleo diet, consisting of a light breakfast, moderate lunch and light dinner. The food is usually vegan plus wild-caught fish, or vegan plus organically-raised poultry and fish (from relatively unpolluted waters). Some people can handle raw dairy products (ideally from sheep or goats). Homogenized, pasteurized cow's milk is junk food in this author's opinion. The little bit of mineral content is grossly offset by the excess mucus, antibiotics and growth hormones usually found in such products. Milk is the perfect food — for baby cows. Humans are the only species that drink the milk of other animals (aside from domesticated pets).

Note also that we did not include breads and grains in the above recommendations. A little bit of certain grains might be okay, but most diets have way too many complex carbohydrates.

A Brief, Condensed Section on Nutrition and Health

Although this could rightfully be placed in the science section, we have included nutrition in the psychology of unlimited energy because this is really a psychological problem. Almost everyone knows basically the difference between healthy and unhealthy food, at least in the Western world. Yet people continue to make poor dietary choices, or they eat a relatively healthy diet but still have numerous health problems.

Approximately 80% of all illness and disease originates in the emotional and mental bodies, not the physical. Only about 20% of all maladies are physically based, and most of these are from environmental pollution. Note: Contained within the 80% of disease that is emotionally based is the popular idea of stress-related illness. The pace of modern life certainly contributes to overall levels of stress, but a more accurate definition of stress would be the inability to process or respond adequately to the complexities of the environment.

Two different people can have the same basic level of workplace challenges, complicated home life interactions, peer pressure, deadlines, bills to pay, etc. Yet one of them will manifest signs of stress and health depletion while the other one might seem to thrive.

It is certainly more difficult to stay calm and centered when numerous people are demanding things from you, but it is not impossible. The key, of course, lies in your overall state of consciousness.

Let's look at the factors behind those who make poor choices regarding diet and lifestyle.

The number-one reason a human being becomes overweight or otherwise unhealthy is due to the desire to get rid of unpleasant feelings (emotions). Emotional eating is rampant in our society. Comfort food sells well in any economic climate (especially during downturns). Poor people have the worst diets. You might think this is because they cannot afford high-quality food. That is only part of the reason. A bigger issue is the stuffing of unpleasant feelings with cheap, easy-to-fix fast food. After a hard day working at minimum wage, a big juicy burger with fries sounds mighty good.

People who are extremely busy are not likely to make wise food choices. They will grab something on the run, or make a meal that takes only a few minutes, and they don't have time to read the ingredients on the brightly colored packages. (Generally, the brighter the package, the worse the quality.)

It takes a lot of energy to digest (break down and process) the synthetic chemicals and additives common to most fast foods. There might be an initial feeling of satisfaction after eating a large, unhealthy meal, but within one to two hours a feeling of drowsiness, heaviness, bloating, etc., will inevitably set in. Why this low energy? Quite simply, all the body's resources are going to help dissolve and assimilate the complex ingredients in the recent meal. In addition, the emotional issues that drove you to purchase the unhealthy meal are still there, festering under the surface. As the "high" of the food wears off, you are back to square one with the emotions.

So far, we are only talking about food. We have not even mentioned the myriad of drugs that often accompany a stressed-out lifestyle, such as those two cups of coffee at Starbucks early in the morning, that doughnut or muffin during the first break, the candy bar during the afternoon break, and the two drinks before and after dinner. That's a lot of caffeine, sugar and alcohol. Multiply this routine by 250 to 300 times per year and you have a formula for disaster.

Since this book is about how to harness unlimited energy, the first thing you can do regarding diet and nutrition is to pay attention to how you feel one to two hours after each meal. Also, note your high and low energy cycles. We all have them. Perhaps you are normally "up" during the late morning and "down" during the mid-afternoon. Plan your life accordingly. Do the most challenging things during your natural "up" cycles. Take your cycles into account when analyzing how you feel after eating. If you eat a heavy, unhealthy meal right before your normal "down" time, you are reinforcing your negative cycle.

Use the "bell curve" diet as much as possible. That means a light breakfast, moderate lunch and light dinner.

One example of a high-energy regimen would be a supergreen smoothie for breakfast with fresh, whole blended fruit and numerous healthy additives (such as chia seeds, flax seeds, spirulina, chlorella, maca, ginseng, etc.); a salad with some sort of healthy protein for lunch, adding cooked vegetables and whole grains in moderation; and a vegetable smoothie or nut snack for dinner. If you need a snack, organic raw chocolate or a handful of nuts are probably best.

Limit your fruit and fruit juice intake. A couple of pieces of fruit plus a half glass of juice in the morning is probably enough for the day. If you eat dairy products, make it an unsweetened small yogurt once a day, a little raw cottage cheese, or a tiny bit of hard cheese sprinkled over your main meal. Avoid processed grains, such as white rice and white flour. A little bit of jasmine rice overlaid with vegetables is okay once in a while.

Do not eat within two hours of bedtime. Avoid nighttime snacks unless it has been several hours since your last meal and you are working late. Then a light healthy snack before bedtime is okay.

Learn to recognize the many forms of dangerous additives. Discover how certain combinations of ingredients can combine to form unhealthy compounds. For example, Bragg's amino acids are about 10% glutamic acid, which converts to monosodium glutamate in the body. Soy sauce is about 4% MSG and is ridiculously high in sodium.

Returning to the analysis of how much energy is generated from food, be aware of false energy cycles. For example, eating sugar seems to initially produce a burst of energy (the sugar rush), but eventually leaves you feeling weak (the sugar crash). Map your up and down cycles. Experiment. Which foods leave your mind in a fog? What keeps you clear and lucid all day?

What are the effects of occasional fasting? Is a fruit-smoothie fast different from a lemon-water fast? Is fasting one day a week giving you more overall energy? What about a seven-day fast once a month? You might quickly discover the optimum level of fasting, and it could be more or less than what you are already doing.

Most people eat way too much. If your food is highly nutritious and supplemented with vitamins and minerals, you probably do not need more than 1,500 calories per day, yet modern "nutritionists" say you should have 2,000 to 3,000 calories per day.

Avoid water with a pH above 8.5. There are a lot of people promoting Kangen water machines that make pH 9.5 water. However, the body is going to react by producing more acid to counteract the high alkalinity. It's better to mix high-alkaline water using Kangen 8.5 setting with balanced pH spring water in the 7.0 to 7.5 range. The overall level of 7.5 to 8.0 pH is probably best. You want a slightly alkaline blood stream (about 7.3 to 7.4), but a highly acidic stomach for good digestion. The right balance of electrolytes makes your body like a high-performance battery. It will keep going a long time before it needs a charge (more food).

Avoid the temptation to salt your food. Although some salt is essential for creating proper electrolytes, most modern processed food has way too much salt (usually in the form of sodium). If you are excessively dehydrated after eating or cannot seem to quench your thirst even with good quality water, you are probably consuming too much salt.

Handle food addictions with love and compassion. After all, most problems involve judgment and criticism of self. If you have a sugar craving, send love and acceptance to the part of the self that believes eating sugar will cover up the negative feelings below the surface. It might be the judgment and criticism itself that led to the addiction, or it could be that you were rewarded with ice cream when you were a good little boy or girl, and so you associate sugar with parental love.

We hope this practical guide to increasing your overall energy through diet is useful. Although there are a lot of nutritional programs and publications, we felt it would be good to give this brief summary based on how diet affects your ability to channel energy.

Clean Environment

The cleanest places on Earth are in the most sparsely populated regions. This makes complete sense. However, it is wise to consider the wind and storm patterns in such places. Does the location where you live have temperature inversions in the winter? Do pollutants from far-away cities settle in a basin or valley near you? Are you high enough in altitude to avoid some of the pollution but low enough to grow food? Has there been, or is there likely to be, mining or industry near you?

Obviously, a clean environment means fewer impurities in the air, water and soil, which means less energy expended trying to rid the body of toxins. Every place on Earth is polluted. In fact, every human being has toxic chemicals in the blood stream. If you are alive in a human body on this planet, you have plastic in your bodily systems. Our biological systems have adapted to this invader or we would all be dead. This does not mean there are no consequences of plastic pollution. Many cancers, allergies and autoimmune diseases are caused by toxic chemicals. There are various factors that decide whether or not your body can withstand the constant assault of chemicals in the environment.

If you are fortunate enough to have the means to move to a relatively clean place, then by all means do so. You might need to change your work/business to accommodate living away from a large city. It could be difficult at first, but in the long run you will find a richly rewarding lifestyle.

You must be willing to give up your attachment to constant distraction. Sure, you can find addictive substances and processes even in a remote area, but it is more difficult. You will come face to face with yourself when it is just you and nature (and a few close family members and friends).

Most parts of the world, even far from major cities, are connected to the Internet. A lot of souls are moving out of the city and conducting business online. As telecommunications become more refined, the number of online businesses will continue to grow.

Balancing your time between farming, gardening, hiking, socializing and one or two online businesses might be the lifestyle you have been longing for.

Alignment with Natural Rhythms

Everyone has biorhythms. These are more complex than just the rising and falling of energy levels throughout the day. Being aware of your natural cycles is a good idea. This has practical benefits, such as knowing when you are most and least alert. It makes sense to plan your more difficult tasks during your "up" cycles and your less-intensive work during your "down" cycles. Of course, if you work for someone else or have pressure and deadlines, it is not easy to observe your natural cycles.

Sleep patterns do not always align with society's dictates. Your body might want to rest when you are expected to work and work when you are expected to rest. If you have your own business, it could be easier to honor your body's rhythms.

How do you get in touch with your biorhythms and circadian cycles? One way is to observe nature. Tune into the natural world. Tune into your body. When you are in harmony with your rhythms, you feel good. When you are out of balance, you will feel as though you are pushing your body to do something it does not want to do.

The science of superstring theory suggests that everything is vibration. When you are in harmony with the natural vibrations of your body and environment, you set up a resonant field which lowers resistance and, hence, unblocks the flow of energy from higher dimensions. In other words, you reduce entropy and increase centropy.

Harmonious Color and Sound Frequencies

Harmonious vibrations can take many forms, including music, tones, chants, and colors. Your body produces several different types of vibratory frequencies. Certain pieces of music can not only evoke strong emotions, but also harmonize with your natural frequencies. This author has had many incredible experiences while listening to harmonious melodies. Certain classical, New Age and meditation music can transmit higher vibrations into the cellular structure of the human body. It can lower resistance, thereby increasing access to centropy.

Some mantras and chants can also attune the body and mind to higher consciousness. You have the ability to keep your vibration high by immersing yourself in a high-vibrational environment. Your body is a lot like a tuning fork. It's easy to tune yourself to high frequencies because there are a lot of beautiful songs and instrumental pieces available online. There are 432Hz, 512Hz and other sound frequencies available. Do some research. Listen for a while and see if you feel a difference in your overall energy level. Not all frequencies will trigger a more positive response, but some probably will.

Like sound, visuals exist that are in harmony with the colors and patterns of the higher dimensions. Although you may not be able to see these dimensions directly with your physical eyes, certain patterns, textures and tones of light can attune you to color harmonics of the higher frequencies. There are various color-sound therapies being practiced worldwide. Again, do some research and try some video-sound combinations. There are mandalas and sacred geometric progressions with accompanying background music on YouTube and other Internet locations. A daily dose of 30 minutes of color, light and

222 THE SECRETS OF UNLIMITED ENERGY

sound therapy, at the proper frequencies, can increase your overall energy significantly.

High-Vibrational Music

There are hundreds of beautiful melodies you can find on the Internet and listen to at your leisure. We are going to list just a few below. We know we are omitting some important works, so we apologize in advance if we left out an important artist or title. Not all of these will easily raise your vibration, but some of them probably will.

From the classics: Pachelbel's Canon in D, Wagner's preludes to several operas, including *Lohengrin*, *Parsifal*, *Tannhäuser* and *Tristan und Isolde*, Barber's *Adagio for Strings*, many of Mozart's concertos and symphonies, Beethoven's concertos and symphonies, and parts of Handel's *Messiah*.

From New Age music: Anything by Asha (Denis Quinn, Asher Quinn or Asher Elijah), Patrick Bernhardt (Patrick Bernard), Gerald Jay Markoe, Deuter, Aeoliah, Sacred Earth, Ananda Vdovic, Ashana and some Pavarotti.

A few rock and Celtic pieces can also lift vibrations, including much of Blackmore's Night, David & Diane Arkenstone, some Moody Blues and Pink Floyd.

In addition, YouTube features certain frequencies of background music, including 432Hz and 512Hz meditations. Some of them are up to eight hours in duration.

DNA Immortality Sequence (Stem Cells)

Since this is a section on immortality, we would be remiss to not bring you up to date on the latest genetic research into life extension and stopping the aging process.

Of course, nobody wants to stay in a human body forever. That would be quite boring and eventually unproductive. But why not stay in a completely healthy and youthful body for as long as you desire to be on Earth? In addition to practicing the various healing techniques offered here and elsewhere, it is a good idea to become familiar with the different types of cells and how they relate to your overall DNA aging program.

Despite what most scientists think, aging is not natural. Degeneration and regeneration, once every Planck second, is natural. Some of your cells seem to have built-in mortality. That is because once they have fulfilled their function, they are no longer necessary. Nature is efficient. She does not make junk. There is no such thing as junk DNA. There is simply some DNA for which the purpose has not yet been determined by genetic scientists.

Telomeres, stem cells and certain other cell types have strong regenerative properties such that they do not appear to age, decay or break. In medical procedures, stem cells are already being used to stimulate the repair of tissues and organs, especially in the muscular and skeletal systems (joints, torn cartilage, etc.).

There are moral issues around the use of stem cells, since some people believe geneticists are "playing God," but it is only a matter of time before modern genetics creates a way to indefinitely postpone the death of the physical body.

Of course, living a long time is only desirable if you have a beautiful, peaceful environment. Why would anyone want to prolong a lifetime of stress and unhappiness? Using genetic technologies in association with the other suggestions given in this section, can greatly enhance the longevity effects of such methods and practices.

We are not encouraging you to run out and spend a fortune on stem-cell treatments, but it is possible to stimulate the growth of new organs or at least postpone their degeneration. Genetic engineering is not going to solve humanity's problems, but it can be a positive contributor when used appropriately.

As of this writing, new advances in genetic editing and genetically modified embryos have been introduced, despite all the opposition. Scientists now believe it will be possible to extend life indefinitely within the next 10 to 20 years.

We are not sure where the opposition to stem-cell research comes from. In the Bible, Genesis Chapter 1, it states we are created in the image and likeness of God. If that is so, then what is wrong with being co-creators with God and learning how to change our bodies to more completely meet our needs while on Earth? This should not be done in vanity. Attempting to extend life because you are afraid of death will not work. Being attached to having a youthful body is also not the answer. However, if you desire to extend your time of service on Earth and have greater enjoyment while being a positive contributor to other human beings, then what is wrong with changing your cells?

Essentially, genetic technologies will reduce or eliminate cells that have a built-in aging program and replace them with cells that are programmed for longevity. Such cells are receptive to the centropic energies. By working with stem cells and related genetics, you can open yourself more fully to the unlimited abundance of the universe.

Assistance/Downloads from Higher Beings

The universe is filled with intelligent life. Very soon, scientists will have proof of this. In the meantime, it is up to you to learn how to contact those souls who are more evolved than you. They reside in the upper dimensions. You have access to these realms, but only if you direct your consciousness or activate the part of yourself that already resides in these planes. Spirit guides and ascended masters are here to help you access your unlimited Beingness. They seem to have boundless energy because they remember who they are. They long ago put away the childish ideas of competition, greed, hoarding or control of resources. They know who they are, and their mission is to help you remember who you are.

There are many publications that teach you how to contact higher beings, including earlier books by this author. There are invocations you can use to call forth various levels of intelligence. This author uses a three-step process when assisting clients in contacting higher beings. The first step is to use protection, the second is to call in the Higher Self and *become* the Higher Self, and the third is to call in the guardian angels and spirit guides that are perfect, right and appropriate to assist with a given task or share wisdom regarding a desired topic.

Like everything else in life, calling in higher beings takes practice. Some souls will not experience very much the first few times they call in their spirit guides, but eventually you will learn to see, hear and feel the presence of higher beings.

A field of flowers does not grow in uniformity. Some plants are taller, stronger or thicker than others. Human beings are that way as well. Your talents and abilities are naturally different those of your friend's and associate's. Some of you seem to be naturally clairvoyant while others appear to have trouble visualizing, etc. You might be one of those who needs to work really hard to develop your ability to see, hear or feel spirit guides. If so, simply recognize that it is okay to have different abilities.

Everyone is clairvoyant. Everyone is capable of contacting higher beings and having a direct experience of them. If they are above seventh density, your mind will not be able to perceive them exactly as they are. It will interpret them based on existing knowledge. For example, Lord Sananda, the oversoul of Jesus, is an eighth density being. If you try and contact him, you might see an image of Jesus, or hear messages that sound like they are coming from Jesus.

This is the mind's attempt to understand the look, feel and sound of a being in the 8th level. In reality, Lord Sananda is a being of immense bright light. Beyond seventh density, you do not have a body that looks human. You might be able to have a direct experience of such a being because you also have an eighth-density self, but it will not resemble a normal human appearance.

It is possible to channel higher beings by merging a part of your energy with that of the soul or souls you wish to bring forth. Unless you have a specific karmic contract to be a trance channel (trance medium), we do not generally recommend entering into that type of relationship with a higher being or group of higher souls. The reason is that it is very hard on the physical body to accommodate the frequencies of beings from other dimensions and levels of vibration. Every time the entity comes in, the body must adjust suddenly to the different level.

This author has met a number of trance channels who have difficulty getting in or out of their bodies or who manifest various health problems. The only real advantage of trance channeling is that it reduces the likelihood that the ego will interfere in the transmission of energy and messages from the higher being(s). If you have done a lot of work on your ego and have a relatively high level of vibration, you will likely not feel the need to become a trance channel.

Conscious channeling is more desirable because you are aware of what is taking place and are simply sharing space with another entity or entities. You and the being(s) are able to regulate how much energy is flowing through the physical body and gradually increase or decrease the frequency as appropriate.

One of the main purposes in conscious channeling (aside from bringing forth information from higher dimensions) is to lift the vibration of the channel and those who are listening/attending the channeling event. Symbiotic relationships between channels and entities take time to develop. This author has worked with the same few entities repeatedly over the last 25 to 30 years. He does not channel deceased loved ones of clients or casually fulfill requests to bring through special beings. His body is attuned to the frequency of the beings he has been bringing forth for a long time.

A healthy relationship with spirit guides will increase centropy in your body. The act of allowing an entity to speak through you does require some kinetic energy, but the long-term effect, if the entity is truly benevolent and knowledgeable about sharing energy with human beings, is to raise the frequency/vibration of the channel and those around him/her.

Even if you decide not to channel an entity, you can always just ask for healing and energy transfer. Telepathic transmission is a gentler, less intrusive way of working with higher beings. You are simply communicating mind to mind with those from other levels. Only a small portion of their energy is coming into your six lower bodies. This is especially appropriate if you are working with beings that are much more advanced (several levels above your vibration).

Simple prayer works. Ask that God send you the perfect, right helpers to maximize your soul growth, happiness and well-being. Ask that you attract those beings who can best assist with raising your vibration and lowering your aging index. Your aging index is simply the rate at which your body is aging. An aging index of 50% means you are aging at half the "normal" rate. In other words, for every ten years that go by on the calendar, your body is getting five years older biologically.

Once your physical vibration reaches a certain point, it is possible to stop the aging process altogether. This generally occurs around the same time you get to the point where you no longer require food and water. Using this channel's density calibration scale, that is around 4.75. Of course, consciousness moves faster than the physical body, so your consciousness level will usually far exceed the physical vibration. You can read about levels of vibration in earlier publications.

Understanding/Awareness

There is a difference between knowledge and wisdom. Likewise, there is a difference between understanding and awareness. Knowledge and understanding require some expenditure of energy to maintain, even if it is merely brain waves and the effort to find out the facts required to attain understanding and knowledge. Wisdom and awareness are different states altogether. They do not require expenditure of time and effort; they only require a willingness to transcend memorized facts and experiences. Awareness is instantaneous. It arises from silent observation. Insights arise as a result of looking directly at "what is." This opens the self to higher dimensions and hence, greater energy. Wisdom is the bridge between awareness and understanding. You are putting into practice the insights gained from awareness. Wisdom taps into the higher frequencies and contributes to an increase in centropy.

When you meditate and when you are investigating and exploring higher truths, notice to what degree you are relying on past knowledge and experience. Some of this is obviously necessary since you don't want to reinvent the wheel, but a lot of memory accumulation acts as baggage, slowing you down. Use what you need and discard the rest. It's a lot like packing for a trip: Take only what you need. It will cost you in both energy expended (lugging heavy bags through airports) and in monetary expense (paying penalties for exceeding weight limits).

When focusing on higher dimensions, pay attention to your inner baggage. You will, of course, need language if you want to communicate your experiences to others, but stay open and receptive to the ways your Higher Self uses language and experience to best formulate ideas and concepts. When this author works with a group of people, some in attendance are highly experienced in personal and spiritual growth, while others have more recently begun to awaken to their higher nature.

The author's Higher Self has a way of communicating with this diverse group such that he seldom bores those who are already familiar with the work while at the same time facilitating the newcomers so they do not get lost and confused with the more advanced concepts. The intellectual mind does not know how to do this. It requires a degree of wisdom and cooperation with higher levels.

Enlightened Teachers

The liberated masters of this world are radiators of energy unto themselves. They can tap directly into the Source and its unlimited fountain of wisdom. Higher-order energy transmutes lower-order entropy. The flow is from disorder to greater order because enlightened teachers are channeling the higher dimensions and radiating the centropy from those dimensions into the entropic realms. Instead of causing the ordered information to become disordered as a result of doing this, the centropy "overlays" itself on the entropic levels, pulling them up into greater order.

A being with an awareness of 9.0 on this channel's density scale might have as much power (energy) as one million souls vibrating at level 3.0. This does not mean the enlightened soul is going to violate the free will of lower-density beings or try to force them to wake up. Such a being is not truly enlightened. Truly evolved souls do not force others to adopt certain ideas, no matter how lofty they are. This is one of the reasons why you do not see avatars walking openly through the marketplaces and public squares — at least they do not announce themselves if they are there.

Despite the fact that those with free will can choose to ignore or refuse the transmutational energies of higher beings, enough of the enlightened energy gets through the layers of denial and ignorance that many souls are indeed pulled up into greater centropy as a result of the work of the realized beings.

Younger souls need to learn their lessons — sometimes the hard way. Enlightened beings do not deprive those souls of their need to experience the consequences of their behavior. Illuminated souls teach by example. Once the student is ready, the teacher appears. The liberated one is simply waiting for the neophyte to begin waking up. A soul who is not ready for enlightenment would not recognize an enlightened teacher if he walked up and hugged him. Remember, belief is powerful. If you believe you are not ready for enlightenment, it will tend to evade you.

Enlightened teachers seem to "sacrifice" themselves in order to be in this world. They might subject their bodies and personalities to abuse and ridicule. However, they know they are not of this world, and so they do not identify with the illusions of those who do not understand them. They are not insulted or emotionally injured if someone is critical or judgmental. They simply go into their center and remain calm. They are ready to offer assistance if and when it is appropriate to do so. They conserve energy instead of wasting it on trying to convince a stubborn soul of higher realities. "Do not cast your pearls before swine," it says in the Bible. This means do not invest much time and energy in those who are unable or unwilling to comprehend what you have to teach.

If you are a teacher, ask that the perfect right students appear — those who can best be served by what you have to offer. Know that each one put in front of you represents an opportunity to honor your sacred commitment to pour forth your unconditional love. You are there to help them awaken. By trusting in the Kingdom of God within and the unlimited energy it represents, you automatically do the highest and best service possible to help your fellow human beings.

Dharma (Service to Others)

Being of service to humanity is not something you do in order to be "good" or to prove that you are somehow purer and more righteous than others. Service comes naturally as you raise your vibration beyond the realms of separation (or rather, the illusion of separation). Once you are no longer living in the consciousness of entropy (duality) you realize you are One with all life and, therefore, when you serve others you are serving yourself. If you are truly serving yourself, you are also serving others — it works both ways.

Selfishness is not really serving yourself; it is perpetuating the belief in scarcity, which is a cornerstone of the belief in separation. Instead of truly serving yourself (loving and accepting who you are), you are merely taking from others that which is materially present, with the belief that you now have more and the other person has less.

This identification with form embodies the reality of entropy, disorder and chaos.

When you serve another, your sole purpose is to lift that person into a higher state of consciousness. To do this, you might need to start with the material plane, perhaps in some form of charity or giving. Once you take care of the basic needs of another, you then help that person move into a state whereby he/she can rise above the planes of duality. "First, feed them so they are listening to you and not to their hunger. Then show them how to prevent being hungry in the future." We put that in quotes because it is a composite of a couple of different sayings, such as "Give a man a fish, and he eats for a day. Teach him how to fish, and he eats for a lifetime."

There may be a time and place to give handouts to beggars, but after you drop a few coins in their hats, the cycle repeats the next day and no real progress has been made. However, if you teach them a skill, a method for manifesting, or give them a deep healing, you start them on the path beyond begging.

Centropic energy naturally reaches out and lifts other aspects of Creation. You don't have to try to be "good" or constantly effort to be more generous. Even if you give money or material things to others in ways that society deems "generous," unless you are helping yourself and others out of the illusion of duality, your help is of a temporary nature.

That said, if you begin a life of service while you are still somewhat selfish, the change in lifestyle might be enough to lift you out of your self-absorption and self-obsession. If the opportunity presents itself to do humanitarian work or to serve in some way, take it. Remember that change begins with you. You are the one you have been waiting for.

Order

The opposite of chaos is order. Chaos is the central principle of entropy, just as order is the central condition of centropy. Raising your consciousness is the process of moving from chaos to order. Your higher being assembles seemingly random events and makes them coherent (orderly).

You can practice this in daily life. Start with something simple and basic such as the clutter in your house. Yes, at first it takes energy to organize things, but as you perfect the process, it gets easier and easier (a sign that you are moving into centropy).

Writing a computer program is a good example. You start with a series of instructions, algorithms and logical statements, and pretty soon you have something useful that can be used over and over again with consistent results (if your programming skills are good). If you throw the instructions into random order, the program will not function. But as soon as you assemble them into the right pattern, order emerges.

Acceptance (Self-Love)

The opposite or resistance is acceptance. When you accept "what is," you then have the energy to change it if it is not to your liking. As long as you are fighting and resisting "what is," you are depleting yourself of the needed energy to solve the problem.

The first step in accepting yourself is to look honestly at the problem. First, is it a real problem or are you just imagining it? Let's use the fear of being in a dangerous situation as an example. We went over this earlier in the section about worry and anxiety. Unless someone is pointing a gun at your head or a truck is about to run over you, you are probably not in any real danger. You are worried about a future that may or may not happen. If it does happen, you need energy and strength (and possibly quick action) to deal with it. If you are living in constant fear of this happening, you will not have the necessary energy to deal with it when it arises. (Your energy will be depleted through worry and fear.)

If you are in constant fear of something that might never happen, then you are wasting your energy. How many of the things you worry about actually occur?

Getting back to acceptance, you start by being at peace with the fact that you are both human and Divine at the same time. Part of you is eternally perfect and part is temporarily imperfect. Accept both states. Send love to your little human self while at the same time loving God. Then extend this love and acceptance to others. This covers the first two commandments: to love God and to love your neighbor as yourself.

Remembering God's Eternal Love

We included this entry because it is important to remember that all energy comes from the eternal Source. In our universe, energy is constant; only the form changes. Beyond our universe is the Tao, the Great Mystery, the unknowable. Without beginning and without end, the Godhead is eternal and infinite. Love increases the more it is given away. This goes against the laws of conventional physics. Although God represents infinite energy, in our universe energy is balanced, going into and out of existence every Planck second.

Focusing on God's Eternal Love means opening to the unlimited energy that drives all the universes forever. No matter how many ways you open to receive centropy, all energy belongs to God and returns to God because God is all there is. "With God, all things are possible," is a true statement, with one exception: You cannot actually be separate from God since there is nothing beyond God. There is no opposite to God; therefore, there is no lack anywhere in the universe. Lack, if it really existed, would be the opposite of God's unlimited abundance, but if something is unlimited, it can have no opposite. According to *A Course in Miracles*, "Love is a law without an opposite."

You can believe there is a force that opposes God. You can believe fear is the opposite of love. You can believe darkness is the opposite of Light. However, these beliefs do not change the eternal Truth.

There are two kinds of beings in the world — those who know everything is God and those who believe there is something else besides God. The only real way to open to unlimited energy is to wake up to the truth that God is the only reality.

All the other suggestions for increasing the flow of energy are based on the belief that you are not One with God. Breathing, meditation, eating pure food — these are preparation for the realization that there has never been and will never be a lack of energy, period. When you realize the truth of infinite abundance, you then know that you have never lacked in any way at any time. You were asleep and dreaming of a world of finite resources.

The only requirement for living in a world of unlimited energy is for humanity to wake up to the abundance that is within and everywhere. Remember that most of this book is designed to get you to realize that you were wrong about the lack of energy on Earth. Once you know there is no lack, you will also remember what is beyond all concepts of lack and abundance.

CHAPTER 18

A Review of How to Move from Entropy to Centropy

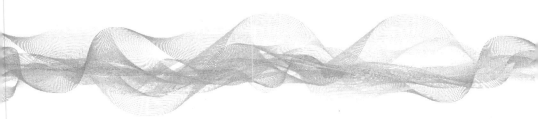

We have talked a great deal about lowering resistance as a key to unlimited energy (using Ohm's Law and other examples). However, we want to make sure you fully understand psychologically how to lower resistance.

What exactly is resistance? In electrical engineering (and electronic components), a material is inserted or embedded between two conducting surfaces or mediums. This material acts as a partial barrier to the flow of electrons by its very nature. The simplest analogy would be erecting concrete barriers on a roadway, such as speed bumps. The higher and more abrupt you make the speed bumps, the slower cars must go to avoid damage.

On a psychological level, negative thoughts, beliefs and programs are like the speed bumps referenced above. The flow of prana enters the physical, emotional and mental bodies of the soul and hits the speed bumps of core negative beliefs and their resulting emotions of fear, anxiety, worry, obsession, guilt, shame, resentment, etc.

Let's look at the various levels of resistance and how they dissipate energy through entropy.

Earlier, we said that the most basic level of resistance could simply be not accepting "what is." We insist that things should be different than the way they are, and we become angry, frustrated or impatient as a result. The reason we don't accept what is, is due to our belief systems, programming and conditioning. In other words, we become attached to certain things and experiences and have expectations regarding future outcomes.

Accepting what is does not mean condoning bad behavior or giving up and resigning oneself to unhealthy or dangerous conditions. However, unless we first fully accept the actual reality of what is taking place, we cannot see clearly the steps that are necessary to create alternatives to bad situations (unhealthy or dangerous conditions). Resisting what is creates a dissipating field of entropy around the soul. We resist because we have belief systems that give rise to fear of what might happen in the future, usually based on what happened in the past. We are, therefore, not present in this moment. Being fully present lowers resistance to what is. Complete acceptance of what is brings us into the present moment.

Being present and accepting what is might mean that we become painfully aware of negative conditions in our lives or in the lives of loved ones. This is uncomfortable due to our negative beliefs and programs. Even if we are aligned with good moral values that are in harmony with universal laws and principles, we still must first accept that we live in a world where war, poverty, misery and suffering are all around us. We must acknowledge that not all souls are ready to move out of these conditions. Some are learning soul lessons that they contracted to experience before they even entered this world. Others have a desire, on a soul level, to experience the results of negative karma. They are learning that when they think negative thoughts and have judgment toward others, negative circumstances will appear in their lives.

We are not here to deprive these souls of their needed lessons. However, love and compassion have a way of overcoming karma and, in fact, dissolving it. By first accepting that things are the way they are, we can then go deep within and access the healing energy (prana) that is everywhere present.

One of the most powerful and practical ways to lower resistance and increase energy is to imagine sending love and compassion out to everyone on Earth, especially those who seem harder to love, such as murderers, rapists, terrorists, and such. At first, this will be quite difficult. You might put on a happy face and say, "I love everyone.

Everything is love and light." But deep inside you know you have not truly realized this.

There is still hate and repulsion every time you see someone being bombed or violently suppressed. This brings us back to acceptance. "I accept that a part of me is not ready to forgive the perpetrators of the 911 attacks." Then send love to the part of you that is angry about that event. Accepting the part of you that feels negative emotions is a great start to tapping into unlimited energy.

Return, again and again, to sending love and compassion to your so-called "enemies." In the Bible, the phrase "love your enemies" does not mean you approve of their bad behavior or that you should put on a plastic smiley face and pretend you are happy when you are not. Sometimes the best way to love someone is to get right in their face and confront them for their inappropriate way of treating other souls. Other times the highest option might be to simply let it go. How do you know what the most enlightened response is to such a situation? On a human level, you probably don't know. Begin with accepting the human self that does not understand the how and why of a negative condition on Earth. "I accept the part of myself that is angry when I observe my government selling weapons to Saudi Arabia knowing such weapons will be used to bomb women and children in Yemen." You are not condoning such bad behavior. You are not justifying the actions of those who prefer making money over being loving and compassionate toward others. You are merely accepting that this is the way things are, and you are accepting your reaction to the situation. Then, you have the necessary energy to respond in the highest and best way.

Feeling helpless to change the world is a direct result of the belief in separation. When such feelings arise, ask yourself, "What is the origin of these feelings?" Not only might you get in touch with your own "Original Cause" issues (those feelings associated with the soul's first descent into the lower worlds), but you also realize that you may have had lifetimes of programming and conditioning that reinforce the idea that you are merely human.

Even if you are a sophisticated self-help guru or psychologist, you might still fall into the trap of using the need for love and acceptance of what is as an excuse to remain locked in your identification with the little self (ego).

"I must love and accept the fact that I cannot do much to change the world." Be careful here. You don't want to move into delusions of grandeur and believe you are farther along on the path than you are, but you also do not want to judge and criticize the gains you have made.

The truth is, you are a powerful, creative, spiritual being, capable of making significant changes to the world. Yet, you may have fallen deeply into the illusion of separation and are being daily influenced by others who are still caught in the drama of duality.

Observe constantly the interplay between the ego and Higher Self, between the part of you that believes the lies and deceptions of this world and the part that knows otherwise. Fighting with the ego is a sure-fire way of dissipating energy. After all, it is really the ego that is at war with itself. And, ultimately, the ego is not real. It is merely a collection of thoughts, an idea of separation. Send love and compassion to the ego. Accept that you have fallen into this illusion, and gently but firmly begin pulling yourself out of the trap. When you fall, pick yourself up, dust yourself off, and continue along the path.

∞ Using Holistic Healing Methods to Lower Resistance

As you know, resistance occurs physically in the form of imbalances and disease in the body, as well as emotionally and mentally, as discussed in the previous chapters. Lowering of the immune system is really just a consequence of resistance. Since the body's overall energy is lower, this lower state allows negative bacteria and viruses to invade and penetrate the body's natural defenses. The purpose of holistic healing techniques is to increase the prana (life-force energy) flowing into, out of and through the body. As you are aware, tension and stress build up in the body and block the vital flow of prana, so meditation, breathing exercises, yoga, and getting away from stressful environments are all integral parts of holistic healing.

In addition to decreasing stress through the methods above, various healing modalities can be useful, such as Reiki, Reconnection, Quantum Touch, acupressure, acupuncture, EFT tapping (Emotional Freedom Technique), and many more.

Most of these techniques simply realign the nadis (energy

meridians) and restore the natural blueprint of the etheric body. As mentioned in previous publications, the etheric body holds the electromagnetic blueprint of the physical body.

When a healthy blueprint is overlaid upon the existing imbalanced energy system, the discordant energy patterns begin to become coherent, aligning themselves with the healthy blueprint. This is because unhealthy energy patterns are not intrinsic to the natural state of the etheric body. Discordance is a form of resistance whereby the harmonic frequencies are out of phase with the natural healthy state of the body. Through holistic healing modalities, the original blueprint can be restored.

This is an overly simplified explanation of how and why holistic healing works, and there are lots of resources online and in libraries that go into far more depth on these subjects, so we encourage you to do more research.

∞ Summary of the Psychological Section and Additional Comments

Let us once again return to the basic energy formula: Energy in equals energy out. Below we review, in itemized format, the factors that increase and decrease your overall energy.

Ways that Increase Overall Potential Energy (Input):

1. Consciously attuning (asking) higher dimensional energies to enter the body/mind
2. Meditating and visualizing higher frequencies/dimensions
3. Breathing techniques, such as Kriya and Kundalini yoga, Rebirthing, primal therapy, etc.
4. Positive affirmations and visualizations
5. Being in the presence of highly evolved souls (physical and in spirit)
6. Sending love to all parts of the self, having total self-acceptance, accepting what is
7. Eating high-quality foods and drinking pure water
8. Taking in the right quantities of multivitamins, multiminerals and supplements

9. Holistic healing techniques that transmit energy into the body/mind
10. Invocation, prayer, and certain rituals (similar to #1 above)

Ways that Decrease Overall Kinetic Energy (Output):

1. Rest, relaxation, meditation and sleep
2. Release of negative thoughts, ideas, beliefs, programs and conditioning
3. Reducing tension and stress in your outer life — balancing work and play
4. Accepting what is — loving the parts of yourself that feel negative
5. Balancing and upgrading your exercise regimen (conscious workouts)
6. Eliminating negative breathing patterns (erratic breathing or holding breath)
7. Eliminating foods and drink that dissipate energy
8. Eliminating bad habits and addictions (substance and process)
9. Choosing to avoid negative people as much as possible
10. Choosing work that is stimulating, not boring and repetitive.

In addition to the steps given above, become aware of the more subtle ways that energy can be increased or decreased, such as eating at certain times and not others. For example, if you eat a high-quality meal and then wait at least two hours before going to sleep, your overall energy will be much better than if you eat a heavy, unhealthy meal just before bedtime. Stress and tension can enter into the dream state. If you have insomnia or are constantly waking up numerous times during the night, you will dissipate energy, even if the reason for the insomnia is that a lot of energy is coming into your body/mind.

Learn to filter the incoming energy. Remember that energy can come in the form of thoughts from others, electromagnetic pollution from Wi-Fi, phone, radio and TV towers, cosmic radiation, and much more. If you have poor filtering capability, all these energies will converge in your body/mind system and possibly wreak havoc.

Some of these are unavoidable, but you can take precautions, such as sleeping with your head away from transmission towers, minimizing light in your room at night, putting radiation screens on phones and computers, turning off devices that are near your bed, etc.

Learn to recognize the power and vibration of certain types of music. Bring high-vibrational, relaxing music into your home and business, if possible. If you work in a place where low-vibrational music is piped in and you have no say in the matter, put up protection fields of golden light around your body as often as possible. Take as many breaks as you can without compromising the quality of your work. If necessary, wear ear plugs or, if you are allowed to, listen to your own music through headphones. Use Bluetooth or speaker mode when talking on the phone to avoid holding it up to your head. Limit the duration of phone calls on your mobile device. Take breaks from sitting in front of a computer. Some of the frequencies coming through the computer might be enhancing your energy field while others are depleting it.

Pay close attention to how you feel before, during and after being in a crowd of people. Sometimes being in a crowd can be energizing, but most of the time it has the opposite effect. Use protection techniques when in train stations, concerts, or sporting events. Remember that when walking down a city street, three out of the four people passing you are likely more negatively polarized than positive. Accept that this is the way it is, send love and compassion to those you pass, and quickly find your way to a more peaceful place.

We hope this psychology section has been helpful in your overall understanding of how to unlock the secrets of unlimited energy.

CHAPTER 19

The Necessary Changes in Society

So far, we have looked at the science, metaphysics, spirituality and psychology of unlimited energy, but this technology will never become a reality on Earth unless there are profound changes to the political, economic and social structure of the world as we know it.

Let's examine first the blocks to the full implementation of unlimited energy. Really, there is only one block, and that is the lack of sufficient consciousness and belief that it is truly possible to have free and abundant energy available to every human being.

Below, we are stating the main obstacles, intentionally using different modes of speech and describing the problem from several different angles. You will note that we are not listing the issues we have already discussed; i.e., the belief in separation, lack of spiritual development, habits and addictions (distractions), etc. In this section, we are getting practical and dealing with the world as it exists today.

Blocks to the Full Manifestation of Abundant Unlimited Energy:

1. Government Suppression and Control
2. Belief in Dark Forces Capable of Oppressing and Enslaving Society
3. Attachment to Fossil Fuels and Nuclear Energy

4. The Necessity to Completely Overhaul the Economic Systems on Earth
5. The Unwillingness to Give Up Identification with the Ego
6. The Reluctance to Speak Out against Tyranny and Mind Control
7. The Lack of Courage to Tell the Truth Openly and Directly
8. Attachment to Religious and Cultural Beliefs and Practices
9. A Perceived Lack of Time and Energy to Devote to Bringing Forth the Technologies
10. Lack of Discipline in Mind and Body

Government Suppression and Control

We have already elaborated on the metaphysical and spiritual reasons for the censorship, intervention and manipulation apparent within the free-energy movement. This includes the system of patents, legal maneuvers and outright prevention of certain technologies from being released to the masses. We all know about inventors who have had their laboratories raided, destroyed or burned. In many cases, those working on the projects have been murdered or "suicided." But what can we do about this from a practical viewpoint? Now that we have the spiritual and metaphysical understandings, what is the next step?

We obviously need to end government suppression and control. The simplest way to do this is to get everyone to raise their consciousness to the point where they no longer believe they need a "big daddy government" to save them from themselves. At that point, the masses will simply refuse to be ruled by an oligarchy of overweight, bloated, bloviated politicos.

Let's review the psychology of why we even believe we need government in the first place. Quite frankly, most of us have never actually grown up and matured. We are still looking for a savior (in religion or government) to solve our problems for us. Or we have become lazy, relying on government grants or handouts, expecting that somehow having the right patent or lawyer will magically allow us to overcome the deeper problems. Let us repeat an important insight (provided by another teacher) regarding the psychology of government. In the West, we have essentially two branches of ruling class (Democrats and Republicans in the USA). The Democrats represent the "mother principle" and the Republicans the "father principle." In a traditional family, both parents provide for the needs of the children, but in different ways. The mother is generally nurturing and provides emotional support, while the father provides material safety and security.

In our society, the mother principle is outpictured as social programs (the favorite of the Democrats) and the father principle is depicted as the need for a strong military and security system (the Republicans). Even though our bodies may be grown up, we still expect government to give us free things (the left wing) and protect us from foreign invaders (the right wing). Therefore, most of the financial resources of our system go to maintaining these two parental processes. Big Mommy government will spend lots of money on welfare, social services, education (indoctrination) and emotionally appealing politicians, while Big Daddy government will spend trillions on the latest weapons, police forces, and surveillance in the guise of keeping us safe and secure from terrorists and such.

Most people have a great fear of anarchy. They believe that if these government programs were removed, there would be lawless chaos. Perhaps that is true if there is insufficient awareness among the masses that the truth is within. Yet how do we provide true education to those who need to raise their consciousness? How do we inform them of the absolute necessity of letting go of outdated beliefs and crippling psychological blocks?

The vast majority of souls on Earth do not even realize they have an internal problem. They blame Darwinism or the devil on their problems. They think it is human nature to fight and compete for limited resources. Even if we somehow manage to convince them that free unlimited energy is a reality, they will immediately dismiss this because they know that human nature will find a way to control it and keep people enslaved. They understandably point out the endless wars for control of resources that have plagued the Earth for millennia.

We live in the time religious people call "Apocalypse." The word "apocalypse" means, "a time of revealing all that has been hidden." That is what we are seeing in the world right now. Everything is coming to the surface — the good, the bad and the ugly. For many, it is overwhelming. It used to be that in the more "developed" countries, the general consensus was that there are a few "bad apples" in government, but that democracy, fairness and justice are the predominant condition. Such fairy tales are now being exposed as delusional.

In the United States, those elected to office typically have a comfortable financial position at the start of their terms (maybe with a financial net worth of half a million to a million dollars). By the time they retire from the House of Representatives or the Senate, their average financial wealth has exploded to between 50 and 500 million dollars. They did not get suddenly rich from their salaries (typically 200,000 to 400,000 dollars per year). Whether it's insider trading, under-the-table deals with lobbyists, or outright bribes by special-interest groups wanting their pet projects to get priority, there is one word that accurately describes the above: *corruption.* Instead of a few "bad apples," there are a few unspoiled ones that have not managed to become infected by the rest of the rotten barrel.

This author once remarked, "If they got rid of all the criminals and corrupt politicians in Washington, DC, it would resemble a ghost town."

It's one thing to realize that both political parties are corrupt. It's quite another to address the psychological and spiritual underpinnings of the problem. Expecting Big Mommy or Big Daddy government to save us comes from an incomplete process of maturation. This is, of course, reinforced by religion and so-called mainstream science, as well as the media. We are expected to believe the media because news comes from "official sources."

As a small child, we relied on the "authority" of our parents to provide for us and nurture our delicate emotions. Parents are not given an instruction manual. There is no such thing as a perfect parent. Every single one has made mistakes. Most have tended toward the opposites — overly permissive or too authoritarian. This is a blatant generalization, but overly permissive parents often bring up souls who become left-wing "socialists," while authoritarian parents usually bring up militaristic, right-wing control freaks. Sometimes the children rebel and take the opposite polarity. This was apparent during the hippie movement of the 1960s, where the offspring became conservatives who voted for Nixon and Reagan.

Polarity in politics is not the only place these imbalances show up. Most souls on Earth are also polarized in religion. The opposite of fundamental religiosity is atheism.

A large number of people "throw the baby out with the bathwater" because they see the fallacies of fundamentalism and reject God altogether in favor of Darwinian science. This author knows several of these souls. Dismissing God because of the grossly distorted version offered by mainstream religions is perhaps understandable, but pretty soon you find yourself on the opposite pole, becoming materialistic and dominated by the survival instinct.

In most areas of life, the key is to find the balance point between extremes. A certain amount of faith is necessary to live a balanced life, but so is a degree of scientific discernment. We will call the majority of religion-rejecting atheists, "pseudo-scientists." Instead of rigorously investigating the so-called spiritual realms with an open mind and heart, they flatly reject all talk of God. How is this any different from the "Flat Earthers" who refuse to look at obvious scientific truths that demonstrate the obloidal shape of the Earth? (Obloids are like spheres that are squeezed or slightly flattened. In the case of the Earth's shape, the equators have greater circumference than the poles. This is why airliners fly near the poles when traveling overseas. They actually travel fewer miles and save fuel.)

We are not suggesting that souls need to reinvent the wheel. Certain facts can be taken for granted in everyday life, such as the existence of gravity. We might not know everything there is to know about gravity, but it makes sense to accept it as a natural law. Beyond a few simple facts, such as the laws of basic mathematics, everything else should be questioned down to its foundation. A true scientist has an open mind and heart, and starts with, "I do not know the truth about this aspect of reality, but I will find out."

The pseudo-scientists in today's world are bought and paid for by large corporations or government grants. If their research falls too far outside the accepted norms, such as Darwinism, their funding is cut off and they are ridiculed by their peers.

The patent process is also corrupt. Just ask Nikola Tesla, who had governmental and corporate entities essentially steal and suppress most of his ideas.

As much as inventors need to be compensated adequately for their inventions (and deserve to be recognized and rewarded), the situation on Earth at this point is such that free-energy systems need to be published and distributed widely on the Internet regardless of the patent process. Some inventors are doing just that. They know that going through the patent process, jumping through the regulatory barriers to forming their own company and manufacturing processes, and trusting that government will cooperate instead of suppressing them, is part of the fairy tale, and they are distributing their schematics and procedures openly online. See the Appendix for a partial list of some of the research and inventions that have made it into the public arena.

Raising consciousness sufficiently to allow Zero-Point devices to work consistently in all environments is necessary, as we pointed out earlier in this book. At the same time, removing our blind faith in government is also necessary. We can no longer sit back and ignore the censorship and suppression of new technologies. We must move forward despite the obstacles.

Let's become aware of all the ways, physically and psychologically, that government interferes in our lives instead of helping us. Returning to the subject of anarchy, we are not suggesting that there should be nobody in charge of various programs, no leadership, or everyone on an equal footing regarding levels of responsibility. Roads still need to be maintained, buildings inspected, etc. However, the overwhelming majority of government can be safely eliminated as long as people are willing to take responsibility for their thoughts, feelings and actions.

The legal system is a big part of the problem. Lawyers get rich defending the guilty and innocent alike. A big corporation, for example, can afford to hire a team of lawyers to find a way to steal new technologies and either suppress or exploit them for profit. The average inventor cannot afford $300-per-hour advice for hundreds of hours in defense of their patent or invention.

While greed, borne out of feelings of powerlessness and inadequacy, is the psychological root of the problem, it takes time to change the machinery of society. As long as people are willing to blame and project their problems onto others or don't want to take responsibility for their behaviors, lawyers will be a necessary evil.

The two-tiered justice system is another cornerstone of the problem. Unless you have been living under a rock, you know that there is one system of justice for the wealthy and another for the rest of us. In some countries, as soon as a company reaches a certain level of success, the government of that country finds a way to seize the company's assets or take it over completely, often coming up with obscure ways that the company supposedly cheated on its taxes or violated some regulation.

Harassing inventors and real scientists is a favorite tactic of the so-called powers that be. Everyone who is seen as a threat, from presidents to basement-dwelling young laboratory enthusiasts, is fair game for harassment. More than one forward-thinking leader or scientist has gotten calls in the middle of the night threatening friends and family if they go ahead with their program.

Even well-meaning associates and people of influence can be obstacles. It's important to be realistic about goals and expectations regarding a project, but there is a fine line between realism and pessimism. What is the quality of the energy being projected by influencers and advisors? Are they merely getting you to cross your "t's" and dot your "i's" or is there a deep underlying belief that your project will not succeed?

Some leading-edge researchers and scientists become paranoid and think that evil entities are lurking in every shadow and orifice. You don't want to close your eyes to government censorship, surveillance and espionage, but at the same time you don't want to blame every laboratory failure on dark astral aliens. The government is all too willing to label you a conspiracy theorist or wacko nut job, so don't give them fuel for their fire by exaggerating the influence of dark forces or negative energies.

Yes, there are opposing energies in anything that threatens the status quo. You can be sure of that. Yet do not go into fear and strengthen their illusion of power. It's possible you can be taken out physically (killed or imprisoned). That is a risk of exploring the unknown and threatening the way of life of the so-called power elite.

Know that you are infinitely more powerful than some government agency that wants to discredit you. Publish as much of your work as you can. Store physical backups in places where they will not be found by adversaries. Confide in people you really trust to keep your work safe. Advise friends, family and associates that no, you are not going to commit suicide and that if you are found "suicided," it is the work of foul play.

At the same time, resist the temptation to open your mouth when it should be closed. Only confide in the right people, those you can truly trust. Keep a low profile. Stay under the radar as much as possible. But do not suppress your ideas or put off doing what you can do today. Ask for help from higher beings, spirit guides and ascended masters. Use protection techniques. Place a powerful shield of protection around your body, your house and your research facilities. Pay your taxes, but find as many loopholes and exemptions as possible. If the government somehow does not get what they think they deserve, that's fine as long as they don't come after you. Pay as little as you can legally get away with. Do you really want to support the apartheid state of Israel or the terrorist government of Saudi Arabia? Do you support regime change in places that refuse to bow down to the central banking system?

Learn how to legally cut off support to the cancerous parasite that is modern government. Learn about different types of trusts and foundations. The wealthy do this and so can you. Refuse to become polarized left or right when it comes to elections and campaign promises. Most promises are immediately broken or cancelled once the person gets elected. Stop expecting things to magically get better every time there is an election. That is fairy-tale thinking.

Learn about the Dark Web and peer-to-peer social networks that respect anonymity. Decentralized Internet platforms are exploding in popularity as of this writing, and for good reason. They are much more difficult to shut down by those who want to uphold the status quo.

You will find all sorts of conspiracy theories and radical viewpoints on the Dark Web, so you will definitely need to keep an open mind and do your research.

A blockchain or peer-to-peer site may be biased in a particular direction, such as supporting or opposing the president. This is fine if all viewpoints are openly expressed. If your view is different, express it even if you are ridiculed by some of the members of the open platform. Be respectful of the beliefs of others, but challenge them.

Mainstream social networks are not good places to express your ideas, due to censorship and the likelihood that they will commit privacy violations. Learn which search engines, browsers and decentralized platforms are the best. Since the list of reputable sites keeps changing, we will not attempt to list them in this book. Many Internet sites have been compromised. As this book was going to press, the search engine DuckDuckGo was discovered joining a consortium of mainstream companies that are dedicated to suppressing and censoring "undesirable" viewpoints. A new one that looks promising is Qwant.

If you are tech savvy, you can explore blockchain and more efficient technologies that are just now making their way to market. Starting your own alternative to mainstream technology is not necessarily expensive if you know your coding.

The point is, you can stay under the radar technologically, as well as psychologically and spiritually. Learning to close down your aura when in the presence of dangerous people is highly desirable. Practicing ways of diverting attention from yourself, especially when going through security at an airport, is useful. Even if you are not carrying anything questionable or illegal, it dissipates energy to have your bags constantly inspected, plus there's the risk of missing your flight.

Some people can draw their auras so tight into the body that people do not even see them. You can learn how to do this (find out about grounding techniques). This can backfire in the case of people constantly bumping into you, but it can be a lifesaver if you are being targeted because of your unorthodox ideas.

Ideally, you are somewhat tech savvy as well as psychologically and spiritually aware, meaning that you have lots of options on how to proceed with your project or program. But if you're not able to keep up with the latest inventions or theories, you can still learn a great deal from those who are willing to share their ideas, and this is why everyone should be doing their own research.

Use the ideas that feel right to you, while respecting the originator(s) and giving credit where it is due. When possible, observe all existing laws and regulations, but you might be called to go outside the legal structure depending on the nature of your project(s). After all, helping humanity break the shackles is more important than blindly following authority and laws designed to protect the status quo.

If you do break one or more laws, ask your higher guidance to keep you safe and alert for the best possible course of action, and remember, you are an agent of God's Laws, not humanity's. In other words, if you are faced with the choice of disobeying either natural law or manmade law, you know which one to choose.

Belief in Dark Forces Capable of Oppressing and Enslaving Society

This belief derives directly from the belief in separation from God. The belief in separation is the natural outcome of identifying with the ego, or material self. Let us review some basic truths. The ego is an illusion. It is a collection of thoughts (small energetic impulses emanating from consciousness), so it has a rudimentary level of reality. These thoughts give rise to the idea of a separate self, or personality. If this separate self is real, where is it? The brain? The heart? Outside the body? Remember the analogy of opening up a radio and looking for a set of tiny musicians playing inside it. In other words, the belief in ego/personality is based on a certain frequency originating within consciousness itself. It is the result of identifying with the physical body and believing it is separate from the rest of the universe.

The Nonlocality Principle of quantum physics has demonstrated that separation is an illusion, just as the appearance of solid objects in the physical universe is also an illusion.

So-called "Dark Forces" are merely those souls who believe in separation to such a degree that they believe there is a force that opposes God. If God is all that is, how can there be anything outside of God? Suffering arises from identification with and attachment to illusions. The Dark Forces are simply souls who have chosen to identify with the material plane and are, therefore, suffering from this attachment. If you believe the philosophy of the Dark Forces, you too will suffer accordingly. If you believe the Dark Forces have control over you, this is what you will experience.

There is an actual possibility that if you endeavor to develop free-energy systems, men in black suits might show up at your door, arrest you, destroy your laboratory, and subject you to all manner of torture and punishment. We are not naïve enough to assume this will not happen.

There is a lot you can do to minimize the chances of this happening, without sacrificing your integrity or watering down your research. Learn the technology of the Dark Web. Use your intuition when selecting business partners, investors and associates. Have backup plans (and physical backups) of all documentation, diagrams, schematics, etc. Have off-site servers and mirror hosting. Develop a "front" business to divert attention from the more controversial projects. Yes, we know this sounds like a Mafia strategy or governmental organized-crime syndicate, but sometimes you need to beat them at their own game. Your most sensitive research is kept compartmentalized, shared with only a few trusted souls, until such time as your project is distributed widespread beyond the possibility of suppression.

For example, some inventors have detailed schematics published to over 30,000 sites on the Internet. Peer-to-peer structures are in place to prevent the destruction of central servers, and physical backups of sensitive data (printed or etched on digital media) will survive a prolonged power blackout.

As you can see, we are taking the middle road between (1) being extremely paranoid and constantly fearing someone will take you and your research out; and (2) naively forging ahead, sharing your most critical data with anyone and everyone you meet. Recall once again our maxim: "Trust God, but look both ways before crossing the street." In this case, ask God, your spirit guides and your friends for as much protection as possible, but release all fear and paranoia regarding opposition to your project.

The Dark Forces are a lot like the Wizard of Oz and the emperor with no clothes. As long as you believe in them, they seem mighty indeed. But withdraw your emotional and mental energy from their shenanigans, and you quickly see that they are but misguided souls masquerading as powerful gods. Of course, their money and military might must be reckoned with, but there are always ways around these obstacles. Remember, you have the advantage if you have developed your higher abilities. Your "army" consists of millions of higher beings all watching your back. Of course, they are not allowed to intervene blatantly in such a way that their cover is blown.

Therefore, you must take care and protect yourself as much as possible. If you are caught up in your own thoughts and emotions and cannot hear their guidance, you might put yourself in danger beyond their ability to help.

Listen within, ask for protection, and pay attention to your surroundings. If something does not feel right about a situation, there is a reason. Be confident, but humble at the same time. Don't assume you know everything about a situation. Get help, both physically and spiritually. Breathe. Relax. Stay in your center. Meditate regularly. The truth is usually somewhere in-between the extremes. You are safer than you fear, but you need to be cautious and aware at all times. Do not underestimate the enemy, but also do not overestimate. Realize that the so-called "enemy" is just a collection of lost souls who believe in separation — nothing more, nothing less. Their impressive weaponry hides the deep insecurity they feel and their overriding fear of powerlessness. As Lao Tzu is credited with saying, "Keep your friends close and your enemies closer." Get to know them psychologically. You will learn their strategies and often their next moves.

Attachment to Fossil Fuels and Nuclear Energy

Retooling equipment is expensive and time-consuming, but it can be done. Although the entire world seems to run on oil, human beings survived before the industrial revolution (although perhaps without so much luxury).

The transition to renewable energy has already been accomplished in a rudimentary sort of way with solar, wind and hydro power. Moving to Zero-Point Energy (ZPE) will necessitate dismantling a lot of pipelines and distillation equipment and building solid-state magnets and motors.

The biggest obstacle, of course, is the need to relinquish the profit motive. Although a small price could be exacted for the setup of ZPE devices, the constant need to fill the tank or heat the home from gas will be gone. Oil executives and their shareholders will temporarily face their personal Armageddon. Of course, they will fight tooth and nail to keep their way of life, as they are doing now. Their main weapon is a mental one — convincing researchers that ZPE is fantasy, or unrealistic, or that somehow the science is wrong.

"How can there be nearly infinite energy in the vacuum of space? Where is it? How come I cannot see it? How come my voltmeter does not measure it?" The biggest and most valid question is: "Why does it seem to work sometimes but not at other times?" We have already answered that question in previous sections.

As soon as mainstream minds become open to the promise of ZPE, the frequencies and vibrations necessary to create a world-wide resonant field of consciousness capable of supporting consistent output of ZPE devices will be achieved. The laws of metaphysics are more universal and encompassing than the physical laws. This has been demonstrated with psychokinetics (mind over matter). A critical frequency in consciousness must be achieved. This cannot happen until people release their attachments to fossil fuels and nuclear energy.

This also means redesigning cities and towns around e-commerce and ZPE transportation systems. Without the constant need for automobiles, their luster and charm will begin to fade. A few will be saved by collectors and displayed in museums. Like the horse and buggy, they will soon fade from memory (except in old films and history books).

The biggest issue here is still the psychological one. Our way of life on Earth will change dramatically for the better, but the word "change" drives terror into the hearts of many. Soothsayers have been pointing out the obvious problems with fossil fuels and nuclear energy for almost a century, yet many are still in denial about the pollution and long-term health effects of breathing automobile exhaust and factory emissions.

This author and his spirit guides concluded quite some time ago that many souls will be unable to make the transition into a world of Zero-Point Energy. Even if there are pockets of higher consciousness where ZPE devices can flourish, some parts of the Earth will simply not accept it. Plagues, exotic viruses and environmental illness will likely consume these regions before they wake up to what is taking place.

This is not to say that the global-warming enthusiasts are entirely correct about having perhaps only a decade left before massive cataclysm. Yet this author, in his personal counseling practice, is seeing a constant increase in the percentage of clients with environmental diseases. The body has an amazing ability to adapt to things like the all-pervasive nature of plastics. It is a fact that every human body has micro-fibers of plastic embedded into the bloodstream and tissues.

How much will be torn down before the new energy systems can be built up? This question applies not only to infrastructure, but to the human body itself. The more humanity resists the ultimate outcome of the end of fossil fuels, the harder the transition will be. If enough people wake up fast enough, the transition can be gentle and swift, not slow and painful.

The Necessity to Completely Overhaul the Economic Systems on Earth

This author has stated ad infinitum that the present economic systems of Earth are almost 180 degrees out of phase with higher spiritual principles. In fact, I doubt it is possible to invent something more at odds with God's limitless love and compassion than the sorry state of affairs labeled capitalism, communism, socialism, fascism, or any other "ism" involving money.

What is the opposite of our current financial system? Very simply, it is:
- abundance instead of scarcity
- prosperity for all and not just for a few
- goods that last instead of planned obsolescence
- incentives to be creative instead of rewards for being lazy (corporate and personal welfare)

There was once a time when we believed it was possible to transition gracefully from the present economic structure into a more enlightened one. That no longer seems possible. The current system is just too broken to salvage much of anything from it. The sooner it dies, the less painful it will be. The longer it continues, the harder it will fall.

Before we can create an enlightened financial structure, we must face the fact that things will be quite rocky for a while. To help you navigate the storm, there are a few basic things to do in preparation. These are listed in order of priority:

1. Buy land you can grow crops on and upon which you can generate solar, wind and hydro power.
2. Invest in gold, silver and other precious metals.
3. Have cold hard cash safely stored.
4. Have liquid assets (credit cards and checking accounts where you can get to your money easily as long as the banks are functioning).
5. Invest in companies and organizations that are helping the Earth, including environmental cleanup and alternative energy.

Once the banking system fails, an economy of barter and trade will temporarily take hold until a new currency can be introduced. The problem with cryptocurrencies is that they produce nothing of real value. If a system is devised whereby cryptos become real currency, then perhaps they are a viable alternative. It is doubtful the banks will allow this if they are functioning. If they are not open, the government will likely nationalize them and issue a new currency (or chop zeroes off the amount on the notes). You may have noticed how inefficient government usually is, so I would not look forward to this option.

An enlightened economic system is one in which creativity is rewarded and everyone has an opportunity to contribute to the well-being of the whole. In such a system, people are compensated for their real contributions to humanity. A farmer is worth more than a lawyer when you get right down to basics. (You cannot eat lawsuits and contracts.) For that matter, the farmer is also worth more than a storehouse of gold and silver. (You cannot eat them, either.) A seed bank or seed vault is worth more than all the gold in Fort Knox (assuming there is actually still gold in that location).

In an enlightened economic system, people are educated to find their calling in life, not to fit into an existing structure. Value is based on how much your contribution uplifts the consciousness of others.

Artists, musicians, teachers, therapists, eco-architects, gardeners and innovative engineers will be emphasized. Insurance executives, stock and bond traders, bankers and accountants will be greatly reduced or eliminated. Right now, over 50% of all jobs have something to do with investing, saving, spending, insuring, storing or counting money. In the new society, the best jobs will be in occupations that make people's lives better in tangible, physical ways. Speculation, options, hedge funds, derivatives and creative financing using compound interest, have no real value other than to make some people rich at the expense of others.

It is inevitable that debt will become so massive in the present system that it will need to be forgiven and a new currency introduced. This is called a financial reset or overhaul. Until human consciousness rises out of the gutter of competition, greed, selfishness and control, the new currency will simply become corrupted like the present currencies. A revolution in consciousness must come before a true financial reset, and a financial reset must come before free unlimited energy can proliferate.

The Unwillingness to Completely Give Up Identification with the Ego

The ego is an illusion. We have been saying this for what seems like forever. We want you to get this on an energetic level, not just intellectually. The ego is simply a collection of thoughts which form the belief in a separate self. There is no separate self. There is a body through which the Creator can express itself in the physical world. That is all. This body you are wearing is a unique and beautiful way for God to express itself (himself/herself) in the world. No one body is worth any more than any other body. Nobody is more valuable or less valuable than someone else. Although bodies appear separate, this is an illusion. The energy field that makes up your body is the same energy field that makes up every other body. Everyone is connected, intimately, throughout the entire universe. What happens to one soul happens to all (although it might not be immediately obvious).

Defending the illusion called the ego has an enormous cost. Is it merely a coincidence that the most expensive thing in this world is military defenses? What are they defending that justifies spending trillions of dollars annually? If the belief in separation were eradicated, the belief in the ego would also end, and you would realize that the thing you are constantly trying to defend is not real. The physical body would actually be safer without extensive police and military. People who own handguns are four times more likely to experience a violent crime than those who do not own handguns.

If the entire universe is within you, if the Kingdom of Heaven is here and now, then what is there to defend? You already have everything. You simply do not realize it. It makes a lot more sense to spend trillions on technologies designed to help you remember who you are.

Today is the best day to let go of your attachment to this insane idea called "ego." Take care of the body and use it as a communications device, for that is what it is. Stop worshiping it and exalting it upon the throne of materialism. The only things worth doing in this world are those that help raise the frequency and vibration of humanity. This does not mean you must forego fun and entertainment, but choose something that is uplifting and genuinely entertaining, something that helps you remember your magnificence.

The Reluctance to Speak Out against Tyranny and Mind Control

There are numerous books and articles available online regarding the increasingly prevalent "police state" that Western countries are experiencing. Although there are a few people speaking out against this and warning about the "boiling frog syndrome," there are far more that are allowing fear of the "deep state" or "dark Illuminati" to keep them from expressing their ideas. As mentioned in the first item above, there is certainly a possibility you could become a target of suppression and harassment, or worse. But if you don't get your ideas out there, you and the world have already lost.

At a high level of vibration, it is possible to invoke a powerful field of protection that keeps you safe at all times regardless of what you are expressing. However, most inventors, true scientists and alternative leaders are not yet at that vibration. This is why doing spiritual work on yourself is of the utmost importance. If you are an inventor or engineer wanting to bring ZPE into the world and you have not done your spiritual "due diligence," then there is a good chance that you will join the ranks of hundreds of visionaries who have not made much headway against suppression.

This author has been told by his spirit guides that the level of consciousness required for ZPE and other technologies to be available to the masses is 4.00 in the aggregate. Right now, the mass consciousness is around 3.70. Yes, there were earlier predictions that this technology would become available around the year 2020. Actually, to be honest, the original prophecy was between 2015 and 2020.

There have been some breakthroughs. Even some governments, such as India's, have indicated, at least on the surface, that they will support such inventions and systems. However, the planned "roll-out" of ZPE has been delayed a couple of times. We are now looking at a high probability that the consciousness of Earth will become sufficient around the year 2025. To get the collective vibration above 4.00, it will likely take an economic crisis big enough to force people to wake up. Only about one-fourth of humanity are trying to better themselves, and far fewer are doing the serious spiritual work required to bring forth ZPE and other new technologies.

The recent "red pill" movement (based on the blue and red pill options given in the movie *The Matrix*) is a beginning, but most "red pillers" have a long way to go before they have truly freed themselves psychologically from the matrix.

The single greatest thing you can do to effectively catalyze the new energy revolution is to raise your consciousness. Higher consciousness needs to go "viral" across the planet. You need to clear ALL your fear of being suppressed or destroyed by the so-called powers that be.

We are not saying you should blindly believe that large corporations or governments have your best interests at heart; trust us, they don't. But becoming gloomy, pessimistic and despondent is also not the best approach.

Withdraw your emotional attachment and belief in the profoundly sick society in which you live (to paraphrase J. Krishnamurti). Love everyone unconditionally even if it appears to be a Pollyanna attitude. You are greater than you realize.

The Lack of Courage to Tell the Truth Openly and Honestly

This is almost identical to the previous topic, but we are going to take a slightly different angle here. We will take this to the personal level. A huge percentage of those embarking upon a road of higher consciousness are dealing with skeptical family and friends. This is also true of unlimited energy philosophies. If you are an alternative scientist, for example, the ridicule you get from conservative colleagues may be dwarfed by the disdain of your own family. Oftentimes, relatives will refuse to even speak to their uncle or brother-in-law that has "gone off the deep end." Of course, it hurts emotionally to be rejected by your own family, but these things are all too common.

Lacking the financial backing of government or industry sources *and* the emotional support of family, you are somehow going to carry on and manifest your visions in the unlimited-energy movement.

The best way to overcome the lack of courage is to spend time with those who have mustered up enough strength to carry on anyway. Find an inventor or scientist who is moving full steam ahead despite ridicule and threats. Visit websites of people who are speaking openly and honestly about the matrix and its philosophy of slavery. Do the necessary psychological work on yourself to overcome your fears. Explore past lifetimes where you had great ideas and they were blocked, or worse, you died for your beliefs.

Ask for help. You can consult with professionals in related fields, and you can talk to your own spirit guides, angels, archangels and ascended masters.

We all have them and they are willing to help. They might protect you as you go about your ZPE business activities or warn you of a potential danger spot. Courage does not mean indiscriminately blabbing everything you are doing to a general audience. Sometimes things really do need to be kept secret or shared only with certain trusted people. But you cannot let fear paralyze your ability to keep going forward.

Attachment to Religious and Cultural Beliefs and Practices

The big majority of humans on Earth are reluctant to accept new technologies and systems due to their ingrained belief systems. The expression, "You can't get something from nothing," has been distorted to cause disbelief that we live in an abundant universe that has more than enough of everything. While it's true that effort must be put into any worthwhile endeavor, it is also true that vast resources are available to those who have the eyes to see and the ears to hear the truth. If science is indeed proving that "The Kingdom of God is within," shouldn't that be the most important guidepost in your journey? Both science and religion are saying that unlimited energy is a reality. The only question then remaining is "How do we tap into this unlimited field?"

To those on the receiving end of this technology, it is difficult to believe that the purveyors of ZPE are not going to want a hefty fee for their services. "If it sounds too good to be true, it usually is," goes through the minds of consumers contemplating converting their home or business to ZPE.

The real litmus test regarding genuine versus fraudulent claims on products is to ask, "What is the state of consciousness of the inventor, salesman, scientist or advertiser?" Unfortunately, at this point, if the government and its agencies are against something, it probably has value (such as new drugs that the FDA opposes, for example). If inventors or engineers have been killed or silenced, it is probably worth looking into their research (if you can get your hands on it).

The so-called powers that be want you to believe that this is a world of struggle and strife and that you cannot get "something for nothing."

Actually, you already have everything (from a spiritual point of view), so you are not really gaining or losing anything. All you are doing is waking up to the fact that you are a powerful, creative, unlimited spiritual being living in a powerful, creative and unlimited universe. This waking up does indeed take effort and discipline. You must guard your mind against the demons of laziness, vice, doubt, fear, guilt, shame and such.

A Perceived Lack of Time and Energy to Devote to Bringing Forth the Technologies

Over half of the general populace in the United States is living from paycheck to paycheck. The situation is even worse in a lot of other countries. Many people are working two jobs just to make ends meet. Add to this the responsibilities of raising children, taking care of the house, etc., and it's a wonder there is any time left for pursuing alternative-energy projects.

Fortunately, more and more business is being conducted online, which frees up the time normally spent commuting to the office. Applications such as Zoom bring video conferencing to everyday people at very little cost. This means less time spent flying to business meetings in distant cities.

Nevertheless, it is challenging to find the time to work on complicated mechanical and electrical projects or to do the research necessary to calculate the exact values needed regarding resistance, capacitance, inductance, etc. We've all heard the stories of inventors down in their basement only coming up at bedtime. Usually there is someone bringing down their dinner, if they remember to eat at all.

In a previous publication, *The Mystery of Time*, we discussed time management and how crucial it is to the creation of new ideas and projects, such as ZPE and related technologies. It is suggested you read that book or find another on the subject. There are 168 hours in a week. About a third of them are normally spent sleeping. If you are not working a regular job, that leaves about 112 hours to divide between family, spiritual time and your projects.

If you are spending too much time on a specific program, you will likely experience burn-out or exhaustion. Notice the warning signs before it gets to that point. Take breaks. Push yourself a little bit if you have a deadline, but not too much. Quality is more important than speed. It makes no difference if you beat the competition regarding a timetable if you take short-cuts that compromise the quality of your project.

Learn to view time as your friend rather than your enemy. Stop resisting it or trying to control it. Observe how you "waste" time and your feelings about that. Beating yourself up because you watched a murder mystery instead of designing your website will not make things better. Accept the fact that you might have adopted poor work habits from your parents. Then forgive yourself, let it go, and resolve to do things differently.

Know that at a higher level, everything happens in perfect, right timing (despite appearances). Paradoxically, once you accept this truth, things tend to move more quickly or become more productive. Your alignment with the natural unfolding of Creation causes things to happen in a favorable way and at the perfect time.

Remember the example of the farmer who kept digging up his seeds every day to see if they had germinated. Needless to say, he destroyed his crop because he didn't trust in the process of planting, watering and weeding.

It's amazing how much you can accomplish when you are focused and disciplined. Get help if you are a procrastinator. There are many therapists who can assist you. Likewise, if you are impatient and cannot take the time to follow through with things, work on your impatience.

Lack of Discipline in Mind and Body

This is closely related to the previous topic of time management. Since you live in a busy world and have limited time to work on your projects, you must make friends with discipline. Yes, it's a dirty word to a lot of people, but all it really means is creating an environment where learning can take place (since it comes from the root "disciple" which means to learn or one who learns).

Eliminate distractions as best you can. If necessary, install sound barriers in your workspace if there are noisy children or neighbors outside. Turn on soft, high vibrational instrumental music in the background (but only if it helps you concentrate).

Discipline applies to every area of your life, including diet and exercise. Decide how much time you need each day for taking care of the body's needs, and then try to schedule these activities at regular intervals. The body likes routine (although the mind may not). Develop healthy habits that calm and relax the body.

Set realistic goals. Do not try to get things done too quickly. On the other hand, challenge yourself. If you know you can finish a program in three months, commit to that time period. Work a little late, if necessary, but do not obsess and contract a case of insomnia because you are too worried about finishing on time.

Discipline is not about drudgery or a sense of obligation. If you are working on a ZPE device or program, it should be exciting and fun (as well as very challenging).

Be creative. If you don't have enough money to build a prototype the way you envisioned it, see if there are ways you can do it for less without compromising quality.

Remember to network with other scientists, inventors or project managers who are highly motivated and disciplined. Go to trade fairs, symposiums, conferences and seminars. Try to associate with people who are better than you are at time management and discipline.

Keep holding the vision. Do not get discouraged. Know that this book came into your hands for a reason. Read it several times. Then read other books on the subject. Condition yourself to overcome the barriers and obstacles to moving forward with your ideas.

Know that you are a powerful, creative, spiritual being. Yes, we keep repeating this. If you can just understand, at the deepest level, the truth of this one statement, you will not fall into distraction and undisciplined or lazy behavior.

Give yourself credit for the wonderful accomplishments you already have made in your life. Yes, you have done well, despite the ego's rants. Admire how far you have come on your path. You have just read one of the most advanced and mind-stretching books on the planet. Congratulations. Now it's time to apply the ideas herein.

We support you energetically in realizing your dreams. We send you our encouragement and hopefully, inspiration. You are worth it. You are the one you've been waiting for. Claim your magnificence now. Amen.

APPENDIX

Links to Zero-Point Devices
and Research

Note: The author has not reviewed extensively the technical details of these devices and makes no guarantees of accuracy regarding the information given in these reports, abstracts and demonstrations. The Appendix and Bibliography are intentionally kept short, since most of the information in this book comes directly from higher intelligence and not from existing scientists and spiritual teachers.

Many of the links below are portals listing numerous related projects and programs. Use at your own discretion.

Nassim Haramein, "The Schwarzschild Proton" http://hiup.org/wp
-content/uploads/2013/05/AIP_CP_SProton_Haramein.pdf

Bruce DePalma's N-Machine http://www.brucedepalma.com

Thomas Bearden's Motionless Electromagnetic Generator http://www
.cheniere.org/megstatus.htm

Nikola Tesla and radiant energy https://teslaresearch.jimdo.com
/radiant-energy/

A compendium of Zero-Point energy projects https://www.bibliote-
capleyades.net/ciencia/secret_projects/energy.htm

The Institute for New Energy (a bit outdated but still some useful information) http://www.padrak.com/ine

John Bedini's SG Motor (considered one of the best by researchers) https://freeenergy.tech/bedini-motor/

A compendium of Dr. Harold Aspden's work http://www.aetherscience .org/www-aspden-org/papers/bib/refs.htm

In the 1990s, four engineers developed the Lutec device, and in 2010 two other engineers modified it, but it seems to have fallen victim to negative resonant fields and opposition from the status quo. Here is one of the more honest reports: http://panacea-bocaf.org /lutec.htm

Capturing the energy dissipated in electrical circuits (Poynting and Heaviside) as explained by Thomas Bearden http://www.cheniere .org/techpapers/on_extracting_EM%20energy.htm

Still one of the best videos on ZPE: *Free Energy — The Race to Zero Point* https://www.youtube.com/watch?v=hEND8dlUp1Y

Bibliography
and References

Julian Barbour, "The Nature of Time" http://www.platonia.com
/nature_of_time_essay.pdf

There are a lot of books by J. Krishnamurti and Dr. David Bohm. Here
is a link: https://www.amazon.com/krishnamurti-bohm-Books/s?k
=krishnamurti+bohm&rh=n%3A283155

There are too many metaphysical books relevant to our discussion
to name them all. Here are some classics:

Hurtak, J.J., *The Keys of Enoch*, Academy for Future Science, 1973

A Course in Miracles, Foundation for Inner Peace, 1978

Talbot, Michael, *The Holographic Universe*, Harper Perennial, 2011

Yogananda, Paramahansa, *Autobiography of a Yogi*, Self-Realization
Fellowship, 2014

Index

ABOUT THE AUTHOR

Sal Rachele

Sal Rachele is a pioneer in the human potential field. In the mid-1970s, he became interested in developing his psychic and intuitive abilities and took Silva Mind Control training. Sal later developed his own unique method called Alpha-Theta Programming, which is designed to reprogram the subconscious mind and unlock the creative potential within.

Sal became involved in Leonard Orr's Rebirthing and Jim Leonard's Integrative Rebirthing, a yoga of breath and conscious purification. In the 1980s, he did extensive work combining guided meditations, original piano music, and psychic counseling in his work. He recorded several cassettes and one CD of his original New Age classical melodies. He worked with a hypnotherapist in the 1980s to create the Leonard Series of self-hypnosis and self-improvement cassettes.

In 1994, he published his first book, *Life on the Cutting Edge*, a self-help manual with extensive illustrations, diagrams, and charts. Numerous projects later, he became aware of his connection to Leah, a sixth-density Venusian, and the Arcturians, a collective consciousness from seventh-density Arcturus, and he began consciously channeling information from these entities. In 2004, he began developing a type of healing based on the sacred sound current, or Naam, and he was given guidance on creating initiations based on this work.

Most recently, Sal has been guided to help souls heal their past, parallel, and future timelines through a cosmic reframing process that involves merging the conscious self with the God presence. Sal lives in northeastern Arizona but travels extensively around the American Southwest and West Coast. He is developing a 40-acre ranch that is off the grid and has partially constructed a 40-foot geodesic dome for future workshops and retreats.

BOOKS BY SAL RACHELE

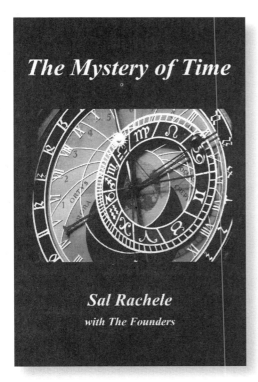

The Mystery of Time

Is time merely a convenient way of measuring the movements of celestial bodies, or is it much more? Why is it important to go beyond the daily clock and calendar? Are the secrets to life hidden within the mystery of time?

This book seeks to answer these questions and many more. The first part explains, through scientific fundamentals, that we are masters of time and space. Within us is the key to creation.

The second part offers practical applications of these ideas, including a powerful new therapy that has already helped transform thousands of lives.

Are you ready to go beyond traditional healing and therapy? Do you have the courage to look at the deepest layers of the subconscious mind?

If you are receptive to the possibilities, then open this book and begin the journey into a wonderful new awareness of self.

Chapters Include
- Linear and Nonlinear Time
- Parallel Realities
- The Nonlocality of Time/Space
- The Nature of Alternate Realities
- A Deeper Look at Free Will and Predestiny
- Time Travel
- Timeline Healing

$19.95 • 275 PP. • Softcover
PRINT ISBN: 978-0-578-20138-2
eISBN: 978-1-62233-808-5

BOOKS BY SAL RACHELE

The Real History of Earth

It is said that knowledge is power. The purpose of this book is to empower you to live an awakened life full of creativity and compassion. Knowing how and why things are the way they are on Earth gives you the power to make effective changes within yourself and the world.

This material will likely challenge your deepest and most cherished ideas of reality, and the author encourages you to thoroughly investigate the ideas he presents.

This book explores the answers to deep metaphysical questions, such as: "Why is there suffering on Earth?" "How do we break out of our self-imposed prison of negative thoughts and beliefs?" and "How did we come to be on this small planet at the edge of a rather average galaxy?"

Chapters Include

- The Nature of God and the Universe
- The Evolution of the Physical Worlds
- Extraterrestrials Who Have Significantly Affected the Earth
- The Early History of Earth, Individual Souls, and the Human Race
- The Rise and Fall of Civilizations in the Solar System

$19.95 • 329 pp. • Softcover
PRINT ISBN: 978-0-578-16430-4
eISBN: 978-1-62233-810-8

⚕ *Light Technology* PUBLISHING *Presents*

TO ORDER PRINT BOOKS
Visit LightTechnology.com, Call 928-526-1345 or 1-800-450-0985,
or Check Amazon.com or Your Favorite Bookstore

BOOKS BY SAL RACHELE

Soul Integration ·

The new Golden Age on Earth you've heard about will not just happen. It is up to all of us to make it happen by healing and transforming our lives through Soul Integration.

Soul Integration is about aligning all parts of the self into a cohesive whole. We then become all-powerful, all-wise, and all-loving and fulfill the promises of the mystics and seers of all ages.

This book shows, step by step, how to access this all-powerful self. Topics include healing the six lower bodies, transcending karma, contacting your soul family in the higher realms, how to reach enlightenment, and how to bring enlightenment down to Earth.

Much more change is on the horizon, both within you and in the outside world. As you go through this material, allow it to assist you in making sense of the chaos and confusion that appear to be all around you.

$19.95 • 336 PP. • Softcover
PRINT ISBN: 978-0-578-12271-7
eISBN: 978-1-62233-809-2

Chapters Include
- The Journey of the Soul
- Soul Mates and Twin Flames
- Soul Fragmentation
- Healing and Restoring the Soul to Wellness
- The Nature of Enlightenment
- Soul Integration in the World

❦ *Light Technology* PUBLISHING *Presents*

TO ORDER PRINT BOOKS
Visit LightTechnology.com, Call 928-526-1345 or 1-800-450-0985,
or Check Amazon.com or Your Favorite Bookstore

eBOOKS BY SAL RACHELE

Earth Awakens: 2012–2030   eISBN: 978-1-62233-812-2

Sal Rachele and his spirit guides, the Founders, take you on a won-
drous journey into the future of our beloved planet — the future you
have always dreamed of. This book shows you tangible, practical ways
of manifesting the new Golden Age of Earth that is destined to occur in
your lifetime.

Earth Changes and Beyond   eISBN: 978-1-62233-807-8

This book answers the who, what, where, when, and even why of current Earth changes with information relating to biology, psychology,
technology, metaphysics, religion, spirituality, economics, and politics.
This is the most significant time in human history. The doorway into
the next step of human evolution is right in front of us.

Life on the Cutting Edge   eISBN: 978-1-62233-806-1

This book takes a no-nonsense look at what is really happening on
Earth — behind the scenes, above the scenes, and beyond the scenes.
It addresses the issues we are facing right now and offers timely
solutions.

BOOKS THROUGH DRUNVALO MELCHIZEDEK

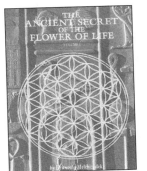

THE ANCIENT SECRET OF THE FLOWER OF LIFE, VOLUME 1

Also available in Spanish as *Antiguo Secreto Flor de la Vida, Volumen 1*

Once, all life in the universe knew the Flower of Life as the creation pattern, the geometrical design leading us into and out of physical existence. Then from a very high state of consciousness, we fell into darkness, and the secret was hidden for thousands of years, encoded in the cells of all life.

$25.00 • 240 PP. • Softcover • ISBN 978-1-891824-17-3

THE ANCIENT SECRET OF THE FLOWER OF LIFE, VOLUME 2

Also available in Spanish as *Antiguo Secreto Flor de la Vida, Volumen 2*

Drunvalo shares the instructions for the Mer-Ka-Ba meditation, step-by-step techniques for the re-creation of the energy field of the evolved human, which is the key to ascension and the next dimensional world. If done from love, this ancient process of breathing prana opens up for us a world of tantalizing possibility in this dimension, from protective powers to the healing of oneself, others, and even the planet.

$25.00 • 272 PP. • Softcover • ISBN 978-1-891824-21-0

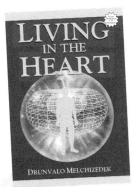

Includes
Heart
Meditation CD

LIVING IN THE HEART

Also available in Spanish as *Viviendo en el Corazón*

Long ago we humans used a form of communication and sensing that did not involve the brain in any way; rather, it came from a sacred place within our hearts. What good would it do to find this place again in a world where the greatest religion is science and the logic of the mind? Don't I know this world where emotions and feelings are second-class citizens? Yes, I do. But my teachers have asked me to remind you who you really are. You are more than a human being, much more. Within your heart is a place, a sacred place, where the world can literally be remade through conscious cocreation. If you give me permission, I will show you what has been shown to me.

— Drunvalo Melchizedek

$25.00 • 144 PP. • Softcover • ISBN 978-1-891824-43-2

BOOKS THROUGH DAVID K. MILLER

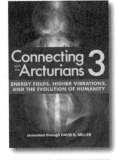

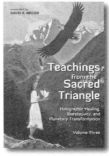

BOOKS THROUGH TINA LOUISE SPALDING

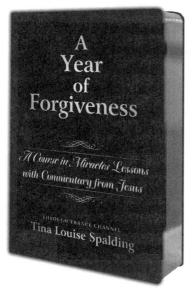

Features gold foil on cover and edges,
plus hundreds of full-color illustrations
by Renée Phillips

A Year of Forgiveness

A Course in Miracles Lessons with Commentary from Jesus

Keep this book close at hand with your *A Course in Miracles* manual, and read Jesus's commentaries after practicing the lesson as described in that text. Allow Jesus's simple and direct discussion of the topic to aid your understanding of these wonderful teachings.

This book is made even more appealing by the whimsical art of Renee Phillips, who has contributed beautiful illustrations for each lesson.

A Course in Miracles will change your life. With this companion book, find help and a clearer understanding of the lessons through these 365 channeled messages from Jesus.

$29.95 • 496 PP. • 978-1-62233-076-8

Jesus: My Autobiography
$16.95 • Softcover • 304 PP.
978-1-62233-030-0

Love and a Map to the Unaltered Soul
$16.95 • Softcover • 240 PP.
ISBN 978-1-62233-047-8

Making Love to God: The Path to Divine Sex
$19.95 • Softcover • 416 PP.
978-1-62233-009-6

Spirit of the Western Way
$16.95 • Softcover • 176 PP.
978-1-62233-051-5

You Can Free Yourself from the Karma of Chaos
$16.95 • Softcover • 224 PP.
978-1-62233-051-5

Great Minds Speak to You
$19.95 • Softcover • 192 PP.
Includes CD
978-1-62233-010-2

CD included!

✷ Light Technology PUBLISHING Presents

TO ORDER PRINT BOOKS
Visit LightTechnology.com, Call 928-526-1345 or 1-800-450-0985,
or Check Amazon.com or Your Favorite Bookstore

PRODUCTS BY LYSSA ROYAL-HOLT

Galactic Heritage Cards

THE FIRST AND ONLY OF THEIR KIND:
This 108-card divination system, based
on material from Lyssa Royal-Holt's
groundbreaking book *The Prism of
Lyra*, is **designed to help you tap into
your star lineage and karmic patterns**
while revealing lessons brought to
Earth from the stars and how those
lessons can be used in your life on
Earth now. Includes a 156-page book of
instruction and additional information.

Illustrations by David Cow • 108 cards (2.75 x 4.5 inches)
156-page softcover book (4.5 x 5.5 inches) • $34.95 • 978-1-891824-88-3

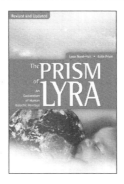

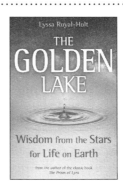

Preparing for Contact
In this book, you will take an
inner journey through your
own psyche and discover a
whole new dimension to your
unexplained experiences.
$16.95 • Softcover • 320 PP.
978-1-891824-90-6

The Prism of Lyra
This text explores the idea
that collective humanoid
consciousness created this
universe for specific purposes.
$16.95 • Softcover • 192 PP.
978-1-891824-87-6

The Golden Lake
This book features Pleiadian
and Sirian awakening teachings
that together provide a road
map for the next phase of
human evolution — the
integration of polarity
and the awakening of our
consciousness beyond duality.
$19.95 • Softcover • 240 PP.
978-1-62233-070-6

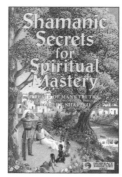

TO ORDER PRINT BOOKS
Visit LightTechnology.com, Call 928-526-1345 or 1-800-450-0985,
or Check Amazon.com or Your Favorite Bookstore

BOOKS THROUGH JAAP VAN ETTEN

$19.95 • Softcover • 352 PP. • 6 x 9
978-1-62233-066-9

DRAGONS
GUARDIANS OF CREATIVE POWERS
BECOMING A CONSCIOUS CREATOR

The elemental (fire, water, air, and earth) powers are the basis of all creation. Understanding the different aspects of these creative powers will help you to become a conscious creator.

Guardians are connected with every aspect of the elemental powers. They are known as dragons; however, different traditions use different names for them, such as angels or nature spirits. They are among the strongest allies we can ask for.

This book offers information to help you reconnect with these creative powers and their guardian dragons. Through this connection, you will become a conscious creator and change your life in ways that lead to success, joy, happiness, and abundance. Thereby, you will contribute optimally to the creation of a new world.

Birth of a New Consciousness: Dialogues with the Sidhe
$16.95 • 192 PP.
978-1-62233-033-1

The Gifts of Mother Earth
$16.95 • 256 PP.
978-1-891824-86-9

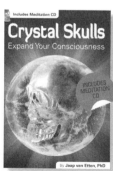

Crystal Skulls: Expand Your Consciousness
$25.00 • 256 PP.
978-1-62233-000-3

Crystal Skulls: Interacting with a Phenomenon
$19.95 • 240 PP.
978-1-891824-64-7